D0073328

Conscientious Objectors and the Second World War

Conscientious Objectors and the Second World War

Moral and Religious Arguments in Support of Pacifism

Cynthia Eller

New York
Westport, Connecticut
London

Library of Congress Cataloging-in-Publication Data

Eller, Cynthia.
Conscientious objectors and the Second World War : moral and religious arguments in support of pacifism / Cynthia Eller.
p. cm.
Includes bibliographical references and index.
ISBN 0-275-93805-0 (alk. paper)
1. World War, 1939-1945—Conscientious objectors—United States.
2. World War, 1939-1945—Moral and religious aspects. 3. Pacifism.
I. Title.
D810.C82E45 1991
940.53'162—dc20 90-21594

British Library Cataloguing in Publication Data is available.

Library of Congress Catalog Card Number: 90-21594
ISBN: 0-275-93805-0

First published in 1991

Praeger Publishers, One Madison Avenue, New York, NY 10010
An imprint of Greenwood Publishing Group, Inc.

Printed in the United States of America

The paper used in this book complies with the Permanent Paper Standard issued by the National Information Standards Organization (Z39.48-1984).

10 9 8 7 6 5 4 3 2 1

Contents

Preface

My interest in World War II pacifism dates back to my childhood. From my earliest years, I was raised as a pacifist in the Church of the Brethren. It was easy to be a pacifist in the era in which I grew up. In the midst of anti-Vietnam War protests, to say one was a pacifist—and moreover, part of a pacifist tradition that reached centuries into the past—was almost a point of pride. But I was aware that in other eras and under different circumstances, pacifism could be a very difficult and unpopular position to hold, and I was always curious to know what it was like to be a pacifist in more trying times.

However, my interest in World War II pacifism stems from deeper sources as well: I know of no stronger challenge to pacifism than a fascist dictatorship engaged in the wholesale murder of entire populations. Time and time again, I have had to ask myself "what about Hitler?" and the answer has never been clear. Part of the motivation for this study was to see how individuals who faced the situation of World War II and who chose not to fight have rationalized their position over the years: why, and whether or not they believe that pacifism was an acceptable response to Hitler. Their answers have intrigued, offended, and inspired me and I hope they will prove interesting to the reader as well.

I would like to thank a number of individuals who have given their assistance and support to this project. Hazel Peters and Mel Zuck were helpful in providing names and addresses for conscientious objectors who served in alternative service; Jean Soderlund of the Swarthmore College Peace Collection and David Haury of the Mennonite Library and Archives directed me to a number of useful sources and were always ready to be of assistance. Sylvia Eller, Robert Spero, Carol Hansen and Kevin Collins, Debbie and Al Habina, Marwin and Barbara Brubaker, Ed and Mary Brubaker, Karen and Stewart Hoover, Mildred Stucky, and Diane Woodruff all provided low-cost housing and good company during my research travels. Barry Seltser, Don Miller, and Frank Mitchell were generous with advice and support. John Tonry developed an invaluable computer program for my data. I relied on Jonathan Greene's computer typesetting expertise in preparing the final copy, as well as Margaret Eller's proofreading skills. Finally, I would like to give my special thanks to all those men who participated in this project, who spoke with me, wrote me letters, and shared their lives and thoughts so freely. Their faithfulness to pacifism in a time of adversity is an inspiration to those of us who try to carry forward their good work. To them this book is dedicated.

Conscientious Objectors and the Second World War

1

Pacifist Moral Argument

World War II stands in the common memory as the last "good" war, a war that weighed so heavily in the balance of relative goods and evils as to leave little moral doubt about the righteousness of the Allied cause. From the bombing of Pearl Harbor to the systematic murder of the European Jews, Americans have been given ample reason to portray World War II as the quintessential just war. As Michael Walzer states in his article, "World War II: Why This War Was Different":

> Many of us . . . believed at the time and still believe a quarter of a century later that Nazism was an ultimate threat to everything decent in our lives, an ideology and a practice of political domination so murderous, so degrading even to those who might survive, that the consequences of its final victory in World War II were literally beyond calculation, immeasurably awful. We see it—and I don't use the phrase lightly—as evil objectified in the world, and in a form so potent and apparent that there could never have been anything to do but fight against it.[1]

Pacifism, a robust movement in the 1930s, was dealt a serious blow by World War II. Prominent pre-war pacifists such as Albert Einstein and Romain Rolland reversed their positions with the rise of fascism in Germany. A. A. Milne, who in 1934 had written his first book for adults, *Peace with Honour,* wrote a sequel in 1940 entitled *War with Honour,* saying, "If anybody reads *Peace with Honour* now, he must read it with that one word 'HITLER' scrawled across every page. Before every irresistible conclusion to which I seek to draw him he must insert another premise: HITLER."[2]

All would-be pacifists of the latter half of the twentieth century are constrained to find a response to this challenge: What about Hitler? Some respond by leaving World War II its glow of moral approbation, but call into question other wars past, present, and future, carefully delineating the features that made this one war just. Others attack the American consensus which has erected World War II as the archetypal good war and present revisionist versions of World War II history. Still others accept the conventional history of World War II, but nevertheless offer reasons why war was an inappropriate response to the situation.

One group of people has been led by circumstance to consider very carefully the issue of World War II: those men who were conscientious objectors to World War II. Each of them found convincing reasons to reject the viewpoint of larger American society. From their initial decision to object, through nearly fifty years of reflection, these individuals have been forced to articulate their beliefs and motivations for standing apart from this "best of all possible wars."[3] They, like us, have had to come to terms with the legacy of World War II, but on a more personal level.

There can be no question that the problem of responding to military conscription produced real tension for the conscientious objectors (COs) of World War II. Though some COs did not experience paralyzing indecision, indeed were convinced as to the path they should take even before the Selective Service Act was passed by Congress, all COs were setting themselves apart from societal norms, and in some cases from U.S. law. Such actions were rarely taken lightly. More importantly, the marginal position COs adopted required them to be well rehearsed in explaining themselves to the unknowing and sometimes hostile majority. Often the "majority" took the form of family and friends struggling to understand the CO; sometimes the majority was an inner voice persistently arguing the merits of entering the military. In spite of a later expressed certainty, most COs did carry on this internal debate. As one CO describes it:

> Maybe the decision isn't necessarily yes or no. There might be some variables there, but basically it's a yes or no situation: Do I or don't I? And you may feel the validity of some of the discussion here, and you may feel the validity over here. But then one becomes stronger, and you make your decision. And I think a person has a tendency to, once he makes a decision, he then tries to reinforce that decision by emphasizing, and building upon, and strengthening the decision that was made, and having the tendency to reduce in importance the information that was discussed on the other side of the fence.[4]

In any case, even the most cloistered of COs felt some tension associated with choosing a response to the government's demand that he register with the Selective Service, apply for CO status, and accept some form of alternate service, or be imprisoned. The decision to be a conscientious objector brought definite consequences in its wake. As with those who accepted conscription into the army, no one emerged from the CO experience unchanged.

However, the choice to be a CO was not just a difficult decision, but a *moral* decision. The issues at stake were moral ones and were discussed in explicitly moral language. Conscientious objection was defended as the right thing to do, and not merely as a more convenient or personally satisfying way of spending the war years. From the beginning, the debate as it took place with the Selective Service System was framed in ethical terms: Those applying for conscientious objector status via Form 47, the "Special Form for Conscientious Objector," were required to substantiate the claim that they were "conscientiously opposed by reason of . . . religious training and belief" to combatant and/or noncombatant military service, and to answer questions such as "under what circumstances, if any, do you believe in the use of force?"[5] Answers were also moral in tone. For example, from the Form 47 of a Catholic CO comes this statement: "A Catholic is morally bound to consider any war in light of these principles [just war principles] before taking part in it. If he takes part, while believing in his heart and mind that it is unjust, he is aiding and abetting murder, and as a consequence is in danger of eternal damnation."[6]

The objection has been raised that whatever a man may say about his good moral reasons for being a CO, his true motivations lie deeper and are probably unrelated to morality. To this view, morality is a thin veneer of rhetoric concealing a personality directed by psychological needs and desires and sociological pressures. This objection is in principle unanswerable, since it posits a theory of human psychology that cannot be disproven. In a World War II-era article about COs, two psychologists discuss this problem:

> The attempt to discover why a young man refuses to go to war presents serious difficulties, unless of course, we are satisfied to say that the cause is blood squeamishness, or merely that he is a coward. Intellectual conceptions might be secured from questionnaires, rational opinions might be tabulated statistically, but usually the subject himself does not know the real cause of his course of action. To ask him why he became a pacifist or to study his answers on Form 47 would yield only the good reasons and the defense of his stand, not necessarily the real reasons for having taken the stand he did. Nor can those reasons be discovered by psychological tests of attitudes and feelings, for the tests available do not reveal the exact information desired.[7]

However, allowing that there are undoubtedly some and perhaps many non-moral factors operating in the decision to be a conscientious objector need not lead one to discount moral factors altogether. Certainly World War II COs are quick to offer their own psychosocial theories about their pacifism, explaining their objection in terms of temperamental factors such as nonconformity or tenderheartedness, or sociological factors such as family influence or religious training. But alongside these theories, most COs offer some account of their moral beliefs and the actions dictated by these beliefs, and quite often these accounts are offered as the determining factor in their decision to be a CO. Regardless of what their "true" motivations may be, moral considerations are believed to be important—even crucial—at the conscious level, and it is at least plausible that this extends to the subconscious and thus qualifies as underlying or "true" motivation.

This study proceeds under the assumption that both non-moral and moral factors motivate individuals to be pacifists in time of war, that morality can influence action. As Michael Walzer says, "We don't have to translate moral talk into interest talk in order to understand it; morality refers in its own way to the real world."[8] But even under the assumption that all moral talk is veiled interest talk, the moral justification of World War II pacifism is still of interest. If morality is truly a world of insubstantial shadows, it is nevertheless a world that people commonly take to be real. How people justify their behavior in moral terms can teach us much about what people value, how they wish to be viewed, and how they perceive the world around them. We may never know the real springs of action, but we can come to understand how people reason about moral issues, how they resolve and rationalize the moral dilemmas they encounter in their lives.

There are few better places to begin a study of moral reasoning generally than the study of attitudes toward war and peace. The power we have as human beings to destroy our fellow creatures is an enormous and frightening capability, one which every known moral system attempts to curb or prohibit. The enterprise of war seeks to legitimate killing within some prescribed arena, and thus is constantly pushing against the limits of our moral sensibilities. Where the lines are drawn is a matter of paramount importance for any ethical system, for as Michael Walzer says in *Just and Unjust Wars,* "War is the hardest place: if comprehensive and consistent moral judgments are possible there, they are possible everywhere."[9]

Because it deals directly with issues that lie at the heart of any ethical system, pacifist moral thought can illuminate the nature of moral reasoning in general. Pacifism has long been understood to illustrate a particular type of moral reasoning: that of deontology, of deciding right and wrong based on qualities inherent in an action rather than on the consequences this action brings. Yet as shown in this study, pacifists display a real moral concern for the consequences of their actions. In being an anomaly to traditional moral theory, pacifist moral thought challenges the adequacy of that theory.

Pacifist moral thought is of course not nearly so unitary as the term may make it sound. This is especially the case for World War II COs, who span the spectrum from the political far left to the religious far right, including in their varied ranks most positions in between. Nevertheless, pacifism is an identifiable phenomenon and can be described and analyzed as such. In spite of enormous variation and the occasional marginal case, pacifism and the arguments enlisted in its support have a definite flavor and texture that we give the name pacifism. Through the study of World War II COs and the moral justifications they offer, we can gain an appreciation of this phenomenon and the kind of thinking that is characteristic of it.

METHODOLOGY

There are a variety of ways in which one could investigate pacifist moral thought. Pacifists have never been parsimonious with their words, and a vast number of texts advocating pacifism exist decades and centuries into the past, including a large concentration of sources from the World War II era. Alternatively, one could do one's own pacifist moral thinking, attempting to elaborate the best and most consistent pacifist justifications available without reference to pacifism as it is found empirically. Rather than developing pacifist justifications from the ground up, or analyzing how literate pacifists have presented themselves in writing, this study relies primarily on oral interviews with World War II COs to reveal to us the world of practical morality. Its interest is in learning how ordinary people rationalize the decisions they make when faced with a painful moral dilemma, to see what sources they draw on, whose authority they appeal to, and finally, which arguments they find most compelling.

This approach is naturally of limited use. There are many questions we could legitimately ask about pacifism that this type of study will fail to answer. We will not learn how pacifists are born or made, what is the most philosophically consistent defense of pacifism, whether pacifism works in the international realm, or whether pacifists could have stopped Hitler. Since this is not a statistical study, it is even impossible to say which pacifist arguments are most widely held to be convincing. However, it does begin a description and open up a discussion, shedding new light on why pacifists feel the way they do, and casting doubt on the empirical adequacy of established moral theory.

The basis of this study is a set of interviews with sixty men who were conscientious objectors during the Second World War. (For details on how the sample was obtained, see Appendix A.) The pacifism of the World War II era was of course not limited to conscientious objectors (women and older men never faced the draft), but COs make a particularly interesting and well-defined group for study. Because conscription applied to all male citizens of draft age equally, the men who emerged as COs during World War II included many who would not otherwise be recognized as pacifists. Many men active in pacifist organizations prior to the war felt driven to accept active service in the military, seeing World War II as presenting exceptional circumstances. On the other hand, men who had never had any pacifist affiliations at all found themselves before their draft boards pleading for exemption from the military on the basis of their conscientious scruples. Conscription worked as a sieve on the pacifist movement, leaving only a small residue of objectors who had the combination of pacifist principles and social nonconformity that characterized the CO of World War II. In the process, it uncovered the quiet pacifists whose versions of pacifism were not always represented in the organized peace movement, and thus added to the wealth of pacifist arguments present in the World War II environment.

In the interest of simplicity, the research sample was limited to conscientious objection in the United States. A further line was drawn in that all COs included in this study "served time" for the cause. They either served in the military in a noncombatant capacity, performed alternative service in the United States, or served prison sentences for running afoul of Selective Service law. Men who were draft age pacifists but were exempt from the draft on the basis of health, farming, or ministry deferments were not included in the research sample. It is also important to note that the term "pacifist" is being used here in a special sense. A significant number of World War II COs object to having this term applied to them, preferring to be thought of as "nonresistants," "war objectors," or "conscientious cooperators." "Pacifist" has taken on a pejorative meaning in the minds of some COs: Those on the left regard the term as too passive in connotation, while those on the right feel that it implies political activism and suggests an anti-governmental attitude. Still others believe that pacifism is an ideal so high or so absolute that they feel it presumptuous to identify themselves with the term.

For the purposes of this study, I will adopt the definition of pacifism used by Gordon Zahn in his dissertation on World War II COs: "[pacifism is] any opposition to war that is based on some higher principle or principles than mere personal expediency. . . . Excluded under this definition are individuals and groups motivated by considerations of political expediency or sympathy for the enemy cause."[10] I modify this definition slightly to indicate opposition to *participation* in war, but not necessarily to war itself, since some pacifists applaud others for fighting while feeling that they cannot themselves do so because of their conscientious scruples. I believe this is the broadest possible definition of pacifism that is still sufficiently narrow to capture our intuitive sense of the word's meaning.

Of the sixty interviews conducted for this study, fifty-four were in person, three were by telephone, and three were self-interviews (i.e., the interviewee was sent a list of questions and he responded to them orally on tape). Two COs responded to a list of questions in writing. My aim in selecting interviewees was to assure a maximum of variety; however, no attempt was made to be representative. The CO provisions of the 1940 Selective Service Act were designed to protect persons who "by reason of religious training and belief" were "conscientiously opposed to participation in war in any form,"[11] so reliable records of COs' religious affiliations were kept. Though far from precise, I felt that this would be the best index to the moral justifications a CO offered for his position. Variety was also sought by choosing men who responded to the draft in different ways—refusal to register, acceptance of alternative service, acceptance of noncombatant military service—and men who underwent a change of heart during the war and either abandoned alternative service and were subsequently jailed, or gave up CO status and went into the military. I believed that these men, having faced the moral dilemma of pacifism in wartime more than once and having come to different conclusions each time might be especially rich sources of moral justification. (See Appendix B for religious affiliation and wartime status of the interview sample.) Finally, some effort was made to secure interviews with men from a variety of geographical locations. Though the preponderance of the interviews were done in California, most of these men were reared elsewhere; the remaining interviews were done on the East Coast or by mail or telephone. (The location of the interviews can be found in the bibliography.)

This method of taping interviews with individuals who had historically interesting experiences is characteristic of the discipline of oral history. Yet oral history is frequently thought of as a method of adding to our store of historical knowledge, and while this is certainly a side effect of this study, it is not its main intent. The history of conscientious objection in World War II is already well documented.[12] The historical material presented in the existing sources is likely to be more reliable than that elicited in interviews with individual COs who were chosen not for their fine memories or important roles as pacifists during World War II, but for their interesting perspective on the moral basis of pacifism. However, I am not seeking to discover what really happened with World War II COs, but rather how they perceive their experiences and reflect on them some fifty years later. In fact, the entire question of the actual events of World War II pacifism is bracketed and set aside as irrelevant to the goal of securing the contemporary moral justification of this long ago experience.

In the course of interviews, I gave COs the opportunity to discuss their World War II experiences apart from the moral dilemmas they faced and how they resolved them, so that this information might be available to future researchers.[13] In the main, however, I directed my questions to the interviewee's beliefs and training, his decision to be a CO, and his *ex post facto* reflections on the rightness of his stand, especially in the light of what we now know about the Second World War. The interviews generally proceeded chronologically, from childhood through the draft, to the war years and the years since. I did not follow a rigidly ordered set of questions, but let the interview wander so that I could get a sense of what the individual felt was of greatest importance about his World War II experience. However, all questions were eventually asked in each interview, so fairly comprehensive data are available across the board. (A copy of my interview guide can be found in Appendix C.)

In addition to my own interviews I was able to draw on interviews from several other oral history projects. The largest of these is a collection of interviews with World War II COs stored at the Mennonite Library and Archives in North Newton, Kansas.[14] This collection consists of approximately ninety interviews with World War II COs, and all but a very few of these were with Mennonites (the only others were with individuals who went to Mennonite colleges or joined the Mennonite church after the war). A second oral history was conducted by Deena Hurwitz and Craig Simpson and used as the text for a

1984 War Resisters League calendar titled *Against the Tide.*[15] Hurwitz and Simpson interviewed approximately forty people, not all of whom were COs (many women were included, along with some pacifist leaders over draft age), and I was able to use the material they published in the calendar as well as complete transcripts of two of the interviews. The last oral history I consulted was a series of nine self-interviews collected by Murray Polner of the Jewish Peace Fellowship.[16] These focused strongly on moral justification, perhaps unsurprising in that Jewish pacifists were confronted with a more heavily weighted moral dilemma in World War II than the average American CO, since even before the Holocaust became general knowledge, the anti-Semitism of Nazi Germany was widely publicized. I also consulted a number of archival sources to strengthen the interview material, including letters, speeches, and articles written by COs during the war. Many of these contain ruminations about pacifism and the war, and provide an interesting contrast to the retrospective tone of the interviews. Finally, I did an extensive review of pacifist materials that were influential to World War II COs and of pacifist pamphlets and articles produced during the war. This material is used primarily as background, but is brought in occasionally to give structure or clarity to the moral arguments made by World War II conscientious objectors themselves.

Although the men I interviewed spoke from the point of view of the present, their actions and justifications can only be adequately understood in light of the past. The war we remember today is not the same one that was fought in 1940–1945. The former is the war to which COs are reacting when they offer moral justifications for pacifism today, but the latter is the war that formed the context for their decision to object. Before embarking on a description and analysis of pacifist moral justification, we must gain an appreciation of who the COs were, how they came to be pacifists, and how they fared during the war years.

NOTES

1. Michael Walzer, "World War II: Why Was This War Different?" in *War and Moral Responsibility,* Marshall Cohen, Thomas Nagel, and Thomas Scanlon, eds. (Princeton, NJ: Princeton University Press, 1974), 86.

2. A. A. Milne, *War With Honour,* Macmillan War Pamphlets, no. 2 (London: Macmillan and Co., Ltd., 1940), 12.

3. Lawrence Wittner, *Rebels Against War: The American Peace Movement, 1933–1983* (Philadelphia: Temple University Press, 1984), 97.

4. J. Edwin Jones, interview with author, 6 September 1986, La Verne, California.

5. U.S. Department of Selective Service, Form 47, "Special Form for Conscientious Objector" (Washington D.C.: Government Printing Office, 1940). A copy of Form 47 can be found in Mulford Q. Sibley and Philip Jacob, *Conscription of Conscience: The American State and the Conscientious Objector, 1940–1947* (Ithaca, NY: Cornell University Press, 1952), 488–92 (Appendix D).

6. Gordon C. Zahn, "A Study of the Social Backgrounds of Catholic Conscientious Objectors in Civilian Public Service During World War II" (M.A. thesis, Catholic University of America, 1950), 104.

7. Ray R. Kelley and Paul E. Johnson, "Emotional Traits in Pacifists," *Journal of Social Psychology* 28 (November 1948): 277.

8. Michael Walzer, *Just and Unjust Wars: A Moral Argument with Historical Illustrations* (New York: Basic Books, 1977), 12.

9. Ibid., xvii.

10. Gordon C. Zahn, "A Descriptive Study of the Sociological Backgrounds of Conscientious Objectors in Civilian Public Service During World War II" (Ph.D. dissertation, Catholic University of America, 1953), 10.

11. Section 5(g) of the Selective Training and Service Act of 1940, quoted in Sibley and Jacob, *Conscription of Conscience,* 487 (Appendix C).

12. The authoritative work on conscientious objection during World War II is Mulford Sibley and Philip Jacob, *Conscription of Conscience: The American State and the Conscientious Objector, 1940–1947* (Ithaca, NY: Cornell University Press, 1952), along with a supporting pamphlet, Mulford Sibley and Ada Wardlaw, *Conscientious Objectors in Prison, 1940–45* (Philadelphia: Pacifist Research Bureau, 1945). World War II conscientious objection is given lengthy treatment in a number of other sources, including Lawrence Wittner, *Rebels Against War: The American Peace Movement, 1933–1983* (Philadelphia: Temple University Press, 1984); Charles Chatfield, *For Peace and Justice: Pacifism in America, 1914–1941* (Boston: Beacon Press, 1973); Charles DeBenedetti, *The Peace Reform in American History* (Bloomington, IN: Indiana University Press, 1980); Peter Brock, *Twentieth-Century Pacifism* (New York: Van Nostrand Reinhold Company, 1970); and Theodore Wachs, "Conscription, Conscientious Objection, and the Context of American Pacifism 1940–45" (Ph.D. dissertation, University of Illinois at Champaign-Urbana, 1976). Two denominational studies give great detail on the alternative service program administered by the peace churches: Leslie Eisan, *Pathways of Peace: A History of the Civilian Public Service Program Administered by the Brethren Service Committee* (Elgin, IL: Brethren Publishing House, 1948) and Melvin Gingerich, *Service for Peace: A History of Mennonite Civilian Public Service* (Akron, PA: Mennonite Central Committee, 1949).

13. The tapes and transcripts of the interviews recorded for this study have been deposited in the Swarthmore College Peace Collection in Swarthmore, Pennsylvania.

14. Keith Sprunger and James Juhnke, coordinators, "Schowalter Oral History Collection—World War II Conscientious Objectors," 122 cassette tapes, Mennonite Library and Archives, North Newton, Kansas. Keith Sprunger and James Juhnke, history professors at Bethel College, supervised this project, but most of the interviews were conducted by their students in the late 1970s. All interviewers worked with the same interview guide. The questions were clearly intended to give a complete and general coverage of the World War II CO experience so that future scholars with a variety of research interests could make use of them. Several questions invited interviewees to discuss what influenced them to be a CO, what they thought about the war at the time, and whether they feel now that they made the right decision, so this collection was very helpful in broadening my sample to include Mennonite conscientious objection.

15. Deena Hurwitz and Craig Simpson, eds., *Against the Tide: Pacifist Resistance in the Second World War, an Oral History* (New York: War Resisters League, 1984).

16. Murray Polner, "An Oral History of American Jews who Chose to Become Conscientious Objectors or Resisted Serving in the Military from World War II—Korean War," ten cassette tapes, Swarthmore College Peace Collection, Swarthmore, Pennsylvania.

2

Pacifism and the Selective Service Act of 1940

Though it would later be remembered as a just war, World War II was not an easy war for the United States to enter in the early years of the European conflict. The 1940 draft was passed only after long and harrowing debate in Congress. Up until June 1940, the month in which the Burke-Wadsworth conscription bill was introduced in Congress, public opinion polls showed a majority of Americans opposing conscription of all twenty-year-old males for one year of military service.[1] When the bill was finally passed on September 16, 1940, by a narrow margin, it limited draftees to a total of nine hundred thousand at any one time, called for service of one year or less, and required that draftees not be posted outside the Western Hemisphere, except in American territories or possessions. On August 18, 1941, less than four months before the Japanese attack on Pearl Harbor, Congress voted to extend the length of service to eighteen months, passing this bill in the House of Representatives by only one vote.[2]

Gaining public acceptance of the 1940 draft was an uphill battle for several reasons: to begin with, it was the first peacetime draft in American history, and thus offended against a long tradition of American voluntarism. During the war of 1812, a military conscription bill was defeated in Congress following a speech from Daniel Webster that challenged:

> Is this, sir, consistent with the character of free government? Is this civil liberty? Is this the real Character of our Constitution? No, sir, indeed it is not. The Constitution is libelled, foully libelled. The people of this country have not established for themselves such a fabric of despotism. They have not purchased at a vast expense of their own treasure and their own blood a Magna Charta to be slaves.[3]

Conscription was instituted by both the Union and the Confederacy during the Civil War, though not without resistance. In New York City in particular, the

1863 introduction of conscription was greeted with a four-day riot that was quelled only when armed forces were brought in and conscription temporarily suspended.[4] Conscription was later accepted by the public in World War I, but Americans continued to take pride in their peacetime volunteer army (especially as they compared it to the universal military training by then common in Europe), and this lack of compulsion was viewed as proof of American liberties. Indeed, many of America's nineteenth- and twentieth-century immigrants from Europe left in part to avoid military conscription in their homelands.

But a far more important factor creating opposition to the 1940 draft was a widespread isolationist sentiment born of Americans' unfavorable evaluation of World War I. Regret over United States involvement in World War I was by no means restricted to pacifist circles: in February of 1937, a poll asked Americans, "If another war like the World War [I] develops in Europe, should America take part again?" The consensus was overwhelming: 95 percent answered no.[5] Revisionist history of World War I even found its way into high school textbooks of the interwar years. Students were taught that the war to "make the world safe for democracy" had really been a mindless power struggle that was exploited by munitions manufacturers who, seeing a profit in continued warfare, sold weapons to both sides and dispensed propaganda to fuel antagonisms and aggravate the conflict.[6] One CO recalls a popular slogan of the post-World War I era saying, "I wasn't old enough to be fer it or agin it."[7] The average American saw history repeating itself in the late 1930s in Europe, and was determined to learn from past mistakes and stay out of the European mess "this time." Advocates of the Selective Service Act were forced to appeal to this sentiment, and they sold conscription to the American people on the theory that a strong army would discourage potential attackers and allow the United States to sit out the war in happy isolation.[8]

A final roadblock on the path to conscription was the peace movement, a political force to be reckoned with during the interwar years. In 1935 the peace movement was estimated to have twelve million adherents and an income of over one million dollars.[9] The desire for and belief in the possibility of international peace inspired a whole generation, and this dream was not easily or quickly extinguished. Even the director of Selective Service made a bow to the dream of a peaceful world in his first semiannual report, *The Selective Service in Peacetime:*

> Peace is an aspiration of good men in every generation. A warless world is an aspiration of human idealism. War itself is a stupid way to settle international disputes and has long been recognized as such by rational people. . . . War is the pathology of international relations. It is an acknowledgment of the failure of reason to guide the affairs of men. Peace, constructive peace, peace with her victories no less renowned than war, is the goal of all social effort—even of war itself.[10]

Yet the peace movement grew ever more uncertain and divided in the face of the fascist threat, until Pearl Harbor brought an end to attempts to keep America out of the war and a beginning to a different sort of peace movement: the individual witness of conscientious objection from within a nation at war.

INTERWAR PACIFISM

Pacifism in the 1930s was perhaps most pervasive among the Protestant clergy. Their vehement support of World War I from the pulpit turned to repentance as a different version of World War I came to light, one in which the brave defenders of democracy seemed now to be innocent young boys drafted to fight and die in a pointless war. This revisionist history was accompanied by a theological shift toward the gospels and especially toward the conception of Jesus Christ as moral teacher and servant of God. New Testament instructions to turn the other cheek and bind up the wounds of the world stood in stark contrast to the practices of war, and pacifism within the churches flourished as a consequence. A religious periodical, *The World Tomorrow*, polled Protestant ministers in the United States in 1931 and found that of 19,372 responses, 12,076 declared that the church should never again sanction any war.[11] (It should be stressed that this was not an absolute pacifism; war was not declared to be always and everywhere morally wrong, but rather was seen as an outbreak of human sinfulness from which the church must stand apart. The fear was that the truth and power of the gospel would be watered down if it were associated with war, and thus must be held inviolate against the temptation of the crusade.) The editor of *The Christian Century* exclaimed over the newfound pacifism of the church in December of 1939:

> It can be said without exaggeration that peace has now become an article of the church's creed. War has lost its glory and stands forth as the naked iniquity which it always was. For the church to bless war, now appears to the Christian conscience as the absolute contradiction of the Christian faith and an act of self-stultification by the church.[12]

Within Protestantism but closer to its margins were the historic peace churches (Quakers, Mennonites, and Brethren), so named because of their doctrinal pacifism dating from the inception of their denominations. These groups were pacifist throughout the interwar years, but in spite of popular sentiment in favor of peace both within and without American Protestantism, the peace churches were not always vocal about their pacifism. This was particularly true in the case of the Mennonites, whose tradition of "set-apartness" led them to maintain their pacifism within the confines of their own communities and to be suspicious of the politically liberal pacifism of the mainline Protestants.[13] The Brethren, under the influence of the social gospel movement, were more receptive to the growth of a broadly based Protestant peace movement, but they too tended to avoid the spotlight and content themselves with quietly teaching the peace doctrine. However, for the Society of Friends (Quakers), the 1930s peace movement presented a rich field of opportunity which they did not hesitate to plow. In addition to ecumenical cooperation with mainline Protestant pacifists, the Friends conducted their own summer work camps and seminars, laboring and educating for peace. Individual Quakers came to the forefront of many peace organizations, sensing that the time was ripe to spread pacifism to a wider audience. In her 1947 summary of the Quaker position on peace, Ruth Freeman details this flowering of the Quaker anti-war position in the years from 1920–1945. Among the new emphases she sees during this period are:

> (1) humble recognition of Friends' inadequacy, (2) insistence that refusal to participate in war was but a part of a way of life that touched all social, political and economic issues, (3) a belief that the way for the individual was also the way for the nation, (4) presentation of the peace testimony argumentatively to win support, (5) advice on terms of peace, form of world organization, attitude of peacemakers and other political issues.[14]

These emphases were echoed throughout the Protestant peace movement, though without the Quaker reliance on a long-standing peace tradition or their characteristic humility. The mainline Protestant peace movement saw the churches themselves, and less so the individuals in them, as being a major tool in the effort to usher in an age of peace. If the churches could act together to declare war un-Christian, the hope was that their voice of moral authority would prove a serious deterrent to the waging of war. As Roland Bainton wrote from the perspective of 1945, "Beneath all these programs . . . lay a residuum of optimism from the liberal era. The assumption was that war can rather readily be eliminated."[15]

The organizational hub of Protestant pacifism during the interwar years was the Fellowship of Reconciliation (FOR), an organization formed in England in 1914 and spread to the United States in 1915, and united around a renunciation of force and a commitment to love and reconciliation. The FOR declared itself officially non-sectarian in 1930, but it remained substantially Protestant, and definitely religious.[16] The FOR absorbed another organization, the Fellowship for a Christian Social Order, in 1928, and then spent the early 1930s hashing out differences between the two groups. The central question of the moment was whether violence could be justified in the class struggle; eventually most of those who answered affirmatively left the FOR, and the FOR itself became strengthened in its absolute pacifist stance.

During this time the FOR was very attracted to Gandhian philosophy, which was then being imported to the West. The use of nonviolence to achieve social goals provided an essential link in the chain of Protestant pacifist reasoning, for it gave pacifists a way to avoid charges of passive acquiescence to social injustice. No longer constrained to sit on their pacifist hands in times of social crisis, pitying the oppressed but unable to use force to ease their plight, Gandhian nonviolence freed pacifists to reclaim their relevance to the political order. As pacifist historian Peter Brock describes it, "The idea of nonviolence brought the pacifist philosophy down to earth, changing it from a counsel of perfection to a more perfect method of maintaining terrestrial values than the way of armed force."[17]

Interest in Gandhi's nonviolent campaigns in India spread throughout the peace movement. It was especially prominent in the thought of the War Resisters League (WRL), an organization formed in 1923 and committed to absolute pacifism, but not sharing the religious roots of the FOR. Lacking the luxury of other-worldly religious concerns, the WRL was more pressed to develop a discipline that could reject violence but retain social relevance. However, the celebration of Gandhian nonviolence among pacifists did not turn to action in the interwar years; though much beloved in theory, there had been little occasion to test its mettle.

The college campuses of the United States were another major arena for the interwar peace movement. Both the WRL and the FOR had active youth sections and did much of their organizing in universities and church youth groups. A series of student peace rallies and strikes took place in the mid-1930s, culminating in an "anti-war strike" on April 22, 1936. With the reported participation of five hundred thousand students all over the country, it was the largest student demonstration in American history up to that point. Around the same time a group of undergraduates at Princeton formed an organization they called "Veterans of Future Wars," ostensibly established so that young men could collect their war bonuses in advance. Their motto was "hand outstretched, palm up, expectant." The idea caught on, chapters were established on other campuses, and during the 1936 anti-war strike, the Veterans of Future Wars led the way in creative demonstrations. For example, at the University of Washington, twelve thousand joined in funeral services for "the unknown soldier of tomorrow," with pallbearers dressed as Hitler, Mussolini, and J. P. Morgan.[18]

Clearly, not all college students embraced the peace movement, but considering that a popular war was only five years down the road, the amount of lip service given to peace was impressive. The extent of student pacifist sentiment was quantified in two polls of American college students of the mid-1930s. The first, conducted in 1933 by the Brown University *Daily Herald,* polled 21,725 students in 65 colleges: 8,415 described themselves as absolute pacifists, 7,221 said they would fight only if the United States were invaded, and 6,089 said they would serve in any war in which the United States was involved.[19] A poll of sixty thousand students by the *Literary Digest* in 1935 reported 81 percent refusing to fight if the United States invaded another country, and 16.5 percent refusing even if the United States itself were invaded.[20]

Conceptually, the American student peace movement owed much to its British counterpart, especially in the form of the famous Oxford Pledge, passed by undergraduates at Oxford University in February of 1933. By a vote of 275 to 153, the members of the Oxford Union adopted the resolution that "this House will not fight for King and country in any war." Though its adoption created some controversy, the Oxford Pledge spread quickly through English universities, and then to the United States. With the revised wording, "I pledge myself not to fight in any war in which the United States is involved" (and several other permutations of this statement), the Oxford Pledge became a focal point for student peace advocates, and many thousands of college students recited or signed this Pledge during the 1930s.[21]

The simplicity of the Oxford Pledge disguised a multitude of different anti-war positions. Some groups and individuals read the pledge as an absolute pacifist statement, a promise to refuse to fight all wars at all times. But perhaps more common, and more in keeping with the general mood of revulsion with World War I, was the socialist interpretation of the pledge as a vow not to allow oneself to be a pawn in the power struggles of capitalist, money-mad states. Thus, the pledge was not a straightforward refusal to fight, but a refusal to fight for the United States (or in Great Britain, "for King and country"). As such, the pledge was adopted in the United States by the Socialist Student League for Industrial Democracy and the communist-controlled National Student League.[22]

Outside student circles, as well as within, the political far left was outspoken in its opposition to war. Both socialists and communists saw war as an integral part of the capitalist/imperialist equation. Communists especially revived the idea of a united front against war—first popular prior to World War I—in which members of the working class worldwide would come to see their primary affinity with each other and not with the nation states under which they were compelled to labor. Making common cause across national boundaries, the working class could then prevent imperialist wars through their own refusal to participate. Particularly after the signing of the Nazi-Soviet nonaggression pact in August 1939, American communists worked tirelessly for the cause of peace.[23]

Though socialists and communists represented only a small percentage of the American public, their diagnosis of war as a field day for greedy entrepreneurs at the expense of the lives and wealth of ordinary people found a receptive audience. Beleaguered by a massive economic depression, statistics on the material and human cost of World War I were guaranteed to dismay even those who did not belong to the political left wing. America underwent a thorough indoctrination during the interwar years into the idea that war did not preserve democracy so much as it lined the pockets of the already well-to-do and left the shattered families of ordinary Americans in its wake.[24]

Thus the United States government was faced with a difficult task in the late 1930s and early 1940s as it struggled to gain public support for peacetime conscription and the government's implied desire to enter the European war. American acceptance of World War II was a goal achieved by short steps (and with the help of gradually accumulating pacifist reversals) until the attack on Pearl Harbor in December of 1941 won public approval of the war as nothing else could. Along with the rest of American society, the interwar peace movement entered the furnace of World War II and emerged utterly transformed.

THE PEACE MOVEMENT IN THE SHADOW OF WAR

The first defection from interwar pacifism occurred with the Spanish Civil War in 1936. The question of Loyalist Spain's right to resist Franco and the duty of American socialists to help them splintered the Socialist Party in America. It was here that the test came which would determine whether socialists were opposed to warfare as such, or only to warfare between capitalist, imperialist states. The results were divided: the Socialist Party took no official position, but the New York local recruited socialists to serve with the Eugene V. Debs column on the Loyalist side of the conflict, and in this they acted with the approval of the national executive committee of the Party. Norman Thomas defended this decision to the pacifists of the FOR saying, "The Socialist Party position is that it will use to the uttermost non-violent methods consistent with true democracy. But . . . it will not yield to fascism anywhere without a struggle and . . . nonviolence is not its first and last commandment."[25]

Many socialists did not agree with Thomas and continued to maintain a more absolute stand. But even those who took an interventionist position regarding Spain did not necessarily believe that interventionism was an appropriate response for the Allies in the early years of World War II. Nevertheless, once the exception was made in Spain, and the commitment to resisting fascism was proclaimed, the Socialist Party found it increasingly difficult to maintain a united front against American entrance into the war in Europe. More and more socialists switched to a position of collective security, and those socialists left holding a pacifist viewpoint soon ceased to speak for the party and spoke only for themselves. Some joined the ranks of the conscientious objectors; others joined the army with the intent of radicalizing it from within.[26]

American communists experienced much less angst than the socialists as World War II developed around them, for their position was more doctrinaire. As long as the Nazi-Soviet nonaggression pact was in effect, the communists were organizing for peace, the war in Europe was an "imperialist war," and their slogan was "the Yanks are not coming." In addition to their own organization, the American Peace Mobilization, communists worked through existing pacifist coalitions and through the labor movement in their efforts to keep American soldiers and arms at home. Their position was changed literally overnight when Germany invaded the Soviet Union. The American Peace Mobilization became the American People's Mobilization, the war became a "people's war for national liberation," and their new slogan was "victory over fascism."[27] Dave Dellinger, a conscientious objector who was then serving time in Danbury federal prison for failing to register for the draft relates this story about the communist about-face:

> When I arrived [in Danbury] late in the fall of 1940, a group of Communist tailors and furriers were there on charges not connected with the war. To my embarrassment they treated me as a heroic figure. Then one day, in the course of

> my regular work assignment I walked into the shop where several of them worked to collect its garbage. To my amazement they turned on me, accusing me of cowardice and fascism. One of them literally spat at me. It wasn't until an hour or so later that I learned that Germany had invaded the Soviet Union. They hadn't even bothered to tell me, let alone find out if I would now ask for parole in order to join the army.[28]

Meanwhile, what was left of the Protestant-dominated wing of the peace movement was struggling to exert some influence over the government to remain neutral regarding the European conflict. In so doing, liberal pacifists found themselves working side-by-side with conservative isolationists, with whom they had relatively little in common except for a mutual desire to keep America out of war. Where most isolationists wanted simply to stand aside from battles they believed were the business of decadent Europe alone, liberal pacifists had an active concern with Europe's welfare, but felt they could help Europeans most by remaining neutral in the conflict. Through neutrality, pacifists hoped America could have a role in arbitrating the conflict, maintaining an island of sanity in wartime, and using its resources to heal and rebuild the post-war world.[29]

Many pacifists, however, became uncomfortable with their tacit alliance with the right-wing isolationists of organizations such as America First. As fascism won triumph after triumph in Europe, the mostly left-leaning pacifists felt increasing pressure to do something to resist the much-despised Axis powers. Many former leaders of the interwar peace movement yielded to this pressure, and their highly publicized recantations carried a great deal of weight with wavering pacifists. Especially influential was Reinhold Niebuhr, a former chairman of the FOR who left in 1934 over the issue of appropriate use of violence in the class struggle. Beginning in the late 1930s, Niebuhr decried German fascism, insisted that Hitler would stop at nothing to destroy Christian civilization, and called for American aid to the Allies, eventually including military intervention.[30] The moral certitude that had characterized interwar Protestant pacifism was gradually whittled away by the fascist threat, until even those who maintained their pacifism felt that it had been relativized. As Lawrence Wittner explains in *Rebels Against War:*

> Those with an ethical revulsion to war could not fail to reserve a special shudder for the peculiar horrors of fascism. The destruction of individual liberty, the glorification of hatred, and, perhaps the ugliest of all, a series of anti-Semitic attacks that raised the ancient pogrom to the status of a State religion, sickened American peace activists, and led many to conclude that war represented the lesser of two evils.[31]

Still, up until the attack on Pearl Harbor, pacifists continued trying to stem the tide of war. They lobbied Congress for neutrality legislation and opposed military conscription. The FOR, WRL, their youth sections, and the National Council of Methodist Youth jointly proclaimed the first day of draft registration

(October 16, 1940) a "Day of National Humiliation."[32] But their growing frustration was apparent. Long-time pacifist minister John Haynes Holmes, reviled during World War I for his pacifist views, gloried in the strength of the interwar peace movement only to see it crumble beneath him. In the pages of *The Christian Century* in late 1940 he bemoaned, "We agree to condemn war as a principle of action or a program of statesmanship, and then find reason to approve each and every especial war that comes along."[33] Except for the FOR and WRL, most interwar peace organizations were failing by 1940. The Women's International League for Peace and Freedom (WILPF), a stalwart of 1930s pacifism, began to lose members and income, and was forced to drop several staff members. Others, such as the National Council for the Prevention of War suffered similar hardships.[34]

The Japanese attack on Pearl Harbor, followed immediately by U.S. entrance into war against both Japan and Germany, sounded the death knell for an already dying interwar peace movement. Pacifism was by no means dead, but its constituency and forms of expression were changed dramatically. Pearl Harbor came as a surprise to most Americans—even to pacifists who had been following international events closely and expected eventual American involvement, but thought America would be drawn in from the European and not the Asian side. Dellie Hahne, interviewed for an oral history of World War II titled *The Homefront*, was a college student at the time of Pearl Harbor. She recalls receiving the news:

> In an incredibly short time—it seemed to be almost a matter of moments—a wave of patriotism swept the country. As we drove home we felt, This is our country, and we're going to fight to defend it. When we got home that evening we were glued to the radio. "The Star-Spangled Banner" was played, and everyone in the room automatically rose. And we were disillusioned college students—the 1940s version of the 1960s kids. The outward show of patriotism was something that I had always sneered at, but we all stood and we all tingled. So the fervor started right off the bat. It was like a disease, and we all caught it.[35]

Pearl Harbor ended debate: American involvement in the war was now a fact.

Ironically, American entrance into the war caused more rethinking among liberal pacifists than among their isolationist counterparts. Although they remained a quiet contingent, polls in 1942 showed that 20 percent of adult Americans—the same Americans who were strongly isolationist before the war—were interested in negotiating a peace with Hitler, and believed that Japan, and not Germany, was America's real enemy.* The prewar attitudes of isolationists, including anti-communism and anti-Semitism, continued to

*This feeling was not restricted to former isolationists; a poll taken on April 29, 1942, asked whether it was more important for the United States to concentrate on fighting Germany or Japan: 21 percent answered Germany, 62 percent said Japan.

influence their assessment of the war, and they did not show any regret over their earlier efforts to keep America out of the war.[36]

For partisans of the peace movement, Pearl Harbor merely provided another push in the direction of anti-fascism and away from absolute pacifism, a pattern set in motion well before the war began for America. Dramatic reversals followed in the first year of the war. The Methodist Church, the most strongly pacifist of the mainline Protestant churches in the interwar years, passed a resolution in 1940 that it would never "officially support, endorse, or participate in war." In 1942, the Methodist bishops met in Council and declared their "unreserved support for the war" and pledged themselves "to the destruction of this brutal and unwarranted aggression and to the preservation for all mankind of the sacred liberties of free people." As the war progressed, so did Methodist support for it, and in 1944 the church adopted a statement reading in part, "We are sending over a million young men from Methodist homes to participate in the conflict. God himself has a stake in the struggle and he will uphold them as they fight forces destructive of the moral life of man. In Christ's name we ask for the blessing of God upon the men in the armed forces and we pray for victory."[37]

However, much of pre-war pacifism did not become wartime fervor, but rather wartime pacifism, a breed apart from the pacifism that preceded it. In general, pacifists retreated to the higher ground of individualistic, religiously motivated pacifism. Though they continued to walk a tightrope between their opposition to fascism and their refusal to use violent means to resist it, they took the time during the war to weave a net of religious conscience to protect their precarious position. One indication of this trend can be seen in the growth of the FOR and the WRL, the two peace organizations defending absolute pacifism, throughout the war years. The FOR grew from 5,000 members in 1938 to 6,700 at the time the Selective Service Act was passed. It continued to grow steadily until it reached a membership of 15,000 at the end of the war. The WRL grew from 900 members before the war to 2,300 members afterward. Their budgets also grew accordingly.[38] The continuing development of an absolute pacifism of religion and/or conscience was also apparent in the proliferation of denominational pacifist organizations in the years just prior to and following Pearl Harbor. These included the Episcopal Pacifist Fellowship, formed in 1939, the Baptist and Unitarian Pacifist Fellowships in 1940, the Lutheran Pacifist Fellowship in 1941, and the Christian Science Fellowship in 1942.[39]

The organized peace movement continued to agitate for limited peace aims, including explicitly stated Allied peace terms, a willingness to negotiate with the Axis powers, and an end to saturation bombing.[40] But through a combination of prudence, fear of accusations of treason, and a thinly veiled preference for Allied victory, the peace movement worked inconspicuously during the war years, focusing its attention on the preservation of civil liberties at home and preparation for a more favorable peace than that which concluded World War I.[41]

The fragmentation of the interwar peace movement left many pacifists feeling more closely tied to former pacifists, now interventionists, than to the isolationists with whom they made common cause or to the average draftee responding to the felt indignity of the attack on Pearl Harbor. As Dave Dellinger writes:

> In the spirit of Gandhi, who said it is better to resist injustice violently than not at all, I felt strong bonds of sympathy with those who had come to believe that the only way to get rid of fascism was to go to war. On more than one occasion, between my first and second prison sentences, one or more of my friends and I embraced as they went off to war and I prepared to go back to prison in loyalty to my belief, also Gandhian, that the best way to resist was nonviolently. They always used to say that when they returned (if they did) and I got out of prison (if I did) we would join forces to rid this country of its own forms of blatant injustice and tyranny.[42]

The heartfelt dreams of interwar pacifists of a world dedicated to peace and justice were sadly set aside for the duration, as wartime pacifists tried to prepare themselves for the hard work of reconstruction after the madness ended. Meanwhile, they concerned themselves with maintaining a pacifist witness for conscience's sake, for posterity's sake, and this witness found its most obvious expression in conscientious objection to the draft.

SECURING CO PROVISIONS IN DRAFT LEGISLATION

Provisions for conscientious objectors in the initial draft of the 1940 Selective Service Act of 1940)Burke-Wadsworth bill were copied almost directly from World War I conscription law, and read:

> Nothing contained in this Act shall be construed to require or compel any person to be subject to training or service in a combatant capacity in the land and naval forces who is found to be a member of any well recognized sect whose creed or principles forbid its members to participate in war in any form, if the conscientious holding of such belief by such person shall be established under such regulations as the President may prescribe; but no such person shall be relieved from training or service in such capacity as the President may declare to be noncombatant.[43]

The obvious flaws in this bill created immediate concern among pacifists. However, the major work of influencing Congress toward more liberal provisions was not accomplished by the organized peace movement (although they were certainly involved) but by the historic peace churches. It was their concerns and ideals that gave the final compromise provisions their particular flavor. In order to understand the status Congress granted to COs during the war, it is necessary to gain an appreciation of what motivated the peace churches. Their experience, and perhaps more importantly, their relation to society at large was decidedly different from that of the organized peace movement.

The first and most obvious distinguishing feature was that peace church pacifists held collective memories of military conscription through many wars and in many countries. Because of this history, they had reason to believe that the government would do more or less as it pleased in relation to COs, and that pre-war devotion to peace was no guarantee that pacifists would be treated well once war came. They also knew that if the government chose to be harsh, they would suffer; if it chose to be lenient, they might suffer less. Suffering was anticipated in any event, and the role of pacifists was to endure rather than to protest. Thus when the peace churches approached the government to discuss CO provisions, they were asking favors, not demanding rights. Generally speaking, they acknowledged the government's prerogative to conscript (or at least the fact that it could and would do so) and were interested first in assuring a home for themselves in the conscription law where they would not be asked to violate their consciences.

Although there was great variation on this point, a small but significant fraction of peace church pacifists did not even oppose the war. They were saddened by it, but as members first of the kingdom of God, they did not perceive the war to be their affair. The government would do whatever it felt it must, and pacifists would have to live with the consequences. Of course, many peace church pacifists had been active, often in leadership roles, in the interwar peace movement, and shared most of the movement's liberal assumptions. These pacifists argued against conscription on principle, and tried to convince the government that their foreign policy was not only morally wrong, but also ill-advised on practical grounds. Nevertheless, through their peace church affiliation, they knew that they were committed to pacifism for the long haul and that a pacifist could not reasonably expect miracles in wartime. The best pacifists could do under the adverse conditions of war was to refuse to participate and do what they could to mitigate the suffering of war's victims.

Peace church pacifists were also heavily influenced by the legacy of World War I. While much of the interwar peace movement was composed of those who had supported World War I and lived to regret it, the peace churches were full of individuals who had been pacifists during World War I and who had paid a high price for that position. The lot of COs in World War I was a poor one. As is seen in the above provisions from the initial Burke-Wadsworth bill, only members of peace churches were to be granted CO status, and no one was to be exempted from noncombatant service. COs quite naturally came into conflict with this law. Some refused to wear the uniform, others felt noncombatant service violated their conscience, and of course many men were never granted CO status at all. The situation was complicated by the fact that CO cases were not handled by civil courts in World War I, but by court-martial. All men drafted were sent or forcibly taken to army camps, and if they there declared an unwillingness to cooperate, they were punished, or turned over to the other soldiers as an object of sport. In *The Fight for Peace,* Devere Allen describes this mistreatment:

> Men were beaten; they had their eyes gouged to the point of severe injury; they were stripped and scrubbed with brooms; they were plunged for long periods under cold showers when previously exhausted from forced useless labor; they were prodded with bayonets; they were dragged through latrines; they were chained, in solitary confinement, to the doors of their cells for nine hours a day; they were subjected to a stream of water from a firehose held directly against their faces for two hours at a time.[44]

Some COs received kinder treatment, and were given tasks around camp that did not violate their consciences, such as KP. This was at the discretion of the army officer in charge of the camp, so much depended on his attitude toward COs. When tried in court for their refusal to cooperate with military authority, sentences given to COs were severe: 17 were sentenced to death, 142 to life imprisonment, 3 to fifty years, 4 to forty years, and 57 to twenty-five years. (Most of these sentences were drastically reduced after the end of the war, and no one was executed.)[45] Once the parameters of the CO problem were better understood, the government made it a practice to furlough COs from the peace churches to farm or relief work and treatment of COs improved.

Peace church pacifists of the pre-World War II era were determined to avoid such problems from the outset in the next round of conscription. The Mennonites, Brethren, and Friends first began working together on peace issues in 1935, and in 1937 they made a statement to President Franklin D. Roosevelt about their desire for peace and their hope that in the event of war, alternative service would be arranged for their members. They stressed their patriotism and willingness to serve the state, but appealed to a higher allegiance to God which required them to refuse military service.[46] Though in retrospect their attitude toward the government seems almost servile, it should be remembered that they anticipated serious persecution in the event of war. In 1940, the FOR published a *Pacifist Handbook* which commented:

> When one thinks of what might have been done with the objectors [in World War I], the course of the government might be called lenient. But it must be remembered that the policy of conscription was still on trial, and the administration was careful not to take any action which would make it unpopular. The President and the Secretary of War wished to avoid all unnecessary brutality. In addition, the country did not suffer severely from the war. It was not invaded, its troops were in action for only a brief time, losses were comparatively small, and there were no severe reverses. The combination of favorable circumstances may never occur again in a major war, and if they do not the conscientious objector must be prepared to pay a higher price for his convictions.[47]

The *Handbook* went on to caution prospective COs about the possible consequences of refusing noncombatant service: "In the world war [I] he [the CO] would have been tried, imprisoned, might have been tortured, and might have been sentenced to death. Another war, if long protracted, may bring the concentration camp and even the firing squad."[48]

The peace churches believed that the most promising path toward a compromise with the government was to stress their willingness to do alternative service, so long as it was not military in nature. They told the Congress that it would be gaining their cooperation and their labor by agreeing to such a plan, and they told their members that alternative service would be a witness for peace and the fulfillment of Jesus' exhortation to walk the second mile in service to humanity.[49] The idea of alternative service was not new; as noted above, a makeshift arrangement in World War I allowed COs to be furloughed to farms and to a Quaker ambulance unit in France. Furthermore, in pre-revolutionary Russia, Mennonites had been allowed to fulfill their obligation to the state through forestry work rather than standard military service. In the interwar years, the Friends in particular operated voluntary work camps in the United States and Europe, and thus had a model for civilian service. Lastly, the Depression-era Civilian Conservation Corps (CCC) had given the government an opportunity to administer a work program which was non-military in nature.[50]

In spite of the peace church bias in favor of a program of alternative service, the peace churches were not naive about the many forms of pacifism in existence that did not share this bias, and they made a sincere effort to promote CO provisions that would account for this diversity. They tried to gain recognition of conscience as a general principle, proposing an alternative draft of the CO section of the conscription bill reading:

> Nothing contained in this Act shall be construed to require any person to be subject to training or service in the land or naval forces of the United States who is conscientiously opposed to participation in war in any form, nor to require any person to be subject to training or service in such forces in any capacity to which he is conscientiously opposed.[51]

Specifically, they advocated a liberal set of provisions which contained the following six points: (1) to base conscientious objection on individual belief rather than membership in a peace church; (2) to allow secular objectors to qualify as COs; (3) to grant complete exemption from the draft for those men who could not conscientiously register or cooperate with conscription in any way; (4) to have a register for COs separate from that for regular draftees; (5) to place COs under civilian rather than military control; and (6) to provide opportunity for alternative, non-military service.[52] This proposal was based on the CO provisions then in effect in Great Britain,[53] and on the desires of prospective COs from peace churches and the peace movement.

Congress, the other party in the debate over CO provisions, had a different set of concerns. Its primary goal was to mobilize manpower for the armed forces and to cultivate favorable public opinion. According to a January 1940 Gallup poll, the public thought justice for COs would be met at a much more minimal level than that proposed by the peace churches: the largest percentage in this survey, 37 percent, favored noncombatant service for COs; only 13.2 percent favored exemption from military service. Of the remainder, 24 percent wanted to force COs to fight, and 9 percent recommended that they be shot or put in jail.[54] Congress was inclined to be more lenient than this, if only to avoid the sticky problem of burdening the army with a large number of disciplinary cases. Dr. Howard K. Beale of the ACLU pointed this out in his testimony to the Senate Committee on Military Affairs in 1940: "Gentlemen, does anyone think that men fighting in violation of their consciences and in repudiation of their God as they have honestly conceived Him and believed in Him will make good soldiers? They will make wretched soldiers."[55] The head of Selective Service himself, General Lewis B. Hershey, used this argument in 1943 to oppose an amendment before Congress that would abolish all CO provisions: "It [the proposed amendment] does unload on the army the necessity of knowing what to do with some ten or twelve thousand individuals who are opposed to active participation in war."[56]

Congress was also no doubt motivated to include CO provisions on the basis of precedent: COs from the historic peace churches had long been granted some form of exemption from military service, at least from combatant status. Congress felt bound to honor the freedom of religion clause in the Constitution, and some respect for religious objection to war was believed important. Also, the lobbyists of the historic peace churches were sincerely committed to seeking compromise, and they regularly voiced their appreciation of the difficulty of Congress's task in making provisions for COs without alienating the public or risking general noncompliance with Selective Service law. Thus mollified, Congress was ready to be reasonable. Congress was further motivated to approve liberalized CO provisions because the Selective Service Act of 1940 was a peacetime draft, and not hugely popular. Liberal exemptions for COs, as well as for categories of draftees such as fathers and ministers, would help to make conscription appear non-threatening and non-invasive.

Nevertheless, Congress had to design a law that could be administered effectively, would provoke no public outcry, and that was not so full of loopholes that a large percentage of the male population would plead exemptions. Congress was especially concerned that CO provisions should be able to accurately differentiate between sincere objectors and so-called "slackers." Another fear was that communists would claim CO status, and Congress was not interested in giving exemptions to anyone whose objection was based on political views. Religious objection could be protected because it was not particularly threatening to the status quo, but apparently to disagree with the national consensus on the righteousness of U.S. foreign policy was too subversive a position to be legally sanctioned by Congress. (However, as E. Raymond Wilson, a lobbyist for the Friends, pointed out, it is curious that while communists were not to be allowed CO exemption, it was perfectly all right that these radicals be taken into the army.)[57] In order to separate out the "undesirables," Congress insisted on a requirement that pacifism must be religious in order to qualify an individual for CO status.[58] However, Congress was not determined that all COs should be members of peace churches. It seemed quite willing to grant CO status to all religiously motivated pacifists, but only worried that divining the sincerity of individual conscience would be a more difficult task administratively than basing exemptions strictly on church membership.[59]

After much haggling between the peace churches, members of the organized peace movement, and Congress, the CO provisions voted into law allowed those who "by reason of religious training and belief" were "opposed to war in any form" to either serve as noncombatants in the army or to be engaged in "work of national importance under civilian direction."[60] This represented a significant improvement over World War I legislation in that CO status was no longer tied to membership in a peace church and that alternative civilian service was made available. However, it fell far short of the goals set by the peace churches when they set out to improve CO provisions. Secular conscientious objection went unrecognized, as did absolutist objection (i.e., objection to registration and/or alternative service). The final blow, and an unexpected one, came on September 6, 1940. Greatly desiring civilian administration for COs, the peace churches had convinced the Congress to let the Department of Justice register COs and administer alternative service. Then at the last minute, the entire operation was shifted to Selective Service control. According to those present when the amendment was passed, the change was made at the request of the Department of Justice, who feared that they would be unable to handle the caseload if there were large numbers of COs.[61] As Theodore Wachs sums up in his dissertation on World War II COs, "The conclusion seems inescapable that pressures of time, political concerns, misconceptions about pacifism, and general ignorance about conscientious objection, all combined to defeat the hopes of those who testified."[62]

And so the Selective Service System was established, and within a few months, draftees were being inducted into combatant, noncombatant, and alternative service, and looking forward to their release in one year's time. Unfortunately, this was not to be. Six days after the attack on Pearl Harbor, Congress amended the Selective Service Act to allow draftees to be sent outside the Western Hemisphere and to extend their service from the time of induction until six months after the end of the war.[63]

CO PROVISIONS IN PRACTICE

Draft Boards and Conscientious Objection

Once having made the decision to seek CO classification, the first step for the draftee was to fill out Selective Service Form 47, the "Special Form for

Conscientious Objector." Form 47 asked for applicant history regarding schooling and jobs, a list of references who could comment on the applicant's convictions, and responses to several questions about the applicant's pacifist beliefs and where he acquired them. Also, and in spite of Congress's decision to base CO status on individual conscience, Form 47 requested extensive information on the applicant's church membership, church activities, and the official position of his church on participation in war. Some COs wrote lengthy essays to accompany their Form 47; others were quite terse. Within the peace churches, especially among the Mennonites, COs were sometimes given help and advice in filling out their papers by their ministers or church elders; this occasionally amounted to giving prospective COs formulaic responses to Form 47 questions that could be copied directly by the applicant.[64]

Many COs were awarded their desired status on the basis of their paperwork alone. In *Conscription of Conscience,* Sibley and Jacob estimate that there were oral hearings before the draft board only in about 25 percent of CO cases.[65] Peace church COs in particular were inclined to receive CO status simply by demonstrating that they were church members in good standing, though this varied greatly from one draft board to another.[66]

There was little consistency in the application of Selective Service law between local draft boards. Much depended on who sat on the board, how they conceived of their duty to conscript, and how much experience they had in dealing with COs. Some boards gave CO classification to practically anyone who asked for it, while others refused to give CO status to anyone, no matter how perfectly they conformed to the legal definition of conscientious objection. Draft boards had a strong incentive to give I-A-O (noncombatant) classification instead of IV-E (alternative service), because I-A-Os were counted as regular draftees toward meeting Selective Service quotas while IV-Es were not. For this reason, some draft boards tried to push I-A-O classification on everyone who applied for CO status.[67] COs could appeal the decisions of their local draft boards to the Department of Justice, in which case they were investigated by the FBI prior to an appeals decision.

Part of the difficulty the local draft boards faced was that the "religious training and belief" that Selective Service law stipulated for all legitimate conscientious objectors was a vague term, given to many different interpretations. As the American Civil Liberties Union put it at the time, "The tendency of draft boards is to interpret religious training and belief in the easy terms of church membership."[68] The official interpretation of this phrase varied throughout the war. In 1940, then Director of Selective Service Clarence Dykstra's guidance was that religious training and belief should be given a "broad sociological definition." His statement read in part, "Religious belief signifies sincere conviction as to the supreme worth of that to which one gives his supreme allegiance." This interpretation was narrowed to a supernatural theism in 1942 when General Hershey, successor to Dykstra, advised the Department of Justice hearing officers that "I must be satisfied that the objection is based on 'religious training and belief' which contemplates recognition of some source of all existence, which, whatever the type of conception, is Divine because it is the Source of all things." However, in early 1943, a judge set precedent by granting CO status to a philosophical objector, Mathias Kauten, saying that religious training and belief was broad enough to include "a response of the individual to an inward mentor, call it conscience or God, that is for many persons at the present time the equivalent of what has always been thought a religious impulse."[69] Though certainly there were those whose CO claims were denied on the basis that they were sincere but nonreligious, many COs won their classification through persistence, by appealing local board decisions repeatedly until there was little doubt about their sincerity, or at least their determination. As a rule, the Department of Justice and the regional Board of Appeals were more liberal than the local boards, and they granted CO status in more than 50 percent of the cases they examined.[70]

Noncombatancy

The greatest number of COs in World War II served as noncombatants in the military. Noncombatants were not required to carry arms or to be trained in their use, but outside of this exception, they were in all other ways regular members of the army. They wore the army uniform, received army pay and dependency allowances, and were under army discipline. Noncombatants were initially assigned to many different branches of the service, including the signal corps, engineering, the quartermaster corps, and decontamination units. This practice ceased on January 25, 1943, when the Secretary of War declared that all noncombatants would be assigned to medical units and guaranteed that they would not be transferred outside the medical service except at their own request.[71] The secretary was apparently motivated to do this for two reasons: first, so that noncombatants would not be scattered to branches of service where their status might not be recognized or respected, and second, because many COs held an ideal of service to the victims of war, and it was hoped that if medical service were guaranteed, more COs would accept noncombatant (I-A-O) status.

Many COs specifically requested noncombatant service, feeling that they could serve with the military so long as they were not required to kill. Others were denied their request for an alternative service classification (IV-E) by their draft boards, but were granted noncombatant status instead. While some appealed this decision or refused induction and ended up in prison, others chose to accept I-A-O status as a compromise position. Since noncombatants were interfiled with full service combatant soldiers (I-A), the exact number of men who were granted I-A-O status during World War II is unknown. Selective Service gives the number as twenty-five thousand; others estimate it to be closer to fifty thousand.[72] Estimates are also complicated by the fact that soldiers with I-A status who developed conscientious objections to combat after entering the military were frequently given noncombatant duty by their commanding officers without any formal change in their status.[73]

The largest number of noncombatants (12,000) were Seventh-Day Adventists. The Seventh-Day Adventist denomination advocated noncombatant service for their members from the time of the Civil War as a way of combining duty to country with a literalist interpretation of the sixth commandment, "Thou shalt not kill."[74] Anticipating the coming war, and wanting Adventist boys to be prepared, Everett Dick, an Adventist who served in World War I, founded the Medical Cadet Corps. At first the program was conducted as part of the curriculum at Seventh-Day Adventist colleges, but as the war approached, summer sections were taught for the benefit of non-students. As Everett Dick describes the program:

> The training consisted of that given to medical department soldiers, such as close order drill, organization of the army, physical training, military courtesy, camp hygiene, litter drill, and first aid. It was an orientation that would help the recruit, who would otherwise be entering the service of his country at a handicap, to fit into a place where he could serve God and his country conscientiously.[75]

The effort expended on the cadet corps was rewarded before long, and most Adventists who had received the training were placed in the medical department even before this was general practice for noncombatants.[76]

Noncombatants were by no means kept from the front lines. They faced all the dangers ordinary soldiers did, and their service was recognized in the form of military awards. Seventh-Day Adventists are especially proud of their record of service, which included at least two Legions of Merit, one Croix de Guerre, five silver stars, thirty bronze stars, twelve purple hearts, and one Congressional Medal of Honor, the highest award given a soldier, and the only one ever awarded to a conscientious objector.[77]

Civilian Public Service

The story of securing alternative civilian service from Congress did not end with the passage of the Selective Service Act. The act specified nothing about the alternative service program save that it be "work of national importance under civilian direction"; the rest was left to the discretion of the President of the United States and his duly appointed deputies. The peace churches, by now organized with representatives of other churches and peace groups as the National Service Board for Religious Objectors (NSBRO),[78] expressed an interest in administering the alternative service program, at least for their own young men. They offered to bear all the expense, and intended that those under their administration refuse to accept pay as evidence of their dedication, in effect taking compulsory service and making it voluntary. The NSBRO worked out a detailed proposal by October 22, 1940, suggesting that two types of service be made available: (1) work for governmental agencies with the government paying maintenance and wages for COs, and (2) work for private agencies, with the agencies bearing the cost and assuming responsibility for the men who chose this style of service.[79] A week later, in conjunction with Selective Service officials and the President's Advisory Committee, the NSBRO worked out a three-fold system, including (1) work financed and administered by governmental agencies, (2) work financed and supervised by governmental agencies, but with camps under church administration, and (3) camps financed and operated by the churches, with projects subject to governmental approval and inspection. This version was agreed to by the NSBRO and the then Director of Selective Service, Clarence Dykstra, on November 25, 1940.[80]

The three-fold plan was presented to President Roosevelt by Dykstra on November 29. Dykstra later reported to the NSBRO that Roosevelt expressed vehement opposition to the plan, saying that work camps were too easy for COs, and that COs should be drilled by army officers.[81] Dykstra returned to peace church representatives on December 5, and asked them if they would be willing to administer alternative service for all COs, and not just peace church members, and pay the entire cost except for transportation. He cautioned the NSBRO that if they did not accept this proposal, he would have to ask Congress for an appropriation to cover the costs of the alternative service program, and that Congress would likely insist on complete government administration. Seeing the opportunity to have some control over the program being pulled out from underneath them, the NSBRO agreed on December 10 to handle the entire program on an experimental basis for six months within the limits of their financial ability to do so.[82] Official authority for the alternative service program rested with the President. He delegated this authority to the Selective Service, who in turn delegated part of it, namely the expense and the off-duty hours supervision of the men, to the NSBRO.[83] The alternative service program became known as Civilian Public Service (CPS) and responsibility for it was split among the service agencies of the three peace churches (the American Friends Service Committee [AFSC], the Brethren Service Committee [BSC], and the Mennonite Central Committee [MCC]).[84] Each project was under the control of a single church agency, while the NSBRO handled general administrative issues of CPS and acted as liaison to the government in Washington, D.C.

Approximately twelve thousand COs served in CPS. The first projects were all work camps modeled on the Civilian Conservation Corps (CCC) of the 1930s, and generally they used CCC barracks and tools and carried on the work of the CCC. Each camp's work was supervised by a technical agency (for example, the Forest Service) who directed the project and furnished foremen to train the COs to do the work. The church's responsibility was to feed, clothe, and supervise the men in off-project hours, and to keep records for the Selective Service on such matters as furloughs and sick days. The majority of the camps engaged in forestry or soil conservation projects involving mostly manual labor such as cutting down trees, breaking and maintaining trails, and reseeding forests. The church agencies provided activities for COs after work, and tried to maintain a religious work camp atmosphere. Classes were offered on many topics, including Bible study, relief and reconstruction, and other areas in which COs expressed interest, and pacifist leaders did lecture circuits from camp to camp. Eventually, Selective Service granted permission to transfer men to camps with special educational emphases. For example, Brethren CPS had a camp designated the School of Fine Arts, another the School of Cooperative Living, and several others.[85]

Though the camps remained active throughout the war, there quickly grew up interest in work projects outside the CCC model. These detached units (or "special projects" as they were sometimes called) allowed COs to work in areas which had been depleted by wartime mobilization. COs worked as dairy testers, farm laborers, and attendants in mental hospitals. One of the most publicized jobs COs held was as human guinea pigs for scientific experiments.[86] The detached units became quite popular—by January 1944, there were more men in special projects than in the camps—but all COs inducted into CPS were required to spend ninety days in camp before they could volunteer for special projects.[87] The detached units were still officially administered by the church agencies (including a few non-peace church groups such as the Association for Catholic Conscientious Objectors), but the COs were in much closer contact with the technical agencies using their services (the doctors, farmers, and scientists for whom they worked). Detached service was a financial boon to the peace churches since they were not required to provide room and board for COs on special projects.

Early in CPS, much excitement was generated over the possibility of service abroad. Many COs were eager to work in the war zones, either in ambulance units (such as the one the Friends operated in France in World War I or the one they were operating in China during World War II) or in relief work for civilian populations suffering the effects of the war. Several detached service units trained men for this sort of service, and classes were also offered in some of the camps in areas such as first aid and nutrition. However, service abroad was forbidden to COs in January of 1943 when the Starnes rider, part of a War Department appropriation bill, stipulated that no government funds be used to send COs abroad. Though the churches were quite willing to finance the projects, the legislation was interpreted narrowly such that the time General Hershey spent signing transfer papers for COs heading overseas was government time and therefore government money.[88] The only American COs who became part of the Friends ambulance unit in China during World War II were those who had served time in prison and joined the unit after their release. All COs in alternative service were restricted to the United States and its possessions (e.g., Puerto Rico and the Virgin Islands) until the war ended.

Although the peace churches agreed to administer CPS for all COs, after a few years the government established a few camps of its own. Government camps did not pay COs wages, but they did pay all their expenses. The government camps were founded at the request of COs who did not feel comfortable with peace church administration, or else felt that the upkeep of their conscripted bodies was rightfully the government's, and not the churches', responsibility. The government stepped in not only because of demand from COs, but also because they wanted to gather all the disciplinary problem cases into a few camps. The more radical COs were transferred to government camps where time spent on work projects dwindled to nearly zero, and the climate was that of a concentration camp. The first government camp opened in June of 1943; after May 1944, new CO inductees were sent to government camps unless they specifically requested church administration.[89]

Prison

Those who helped frame the CO provisions in the draft law hoped that more liberal provisions would result in sending fewer COs to prison than in World War I. However, the number actually increased: in World War II, nine times as many COs were imprisoned, and even as a percentage of the total number of men drafted, there were two to three times as many COs in prison in World War II as compared to World War I.[90] A Selective Service monograph written soon after the war reported a total of 15,758 Selective Service delinquents (men evading the draft, but not for reasons of conscience) and 6,086 self-proclaimed conscientious objectors.[91]

COs ended up on the wrong side of the law—some COs would say the right side—in a variety of ways: Some were denied CO classification, others refused to serve in CPS or left CPS after a period of service, some never registered. The largest group of COs, about 75 percent of the total, were Jehovah's Witnesses, most of whom requested and were denied ministerial exemption, and subsequently refused their summons to join the army.[92] Several small groups of COs did not find a hospitable quarter within the draft law for idiosyncratic reasons. For example, Hopi Indians were believed to have not a religious objection but a nationalist one, and thus did not qualify as COs.[93] One small Mennonite sect would not cooperate with the Mennonite Central Committee out of fear that their young men would be corrupted if they joined CPS and came under the influence of other Mennonites not of their sect; their draft-age men refused induction into CPS and were imprisoned.[94] Only 300 men were imprisoned for refusal to register, and of these 100 were Black Muslims who said they had "already registered in Mecca."[95]

The maximum sentence allowable by law for Selective Service violation was five years and ten thousand dollars. When conscription was first passed, sentences were relatively short because peacetime military service was only a year in duration, but after the onset of the war, sentences were generally lengthened. Wartime sentences varied widely from one area of the country to another. The average sentence for Selective Service violators in Vermont for the year ending June 30, 1943, was 1.1 months, while in South Dakota it was 55.7 months; the average sentence nationwide for the entire war was 35 months. In a few areas (notably southern California) and under a few particular judges, COs were routinely released on probation and allowed to continue in their peacetime occupations.[96] In certain jurisdictions where CO cases were common, cases were tried in large batches, as many as thirty or forty at a time, with the same sentence being imposed on all violators. This was especially true with Jehovah's Witnesses, who raised no objection to being tried en masse.[97]

COs in prison were eligible for parole on the same basis as other prisoners. They also fell under the provisions of a special parole established by Presidential Order No. 8641 in January 1941, designed to get Selective Service violators out of prison and into the army. In the case of COs, men who had requested CO classification and been denied could be paroled to CPS after as little as thirty days in prison.[98] Many COs accepted parole, but problems developed over men who refused to apply for parole at all on the basis that they were not criminals and should not be treated as such, or because they were unable to promise in good faith to keep the conditions of parole (one of which was that they had to obey the law in the future—something they had no intention of doing insofar as Selective Service law was concerned).[99]

Once out of prison, having either served their full sentences or been granted parole, COs were still not safe from prosecution. While in prison, their draft boards gave them a routine IV-F (mental or physical disability) classification, but upon release, that classification could be changed to I-A, and they could be called up for military service again. If they refused induction again, as they likely would, they could be tried again for a second offense against the Selective Service Act and be returned to prison.[100] Called "cat and mouse" convictions, this double or even triple sentencing for draft refusal was not uncommon, although most COs served only a single sentence.

TREATMENT OF COs IN WARTIME

The first thing to be said about the treatment of COs during the Second World War is that it was surprisingly good. Whether because of the interwar peace movement or a tolerant mood in American society for ideological minorities, World War II COs were rarely the objects of the kind of scorn experienced by COs in World War I. Still, COs were in an awkward position *vis-à-vis* a nation at war, and their experiences varied from near adulation in certain subcultures to total shunning.

Family

Most COs recall their families being very supportive of their decision to be a CO. Some families were so strongly committed to pacifism that to be a CO was to take the path of least resistance. Peter Bartel, a Mennonite CO, said of his family that "they were all staunch believers. It was much easier for me to be a conscientious objector than not."[101]

Others felt their parents were supportive of them personally, but did not really understand their motivations for becoming a CO. A Japanese-American CO, Saburo Mizutani, experienced this sort of relationship with his parents:

> With my family I could never get my folks nor my family friends who were born in Japan, to really understand what pacifism was all about. Partially it's because I wasn't fluent in Japanese or didn't know enough words in it to really explain what pacifism is all about. But they didn't interfere with me. They said, "if that's the way you feel about it." . . . My dad frankly told me, "I don't understand what you're saying to me, but if that's what you want to do and the government allows it, I'll go along with it."[102]

A number of families were faced with the potentially difficult situation of having one son in the military and another in CPS camp or prison as a CO. Generally this worked out fine, with mutual respect maintained between all parties. One CO whose brother was in the navy said that his mother made a statement at a large Methodist convocation during a debate on conscientious objection, saying that the church should be like her family: all positions represented, and everyone still supporting and respecting each other's differences.[103] Another CO said that his brother in the marines was sympathetic to his point of view; one CO's brother went so far as to tell him, "You're doing the right thing, but I can't do it."[104]

But sometimes COs' immediate families opposed their son's decision to be a CO. This disapproval took a number of different forms. Some COs felt their family's real objection was to the negative publicity they had to endure. While these families may have felt indifferent to their son's choice to refuse participation in the war, they were deeply hurt by the attitude of their neighbors and felt ashamed, particularly if their son was imprisoned.[105] More often COs traced their parents' opposition to a pragmatic concern for their welfare: parents worried that their sons would become pariahs in their home communities, that they would have difficulty finding or keeping jobs after the war, that the stigma of being a CO would follow them the rest of their lives. They urged their sons to join the army in the hopes that with a college education they would secure a desk job and never see the fighting front of the war.[106]

Pragmatism had its flip side too: several COs mentioned that their parents, particularly their mothers, expressed relief that their sons would be safely at work on the home front, and not out in the midst of battle where they could be shot at and killed. Richard Brown's brother, who was in the navy, was stationed at Pearl Harbor when it was attacked by the Japanese and had his ship torpedoed out from under him. The family did not hear that he was safe for many days after the attack. With all this anxiety, it is no surprise that Brown's mother was glad Brown was a CO, saying, "Well, thank God, at least one of my sons isn't going to be killed."[107]

More difficult were the cases of real disagreement between COs and their families. Some COs were disowned for taking the stand they did. Others faced a deep rift between themselves and their families that was only healed many years after the war. Caleb Foote, active as an FOR staff person in the early years of the war, eventually refused induction into CPS and was sent to prison at McNeil Island. His father, a Unitarian minister, favored U.S. participation in the war, and was deeply distressed by Foote's position, especially his decision to reject alternative service knowing he would be imprisoned. Foote tells a story about his father's disapproval:

> My father had retired, and then because of the shortage of ministers during the war [World War II], he went back into the service, so to speak, and he took a church in Charlottesville, Virginia. One day my mother and father were being driven somewhere by a member of the congregation who was a colonel in the army. And on the way out, the colonel, to make conversation, asked my father, "Well, tell me about your children." And my father went through his four children. I'm the fifth. He went through his four children. And the colonel had kept track of the numbers. He said, "What about the fifth?" And my father didn't say anything at all.[108]

Church

COs experienced significant hostility from the church, a fact that tended to surprise and upset them. They may have actually been treated no worse in church than in the community in general, but it was experientially more difficult coming from the church: First, because many of the COs felt that the church was an important influence on their pacifism, and that now this great teacher was turning its back on its most dedicated pupils. Second, COs suffered more from the disapprobation of the church because it was similar to rejection from one's family. If strangers taunted COs, it was less likely to hit home than if church members did so. Third, church members were more inclined to voice their anti-CO sentiments than was the population at large, because the church, as moral authority, felt freer to discipline and correct. James Bristol, employed as a Lutheran minister at the time he chose not to cooperate with conscription by filling out his draft papers, commented: "I had much, much more unpleasantness with the church than I did with the government, even though the government put me in prison."[109]

One might assume that there were no such tensions in the peace churches where conscientious objection was the preferred position, but in fact many peace church COs said that their churches were not supportive of them during the war. One CO theorized that his Mennonite congregation had difficulty encouraging COs because there were young Mennonites in the same congregation who went into the military, and people were confused about how to respond to the situation.[110] One might also guess that those in the peace churches who had relatives in the military or supported the U.S. war effort would feel very defensive about it, and might relieve this tension by casting blame on the COs.

But not all churches discriminated against COs, and some individuals had very positive experiences with the church in wartime. Clearly in the case of the peace churches, however the local congregation may have responded to its COs, the denominations as a whole were aggressive in their support, both financial and spiritual, of COs. COs outside the peace churches were also known to receive financial support from their home congregations, and hospitality from the congregations they worshipped with while in CPS. Even where a congregation was antagonistic to COs, ministers would occasionally defend the right of conscientious objection.[111]

In his wartime article, "The Church and War," Roland Bainton suggests that while the churches had a crusading attitude toward World War I, they were far more restrained in their attitude toward World War II; that while they supported the U.S. war effort both individually and institutionally, they were not "fighting a war for Jesus" but fighting because they saw no other option.[112] Thus the churches were committed to fighting well and winning, but they were willing to be tolerant of those who did not agree with them.

Community

Most COs did not experience problems with their home communities. Either their communities were fairly tolerant or they were unaware of the individual's status as a CO. Frequently COs had left home and were not yet established in a new community, so neighborhood ties did not have a significant impact on them. Those who did experience trouble did so because of their social prominence, either as well-known individuals or as members of a conspicuously pacifist group. Gordon and Gale Nutson, two brothers from the small town of Owosso in Michigan, were, as they described it, "the fair-haired boys in business . . . the nice boys of the Methodist church." They faced a great deal of antagonism from the community, so much so that they were glad to finally sell their business and leave for CPS, just so they could get away from the social pressure. Once in CPS, Gordon received letters saying that if he ever went back to Owosso, he would be shot.[113]

Mennonites probably experienced the greatest degree of community antipathy because they formed a large enough fraction of the population in the areas where they lived so as to be quite noticeable. Mainly a rural people, the Mennonites frequently settled in communities that prided themselves on their patriotism, and where much of community life revolved around organizations such as the American Legion. The most extreme incidents involved vandalism of church property and verbal abuse. In the town of Kalona, Iowa, a group of townspeople having a bon voyage party for departing soldiers concluded their evening by throwing pipe bombs at a Mennonite leader's house and hanging two

Mennonites in effigy in the middle of town. Interestingly enough, the man who related these incidents in Kalona said that they really weren't too bad, that the Mennonites had expected worse (as had been the case in World War I).[114]

Relations with the communities surrounding CPS projects ranged from mutual admiration to barely concealed rage. Many COs spoke of good relations with those they had contact with in CPS, and attributed it mainly to their willingness to give a "good day's work."[115] But some individuals were not so easily won over. COs I interviewed reported that restaurant owners would refuse to serve them, that non-CO hospital workers destroyed their property, and mostly, that they were subject to verbal abuse from townspeople who were not eager to have a camp full of "slackers and cowards" right next door. Duane Windemiller, who was working in a CPS hospital unit in New Hampshire during the war, recalls a time when he was standing on a street corner in town when a couple of men saw him, and one said to the other, "You know what they ought to do with these COs? They ought to grind them up and take them out to Kansas and spread them on the wheatfields where they'd do some good."[116]

COs faced some of their most difficult moments in one-on-one situations with civilians, most often while hitchhiking. Several COs mentioned hitchhiking incidents where they were unceremoniously turned out of a driver's car when they confessed to being COs, but there were also numerous stories of drivers who reacted with interest and toleration. Howard Ten Brink remarked that, "of all the people I met, there probably wasn't more than one percent who had a negative reaction."[117] Gale Nutson tells a memorable story of one of Ten Brink's hitchhiking experiences:

> He was hitchhiking, I think to Lansing or some place, and this man picked him up, and he said, "How come you're not in the service?" And of course Howard wanted the ride very badly, but he said, "Well, I'm a war objector." And then this fella started to challenge him, "Well how in the world did you ever get to think that way?" And he was very critical. And so Howard said right off, "Well, I don't believe in killing a man unless you're gonna eat him." It stopped him cold. The man didn't know what to say. And after that the man became very civil, and the man says, "No, no, seriously now, tell me about it." And it developed into a nice conversation. And the man even went way out of his way across the city of Lansing to let Howard out on his street. When he picked him up, he was so angry; but this remark disarmed him.[118]

There were some organized efforts to discriminate against COs during World War II, conducted mostly at the behest of the American Legion. Just after the Selective Service Act was passed in 1940, Representative J. Thorkelson from Montana introduced a bill to the House legislating that COs remain ineligible for public office and not be allowed to vote (apparently for the rest of their lives), and that a list of COs be open for public inspection and sent out for free distribution every month. Then in 1943, Senator Elmer Thomas of Oklahoma introduced a bill to remove all CO provisions from the Selective Service

Act.[119] Neither of these bills received serious attention. Some American Legion posts forced the cancellation of CPS units in state mental hospitals, although other posts were quite accommodating, in one case even agreeing to a CPS unit in a veteran's hospital.[120]

Generally, the public was quite tolerant of COs in World War II. Leo Crespi, a Princeton psychologist, did a series of public opinion surveys late in the war, trying to determine if the public approved of CO provisions and to what extent they would discriminate against COs because of their views. Although Crespi found widespread disapproval of COs, he also found that most people were willing to deal with COs as individuals and were supportive of continued draft law provisions for COs.[121]

In some ways this toleration is understandable in light of its historic setting. World War II was a good war (if such can exist) for the United States, both for the government and the people. There was relatively little domestic disagreement over the need to fight World War II (as there had been in World War I), so the existence of COs did not threaten the government's task of keeping the population mobilized and unified. Meanwhile, the economy was booming. Unemployment dropped to new lows, as eleven million Americans entered the armed forces and twenty million worked in war production jobs.[122] Even on the war front, America was not doing badly. At the height of the conflict, American battle deaths were only three times the American automobile fatalities for the same period, and the United States suffered far fewer casualties than any other major participant in the war. In fact, in January 1944, the federal government announced that there were more American injuries in war production factories than on the battlefield.[123] Furthermore, while the United States was taking relatively light punishment, it was giving itself most of the credit for winning the war.[124] Thus America did not need scapegoats, and could afford to endure COs as an interesting anomaly.

Nevertheless, COs were constantly aware of their minority status, and for some, it was painful. Sigmund Cohn expressed this by saying, "It was difficult in this sense, that you were so isolated. You know, here was this tremendous war effort going on, and you were saying no to the whole damn thing. And I think in that sense, having gotten the status you wanted, you still felt kind of out of it. You were a very tiny minority."[125] Others were more accustomed to marginal social status, and less disturbed by it; Al Herbst, a Brethren CO, remarked, "I guess being in an unpopular position has never bothered me that much. In the community where I grew up, Brethren were looked upon as very, very strange. They did lots of strange things, like washing people's feet, and they wore funny clothes . . . so I don't remember *not* being a minority."[126]

The Military

A surprise for most COs was the treatment they received at the hands of the military, which was usually quite reasonable. Some COs even encountered soldiers who were apologetic about not being COs themselves. A Mennonite CO, Sam Guhr, recalls meeting a lieutenant on a train who shook his hand, and said he was proud of him and that there ought to be more COs. After a long discussion on the subject, Guhr said the lieutenant "admitted that he was doing wrong."[127] Another CO was in the habit of picking up soldiers hitchhiking from a nearby army camp into town, and he says that when he told them he was a CO, "they'd always blush and they'd say something about, 'Gee, I haven't read the Bible lately.' I couldn't care less, you know, but they were embarrassed, not me. That was the amusing part."[128]

A response frequently given to COs by soldiers was, as CO Wally Nelson remembers it, "That's why I went in, to fight for our freedom to not fight if we wanted to." Some COs appreciated this sentiment; others, predictably, did not. Again, Wally Nelson responds, "I'm sorry, you weren't fighting for that. I don't want to disillusion you, but you already been disillusioned, because you weren't fighting exactly for that."[129] Some COs could scarcely help but be appreciative; Duane Windemiller relates this story:

> The American Legion . . . they'd get a little under their belt, and more than once, came toward the [CPS] camp. They were going to eradicate us, didn't think we ought to be there. And we'd retire to the chapel. And they never did come all the way. I don't know, prayer must have done some good. And one time when the COs went in to attend the Christmas festivities in town, there was a kind of a Christmas tree celebration at the end of it. And there were some of these guys, and they got a little too much to drink, and they started across the circle. I can't remember what they said, but it was kind of violent. And a soldier stepped out, and he was in uniform. He said, "Before you touch them, you gotta walk over me." He just came back from Australia. He said, "We're fighting so that we can be free. This is not freedom if you're gonna come and . . ." He saved our necks, I think.[130]

Part of this kindness on the part of the military stemmed not from ideological principle, but from a certain *esprit de corps* among the young men who had been drafted to do the dirty work of the war. One CO recalls being welcomed into a USO reception by a group of servicemen who said, "You're one of us, you're drafted too."[131] Richard Brown theorized that being in the midst of a war had a humanizing effect on soldiers, such that they tended to be less critical of someone's choice to be a CO:

> A lot of people in town were violently patriotic. Especially if they had never been in a war themselves. And sometimes women, I think, elderly women, were extremely patriotic in that respect. People who'd been shot at, you know, and who'd been in a war and seen all of the things that can happen in a war, tend to be much more moderate in their condemnations.[132]

This then was the environment in which World War II conscientious objection developed and existed. Who became COs, what inspired and motivated them, and what they experienced in the army, alternative service, and prison will be the subject of the next chapter.

NOTES

1. E. Raymond Wilson, "Evolution of the CO Provisions in the 1940 Conscription Bill," *Quaker History* 64 (Spring 1975): 4; Theodore Rickard Wachs, "Conscription, Conscientious Objection, and the Context of American Pacifism, 1940–45" (Ph.D. dissertation, University of Illinois, Champaign-Urbana, 1976), 28.

2. Patricia F. McNeal, "Catholic Conscientious Objection during World War II," *Catholic Historical Review* 61 (April 1975): 226. McNeal reports that the Selective Service Act itself was extended in this vote (and not just the length of service), and that the vote was 293 to 292. James Bristol, who was active in lobbying against Selective Service legislation in the early 1940s tells me that these numbers are in error and that the vote was on extending the length of service (and not on continuing conscription), but that it did pass by a margin of one (James Bristol, letter to author, 31 July 1989).

3. Daniel Webster, speech before the House of Representatives, 9 December 1814; quoted in Harry A. Wallenberg, Jr., *Whither Freedom?: A Study of the Treatment of Conscientious Objectors in the United States during World Wars I and II and Its Relation to the Concept of Freedom* (New York: Fellowship of Reconciliation, 1954), 13.

4. James Barnet Fry, *New York and the Conscription of 1863* (New York: G.P. Putnam's, 1885); Fred Albert Shannon, *The Organization and Administration of the Union Army, 1861–1865*, vol. 2 (Cleveland: Arthur H. Clark Company, 1928), 103–171; James Ford Rhodes, *History of the Civil War, 1861–1865* (New York: Macmillan, 1917), 287–90.

5. Lawrence S. Wittner, *Rebels Against War: The American Peace Movement, 1933–1983* (Philadelphia: Temple University Press, 1984), 3.

6. Fred L. Convers, interview with author, 2 October 1986, Berkeley, California; Sigmund S. Cohn, interview with author, 30 September 1986, Berkeley, California; James Bristol, interview with author, 27 May 1987, Philadelphia, Pennsylvania. The role of munitions makers in arming belligerents and promoting World War I was exposed in George Seldes, *Iron, Blood and Profits: An Exposure of the World-Wide Munitions Racket* (New York: Harper and Bros., 1934), and Helmuth C. Englebrecht and F. C. Hanighen, *Merchants of Death: A Study of the International Armament Industry* (New York: Dodd, Mead & Co., 1934).

7. Anonymous World War II conscientious objector, interview with author, 7 September 1986.

8. James Bristol, interview with author, 27 May 1987, Philadelphia, Pennsylvania.

9. Wittner, *Rebels Against War,* 1.

10. U.S. Director of Selective Service, *Selective Service in Peacetime,* Semiannual Report, vol. 1 (Washington D.C.: Government Printing Office, 1942), 187.

11. Wittner, *Rebels Against War,* 5.

12. Charles Clayton Morrison, "The Church in Wartime," *The Christian Century* 56 (December 1939): 1535.

13. The rationale behind Mennonite reluctance to be associated with liberal pacifists is given in the wartime book, Guy Hershberger, *War, Peace, and Nonresistance* (Scottdale, PA: Herald Press, 1953 [1944]).

14. Ruth Freeman, *Quakers and Peace* (Ithaca, NY: Pacifist Research Bureau, 1947), 48.

15. Roland H. Bainton, "The Church and War," *Social Action* 11 (January 1945): 40.

16. Glen Zeitzer, "The American Peace Movement During World War II" (Ph.D. dissertation, Bryn Mawr, 1978), 9–11.

17. Peter Brock, *Twentieth-Century Pacifism* (New York: Van Nostrand Reinhold Company, 1970), 126.

18. Ralph S. Brax, "When Students First Organized Against War," *New York Historical Society Quarterly* 63 (July 1979): 246–47; Charles Chatfield, *For Peace and Justice: Pacifism in America, 1914–1941* (Boston: Beacon Press, 1973 [1971]), 260.

19. Wittner, *Rebels Against War,* 6.

20. Chatfield, *For Peace and Justice,* 259–60.

21. Ibid., 260.

22. Ibid.

23. Wittner, *Rebels Against War,* 8.

24. Ibid.

25. Norman Thomas, "Norman Thomas Replies," *Fellowship,* 3 (February 1937): 13, quoted in Wittner, *Rebels Against War,* 20, and Chatfield, *For Peace and Justice,* 243. For further elaboration of the Socialist Party's reaction to the Spanish Civil War, see Chatfield, *For Peace and Justice,* 241–45.

26. The classic argument in favor of radicals subverting the army from within is given by Dwight Macdonald in *Politics,* a radical wartime journal he edited, and which was very influential among radical pacifists; see Wittner, *Rebels Against War,* 94.

27. For details on the communist reversal, see Gordon C. Zahn, "Peace Witness in World War II," *Worldview* 18 (February 1975): 50; Chatfield, *For Peace and Justice,* 320; and Wittner, *Rebels Against War,* 23–24.

28. Dave Dellinger, "Introduction," in *Against the Tide: Pacifist Resistance in the Second World War, an Oral History,* Deena Hurwitz and Craig Simpson, eds. (New York: War Resisters League, 1984).

29. Chatfield, *For Peace and Justice,* 252–53, 286.

30. Ibid., 312; a number of Reinhold Niebuhr's anti-pacifist essays were collected in a volume titled *Christianity and Power Politics* (New York: Archon Books, 1969 [originally 1940]).

31. Wittner, *Rebels Against War,* 15.

32. Wachs, "Conscription and American Pacifism," 138.

33. John Haynes Holmes, answer to editor's question "If America is drawn into the war, can you as a Christian, participate in it or support it?" *The Christian Century* 57 (December 1940): 1546.

34. Wachs, "Conscription and American Pacifism," 42; Wittner, *Rebels Against War,* 33, 52–53.

35. Mark Jonathan Harris, Franklin D. Mitchell, and Steven J. Schechter, *The Homefront: America During World War II* (New York: G.P. Putnam's Sons, 1984), 27.

36. Richard W. Steele, "American Popular Opinion and the War Against Germany: The Issue of Negotiated Peace, 1942," *Journal of American History* 65 (December 1978): 705–06.

37. Emerson Keith Ewing, "The Pacifist Movement in the Methodist Church During World War II: A Study of Civilian Public Service Men in a Nonpacifist Church" (M.A. thesis, Florida Atlantic University, 1982), 28, 34; Zahn, "Peace Witness in World War II," 50.

38. Glen Zeitzer, "The FOR on the Eve of World War II: A Peace Organization Prepares," *Peace and Change* 3 (Summer-Fall 1975): 46; Chatfield, *For Peace and Justice,* 327–28.

39. Chatfield, *For Peace and Justice,* 302.

40. Charles DeBenedetti, *The Peace Reform in American History* (Bloomington, IN: Indiana University Press, 1980), 138.

41. Zeitzer, "The American Peace Movement During World War II," 155; for contemporary examples of this, see Jessie Wallace Hughan, *Three Decades of War Resistance* (New York: War Resisters League, 1942), 24, and Richard Gregg, *A Pacifist Program in Time of War, Threatened War, or Fascism,* Pendle Hill pamphlet no. 5 (Wallingford, PA: Pendle Hill, 1939), 31–32.

42. Dellinger, "Introduction," in *Against the Tide,* Hurwitz and Simpson, eds.

43. Burke-Wadsworth bill, quoted in Wilson, "Evolution of CO Provisions," 5.

44. Devere Allen, *The Fight for Peace* (New York: Macmillan, 1930), 597, quoted in Fellowship of Reconciliation, Peace Section, American Friends Service Committee, Brethren Board of Christian Education, Friends Book Committee, General Conference Commission on World Peace, Methodist Church, The Mennonite Peace Society, War Resisters League, and Women's International League for Peace and Freedom, *Pacifist Handbook: Questions and Answers Concerning the Pacifist in Wartime, Prepared as a Basis for Study and Discussion* (Nyack, NY: Fellowship of Reconciliation, 1940), 15.

45. Mulford Q. Sibley and Philip E. Jacob, *Conscription of Conscience: The American State and the Conscientious Objector, 1940–1947* (Ithaca, NY: Cornell University Press, 1952), 14.

46. Wachs, "Conscription and American Pacifism," 48–49.

47. Fellowship of Reconciliation, et al., *Pacifist Handbook,* 15–16.

48. Ibid., 33.

49. The pre-war conception of alternative service within the peace churches can be found in Guy Hershberger, "The Christian's Relation to the State in Time of War: Is Alternative Service Desirable or Possible?" *Mennonite Quarterly Review* 9 (January 1935): 30–31, and Leslie Eisan, *Pathways of Peace: A History of the Civilian Public Service Program Administered by the Brethren Service Committee* (Elgin, IL: Brethren Publishing House, 1948), 38–39. Two pamphlets printed immediately after alternative service arrangements were made and designed to inspire young men in the peace churches to see alternative service as an opportunity to witness for peace are Thomas E. Jones, *Creative Pioneering* (Philadelphia: American Friends Service Committee, 1941), and Paul H. Bowman, *Creative Citizenship* (Elgin, IL: Brethren Service Committee, 1940).

50. Sibley and Jacob, *Conscription of Conscience,* 112–15.

51. Wilson, "Evolution of CO Provisions," 6.

52. Ibid., 4; Wachs, "Conscription and American Pacifism," 63–65.

53. For more detailed accounts of CO provisions in Great Britain during World War II, see Wachs, "Conscription and American Pacifism," 53; Brock, *Twentieth-Century Pacifism,* 155–67; and Sibley and Jacob, *Conscription of Conscience,* 2–7.

54. George Q. Flynn, "Lewis Hershey and the Conscientious Objector: The World War II Experience," *Military Affairs* 47 (February 1983): 1.

55. National Service Board for Religious Objectors (NSBRO), *Congress Looks at the Conscientious Objector* (Washington D.C.: National Service Board for Religious Objectors, 1943), 85. This work includes transcripts of all congressional discussions of conscientious objection in light of the 1940 Selective Service Act up until the time of publication.

56. Ibid., 55.

57. Wilson, "Evolution of CO Provisions," 7.

58. Julien Cornell, *Conscientious Objection and the Law* (New York: John Day, 1943), 12; Wachs, "Conscription and American Pacifism," 54.

59. U.S. Director of Selective Service, *Selective Service in Peacetime,* 193.

60. U.S. Selective Service System, *Conscientious Objection,* Special Monograph no. 11, vol. 1 (Washington D.C.: Government Printing Office, 1950), 86–87.

61. Wachs, "Conscription and American Pacifism," 68–69; Wilson, "Evolution of CO Provisions," 10.

62. Wachs, "Conscription and American Pacifism," 57.

63. McNeal, "Catholic Conscientious Objection," 226.

64. David Jones, interview for "Schowalter Oral History Collection—World War II Conscientious Objectors," Keith Sprunger and James Juhnke, coordinators, 122 cassette tapes, Mennonite Library and Archives, North Newton, Kansas (hereafter abbreviated as SOH interview); Roy Mast, self-interview answering author's questions, May 1987; Gordon C. Zahn, "A Descriptive Study of the Sociological Backgrounds of Conscientious Objectors in Civilian Public Service During World War II" (Ph.D. dissertation, Catholic University of America, 1953), 117, 121.

65. Sibley and Jacob, *Conscription of Conscience,* 60.

66. Dwight Hanawalt, interview with author, 10 September 1986, La Verne, California; Gilbert Grover, interview with author, 24 September 1986, Modesto, California; Seth Gifford, interview with author, 30 April 1987, Providence, Rhode Island; Russell Jarboe, interview with author, 25 February 1987, La Verne, California; Peter Bartel, SOH interview; Albert Herbst, interview with author, 6 September 1986, La Verne, California; Fred Barnes, telephone interview with author, 13 May 1987.

67. Howard Bogen, interview with author, 9 September 1986, Pasadena, California; Gordon W. Nutson, interview with author, 25 September 1986, Modesto, California.

68. American Civil Liberties Union (ACLU), *Conscience and War* (New York: American Civil Liberties Union, 1943), 18.

69. Mulford Q. Sibley and Ada Wardlaw, *Conscientious Objectors in Prison, 1940–45* (Philadelphia: Pacifist Research Bureau, 1945), 2–3; ACLU, *Conscience and War,* 20.

70. Sibley and Jacob, *Conscription of Conscience,* 76; Gerald Rubin, interview with author, 2 October 1986, Corte Madera, California; Robert Cary, interview with

author, 1 October 1986, San Francisco, California; Arthur Bryant, self-interview answering author's questions, May 1987; Robert Vogel, interview with author, 15 September 1986, Pasadena, California; Gordon Zahn, interview with author, 29 April 1987, Charlestown, Massachusetts.

71. ACLU, *Conscience and War*, 9.

72. Sibley and Jacob, *Conscription of Conscience*, 83.

73. Ibid., 104; Brock, *Twentieth-Century Pacifism*, 177–79.

74. Ibid., 86; the history of the Seventh-Day Adventist position on noncombatancy is given in Roger Guinon Davis, "Conscientious Cooperators: The Seventh-Day Adventists and Military Service, 1860–1945" (Ph.D. dissertation, George Washington University, 1970).

75. Everett N. Dick, "The Adventist Medical Cadet Corps as Seen by its Founder," *Adventist Heritage* 1 (July 1974): 19.

76. Ibid., 24.

77. Davis, "Conscientious Cooperators," 217. Tate Zytkoskee, a CO who is very active in the Seventh-Day Adventist denomination, tells me that there were considerably more service awards given to Adventist noncombatants than those reported by Davis, but that precise numbers are not available (Tate Zytkoskee, telephone conversation with author, 21 October 1988).

78. Wachs, "Conscription and American Pacifism," 101. In 1944, the groups affiliated with the NSBRO included Assemblies of God, American Baptist Home Mission Society, Association of Catholic Conscientious Objectors, Christadelphian Central Committee, Christadelphian Service Committee, Church of God—Indiana, Church of God—Seventh Day, Brethren Service Committee, Congregational Christian Committee for Conscientious Objectors, Disciples of Christ Department of Social Welfare, Dunkard Brethren Church, Dutch Reformed Church, Episcopal Pacifist Fellowship, Evangelical Church Board of Christian Social Action, Evangelical and Reformed Church Commission on Christian Social Action, Evangelical Mission Covenant, Federal Council Churches of Christ in America, Fellowship of Reconciliation, First Divine Association in America, Inc., American Friends Service Committee, Central Conference of American Rabbis, Jewish Peace Fellowship, Rabbinical Assembly of America, Augustana Lutheran Fellowship of Reconciliation, Lutheran Peace Fellowship, Megiddo Mission, Methodist Commission on World Peace, Mennonite Central Committee, Molokan Advisory Board, Pacifist Principle Fellowship, Pentecostal Church, Inc., Committee on Presbyterians in CPS, Seventh-Day Adventists Committee on National Service and Medical Cadet Training, Unitarian Pacifist Fellowship, United Brethren, Women's International League for Peace and Freedom, and Young Men's Christian Association (listed in Eisan, *Pathways of Peace*, 392–393). In its early years, the executive committee included representatives for the Quakers, Brethren, and Mennonites, as well as the FOR and WRL.

79. Philip Jacob, *The Origins of CPS* (Washington D.C.: NSBRO, n.d.).

80. Ibid., 6–7; Wachs, "Conscription and American Pacifism," 104–106.

81. Ibid., 7; Wachs, "Conscription and American Pacifism," 109–111.

82. Ibid., 7; Wachs, "Conscription and American Pacifism," 115.

83. Eisan, *Pathways of Peace*, 363.

84. The service committees themselves were cooperative efforts among many different branches of the Friends, Brethren, and Mennonites. For example, the

Brethren Service Committee represented the Church of the Brethren, Brethren Church, German Baptist (Old Order) Brethren, Dunkard Brethren, etc.; the Mennonite Central Committee was supported by such diverse groups as the Old Mennonites, Amish Mennonites, General Conference Mennonites, Old Order Amish, Mennonite Brethren, Brethren in Christ, Conservative Amish, and Church of God in Christ Mennonites (Holdeman). For further information, see, for example, Melvin Gingerich, *Service for Peace* (Akron, PA: Mennonite Central Committee, 1949), 476, 478 (appendices 21 and 23).

85. Eisan, *Pathways of Peace,* 120–22.

86. Ibid., 235–38. For additional information on special projects, see Clarence E. Pickett, *For More Than Bread: An Autobiographical Account of 22 Years' Work with the AFSC* (Boston: Little, Brown and Co., 1953), 328; Sibley and Jacob, *Conscription of Conscience,* 132–49; Gingerich, *Service for Peace,* 177–275.

87. Eisan, *Pathways of Peace,* 188, 195.

88. Wilson, "Evolution of CO Provisions," 14.

89. Eisan, *Pathways of Peace,* 379.

90. Sibley and Jacob, *Conscription of Conscience,* 332.

91. U.S. Selective Service, *Conscientious Objection,* 23–24.

92. Pickett, *For More Than Bread,* 334.

93. American Civil Liberties Union—National Committee on Conscientious Objectors, 1940–1947, Document Group 22, Swarthmore College Peace Collection, Swarthmore, Pennsylvania.

94. Gingerich, *Service for Peace,* 389.

95. Sibley and Jacob, *Conscription of Conscience,* 334.

96. ACLU, *Conscience and War,* 35; Stephen M. Kohn, *Jailed for Peace: The History of American Draft Law Violators, 1658–1985* (Westport, CT: Greenwood Press, 1986), 52; Sibley and Wardlaw, *COs in Prison,* 8.

97. Sibley and Wardlaw, *COs in Prison,* 8.

98. ACLU, *Conscience and War,* 36.

99. Sibley and Wardlaw, *COs in Prison,* 11.

100. Ibid., 63.

101. Peter Bartel, SOH interview. See also Gordon Kaufman, interview with author, 29 April 1987, Cambridge, Massachusetts.

102. Saburo Mizutani, interview with author, 29 September 1986, Sacramento, California. See also George Fischer, interview with author, 22 April 1987, Danvers, Massachusetts.

103. Frank Wright, SOH interview.

104. Malcolm Parker, telephone interview with author, 28 February 1987; James Lowerre, interview with author, 3 March 1987, Orange, California.

105. Howard Ten Brink, interview with author, 24 September 1986, Modesto, California; Fred Barnes, telephone interview with author, 13 May 1987; J. Lloyd Spaulding, SOH interview.

106. Robert Vogel, interview with author, 15 September 1986, Pasadena, California; Rudy Potochnik, interview with author, 26 September 1986, Modesto, California; Ralph DiGia, quoted in *Against the Tide,* Hurwitz and Simpson, eds.

107. Richard Brown, interview with author, 2 October 1986, Berkeley, California. See also Howard Bogen, interview with author, 9 September 1986, Pasadena, California.

108. Caleb Foote, telephone interview with author, 28 February 1987. For similar difficulties with extended family members, see Lawrence Templin, SOH interview; Robert Cary, interview with author, 1 October 1986, San Francisco, California. For difficulties with in-laws, see Henry Blocher, interview with author, 10 September 1986, La Verne, California; Howard Bogen, interview with author, 9 September 1986, Pasadena, California; James Lowerre, interview with author, 3 March 1987, Orange, California.

109. James Bristol, interview with author, 27 May 1987, Philadelphia, Pennsylvania. See also George Fischer, interview with author, 22 April 1987, Danvers, Massachusetts.

110. Eugene Carper, interview with author, 10 September 1986, La Verne, California.

111. See, for example, Hobart Mitchell, *We Would Not Kill* (Richmond, IN: Friends United Press, 1983), 77; James Lowerre, interview with author, 3 March 1987, Orange, California.

112. Bainton, "The Church and War," 40–68. For a confirmation of this argument, see Harmon Wilkinson, interview with author, 23 February 1987, Whittier, California.

113. Gordon W. Nutson, interview with author, 25 September 1986, Modesto, California; Gale O. Nutson, interview with author, 27 September 1986, Modesto, California.

114. J. John J. Miller, SOH interview. See also Varden Loganbill, SOH interview; Gordon Kaufman, interview with author, 29 April 1987, Cambridge, Massachusetts; Marvin Hein, SOH interview; Roy Mast, self-interview answering author's questions, May 1987.

115. Herbert Hogan, interview with author, 11 September 1986, La Verne, California. See also Robert Cary, interview with author, 1 October 1986, San Francisco, California; Russell Jarboe, interview with author, 25 February 1987, La Verne, California; Aretas Boone, interview with author, 24 September 1986, Modesto, California; Carl Paulson, interview with author, 23 April 1987, Upton, Massachusetts.

116. Duane Windemiller, interview with author, 22 April 1987, Hampton Beach, New Hampshire. See also Bill Colburn, interview with author, 5 May 1987, Concord, New Hampshire; Samuel Liskey, interview with author, 11 September 1986, Ontario, California; Paul Ashby, interview with author, 30 September 1986, San Francisco, California; Harris et al., *The Homefront,* 88, 90.

117. Howard Ten Brink, interview with author, 24 September 1986, Modesto, California.

118. Gale O. Nutson, interview with author, 27 September 1986, Modesto, California.

119. NSBRO, *Congress Looks at the CO,* 32, 55.

120. Mitchell, *We Would Not Kill,* xii.

121. Leo P. Crespi, "Public Opinion Toward Conscientious Objectors: III. Intensity of Social Rejection in Stereotype and Attitude," *Journal of Psychology* 19 (April 1945), 274; Leo P. Crespi, "Public Opinion Toward Conscientious Objectors: II. Measurement of National Approval-Disapproval," *Journal of Psychology* 19 (April 1945), 248; Leo P. Crespi, "Attitudes Toward Conscientious Objectors and Some of Their Psychological Correlates," *Journal of Psychology* 18 (July 1944): 115.

122. Wittner, *Rebels Against War,* 110. For an account of the effects of the booming economy on an individual civilian, see Harris et al., *The Homefront,* 151.

123. Wittner, *Rebels Against War,* 110; Harris et al., *The Homefront,* 143.

124. Wittner, *Rebels Against War,* 103.

125. Sigmund Cohn, interview with author, 30 September 1986, Berkeley, California.

126. Albert Herbst, interview with author, 6 September 1986, La Verne, California. Several COs mentioned that the experience of being a CO in wartime sensitized them to the plight of other minorities, particularly blacks, who did not have the same luxury COs did of "passing" when they were in strange territory. See Harmon Wilkinson, interview with author, 23 February 1987, Whittier, California; Dwight Hanawalt, interview with author, 10 September 1986, La Verne, California; Gale O. Nutson, interview with author, 27 September 1986, Modesto, California.

127. Samuel Guhr, SOH interview.

128. Anonymous World War II conscientious objector, interview with author, 21 February 1987.

129. Wallace Nelson, interview by Deena Hurwitz for *Against the Tide,* privately held. See also Delmar Stahly, SOH interview. For a positive interpretation of this sentiment, see Hubert Brubaker, interview with author, 25 September 1986, Modesto, California.

130. Duane Windemiller, interview with author, 22 April 1987, Hampton Beach, New Hampshire.

131. Loris Habegger, SOH interview.

132. Richard Brown, interview with author, 2 October 1986, Berkeley, California.

3

The Conscientious Objector Population

Once Congress and the peace churches had negotiated a set of CO provisions, they had only to wait and see who would come out from among those drafted to request CO status. Certain populations were expected to surface, especially members of the peace churches and the Seventh-Day Adventists (who had already been in communication with the government regarding noncombatant provisions). But many others claimed conscientious objection as well, and the total group of World War II COs was nearly as diverse as the group of men who were inducted into the army.

The total number of men who were COs in World War II (by the definition of this study) is approximately forty-three thousand (twenty-five thousand noncombatants, twelve thousand in Civilian Public Service [CPS], and six thousand in prison). This number is not precise, owing not only to the previously mentioned difficulty in estimating the number of noncombatants, but also because there is some overlap between categories (e.g., a man who left CPS to be a noncombatant in the army is counted twice). It is also not a fair estimate of the strength of pacifism in wartime America. Not only are women and older men excluded, but draft-age pacifists who had other deferments (work, farm, health, or ministerial exemptions) are not included in these numbers. Selective Service estimates that twenty thousand COs were never classified as such because of other deferments; the National Service Board for Religious Objectors (NSBRO) puts this number somewhat higher, suggesting a total of one hundred thousand COs among draft-age males, including those who were inducted into some form of service, those in prison, and those with deferments.[1]

The number of COs in World War II is quite small as a percentage of the total number of men drafted: about one-tenth of 1 percent. There were slightly more men granted IV-E classifications in the first round of conscription in early 1941 than by the second round in June 1941. The percentage of men with IV-E classification stayed quite stable through the early phase of the war, with the exception of a brief drop right after Pearl Harbor.[2] Though COs were a tiny minority in World War II, their ranks swelled to eight or nine times those of COs in World War I. Even accounting for the greater number of men drafted in World War II, there were three to four times as many COs in World War II as in World War I.[3]

Conscientious objection in World War II was, at least to judge by statistics, a religious phenomenon. As many as 93 percent of COs claimed a religious affiliation.[4] There is no way of knowing for certain how many of these COs were truly religious objectors, since anyone who wanted CO status had a strong incentive to describe their objection in the religious terms that draft boards were prepared to legitimate.[5] Nevertheless, the majority of COs were at least exposed to organized religion before making their decision to object. As mentioned earlier, half of the noncombatants were Seventh-Day Adventists, and three-quarters of those imprisoned were Jehovah's Witnesses; 60 percent of the COs who served in CPS were affiliated with the three historic peace churches.[6] An idea of the breadth of CO religious affiliations can be seen in the *Directory of Civilian Public Service,* which lists 230 denominational affiliations for CPS men, ranging from the peace churches to the mainline Protestant and Orthodox churches, to a multitude of tiny sects (such as the Emmissaries of Divine Light and the Overcoming Faith Tabernacle). Most affiliations listed were Jewish or Christian, but a smattering of COs came from Asian or New Thought religious groups, and gave their affiliations as Hindu, Buddhist, Zoroastrian, Taoist, Rosicrucian, and Theosophist.[7]

The peace churches provided most of the COs to CPS, but many, and sometimes most, of their draft-age young men did not claim CO status, accepting full military service instead. In his dissertation on the Church of the Brethren in World War II, Lorell Weiss compared the degree of conscientious objection in the historic peace churches with that of a few mainline Protestant denominations. Taking COs as a percentage of total church members age thirteen and older (the latter constraint serving to ensure some uniformity between denominations since some churches practiced believer's baptism and did not count unbaptized children as members), Weiss found that the figure for Mennonites was roughly 42 percent, for the Friends, 10 percent, and for the Brethren, 8 percent. Though these figures indicate that at least for the Brethren and Friends, many draft-age members were accepting military service, the percentage of their young men who were COs far exceeds the next highest denominations, the Congregational Christians and the Methodists, whose percentage of COs were 0.2 percent and 0.1 percent respectively.[8]

While religious objection to all war predominated in World War II, it was not the only pattern of conscientious objection. Most closely aligned to the religious objectors were men who objected to all war, but for philosophical, political, or humanitarian reasons that were not religious in the usual sense of the word. There were also socialist objectors who were not opposed to all war, but who continued to maintain that the war against Germany and Japan was an imperialist war that could not serve the interests of the working class. Many other types of selective objectors inhabited the margins of the CO population, sometimes being granted CO classification by more liberal draft boards, other times prosecuted as Selective Service violators whom no one—even themselves—considered to be conscientious objectors. These included black men who refused to serve in a jim crow army,[9] Japanese-Americans who had no inclination to join the U.S. military after being kept in concentration camps for the first several years of the war, and Native Americans and Puerto Ricans who felt nationalistic ties to groups other than the United States government.[10]

A final category of objectors were the true fifth columnists, men who supported Nazism and hoped for its victory, or at least hoped that Germany would take communist Russia with it when it was defeated. There may have been a significant proportion of Americans holding such views, but during wartime (and since) they were very quiet. One exception was Father Charles E. Coughlin, a Catholic priest who was outspokenly anti-Semitic and anti-communist in his radio broadcasts from Detroit. Some of his followers found their way into CPS camps where they were the most marginal of all COs, objecting neither to war in principle nor to World War II in particular, but only to America's choice of allies.[11]

Sociological data on the CPS population is available from Selective Service files. Such measures as education, age, and geographical region of origin are included; in addition, COs were given intelligence tests, as were army inductees. The conclusions of sociological research on the CO population can be stated briefly: COs in CPS were more likely than army inductees to be from rural areas (though this measure was skewed greatly by the Mennonite COs, who were 59 percent rural). Both those in CPS and army inductees were obviously in the draft-age bracket of eighteen to thirty-six years old, but COs as a rule were somewhat older (more likely to be in their late twenties than early twenties). Those in CPS also tended to have more years of education than army inductees, though this varied from an average of 14.27 years in Friends CPS (where 20 percent of the COs had education beyond college) to 10.45 years in Mennonite CPS (which still exceeded the army average of 9.4 years). Finally, COs ranked higher on the army intelligence test than did army inductees: 70 percent of the COs tested were placed in army grade I as compared with 9 percent of the army inductees, 27 percent of the COs and 36.4 percent of the army inductees were in grade II, and so on down the scale.[12] In his dissertation on COs in Civilian Public Service, Gordon Zahn concludes that these and similar sociological measures indicate that COs have the age, education, and intelligence one would expect in those who adopt an "intellectually inspired" socially deviant position.[13]

ROOTS OF OBJECTION

The question of what motivated individuals to become COs is a complex one, and one without any definite answer. As Theodore Wachs says in his study of radical COs, "certain influences and motivations are all but impossible to measure by any method. Pacifists themselves are often among the first to caution that even they do not fully understand exactly what combination of forces inspired them to take their particular positions."[14] Certainly the decision to be a CO took place in the language of morality, but everyone recognizes that moral decisions are frequently influenced by non-moral considerations. Conscientious objectors are frank about admitting the non-moral factors in their decision to object, as well as reflecting at length about the moral training that led them to see pacifism as the right choice.

Family

One commonly mentioned influence on COs was that of family members. In many cases, this was an extension of the influence of the church. As Harvey Deckert, a CO from the General Conference Mennonite Church explained: "I had been taught pacifism in the home, in the church, in the Sunday School. We just sort of grew up that way, and there was never no other way. It never entered my mind that I would go as a regular combatant."[15] Or as Wesley Prieb, a Mennonite Brethren CO said:

> I think it was kind of drilled into me by my mother. My mother probably much more than my father shaped my thinking in this regard. . . . I remember in my childhood years she would tell me stories about the *Martyr's Mirror* and so I had all of these images of the martyrs in my mind throughout childhood, and the concept of faithfulness and obedience at all cost was really drilled into my mind.[16]

Fred Convers, an atheist CO, traces his pacifism in part to his mother's aversion to violence:

> I felt that my mother was essentially a pacifist just purely out of emotional reasons. You know, she was just horrified at violence. And it was a broken home. My father had left when I was six years old. And so probably my feelings, my emotional feelings about pacifism, were greatly influenced by being brought up in a feminine family without any masculine role models. There was no macho stuff at all around. I was never in my life taken hunting. I was taken once by a distant uncle fishing. But there was just sort of no masculine contact practically. And I do have the feeling that especially my mother was sort of somehow shocked by violence.[17]

As the war drew closer, COs were influenced by the choices made by male relatives. This was particularly true in large Mennonite families where several brothers were drafted. Younger brothers sometimes attributed their choice to apply for CO status to the example set by their older brothers and the stories their brothers told of CPS.[18] One rather exceptional case was that of Lawrence Templin, who had grown up in India as the son of a Methodist missionary, and returned to the States to attend college. Templin's father, a pacifist who was active in the FOR, refused to register for the draft on April 27, 1942, when all men aged 45 to 65 were required to do so. As it turned out, this age group was never drafted and those men who refused to register were never prosecuted, but the senior Templin's decision inspired his son. Templin refused to register on his twentieth birthday in 1942, and later cited his father's influence as a primary reason for his choice.[19]

Church

Another prominent source of inspiration for COs was the church. This is perhaps most true of COs from the peace churches, where virtually every CO questioned cited the church's teachings as a source of their conscientious objection. In the case of some peace church COs, the pacifism of the church was a stronger social force in their lives than the militarism of American society in general. Some branches of the peace churches disfellowshipped members who went into the military because conscientious objection was considered so basic to the tenets of the church. Among these groups were the German Baptist Brethren and the Amish, which were not only churches, but total communities with distinctive dress and social practices. To risk disfellowship must have felt to these young men comparable to risking banishment from the land and all the people they cared about. Roy Mast, who was raised among the Amish, did not become a member of the church until he was pressured to do so, so that he could more easily qualify as a CO. He reflects that his pacifism was not set in his own mind at that time, and that he was tempted to join the army to enjoy the glory bestowed on soldiers by civilians during World War II, but the weight of his early years finally swayed him to conscientious objection. He explains:

> I was an unregenerated, not born again boy, when I went in church. In our church as young men, some of us young boys did not live a Christian life that was parallel to the Christian walk of life. So I grew up as a boy in the Amish church, and we were involved in some things that we shouldn't have been. Mainly I could say this, and to my shame, with alcohol, card-playing, and some of the things that I don't think was right for a Christian young boy.
>
> I guess I'd say I was a pacifist. I was not interested in fighting. Not for the sake that I really have so much love for my enemies, like the Bible says, but I was just simply taught that it was wrong to kill or steal. So that's why I didn't want to do it. Not that I really was a child of God.[20]

Others in more liberal branches of the peace churches may have felt less direct social pressure, but the lessons of their first eighteen years as churchgoers still carried a great weight. Many peace church COs told of particular ministers or Sunday School teachers who were strong pacifists, and who gave pacifist literature to young men in their congregations.[21]

The same was true for COs from several Protestant denominations which had leaned strongly toward pacifism in the interwar years. Though these denominations ended up dropping their pacifist teachings during World War II, many of their young men were influenced strongly enough to adhere to a CO position throughout the war. Among the denominations cited by the COs I interviewed as sources of their pacifism were the Methodist church, the Christian Church (Disciples of Christ), the Advent Christian church, the Church of God (Anderson, Indiana), and the theosophical movement.[22] John Hampton, an absolutist objector who was imprisoned during World War II, credits the Methodist church with inspiring his pacifism in this excerpt from a letter to his wife Dorothy:

> The Methodist Church is one organization that I owe more to than any individuals outside of my mother and father. With all its mistakes and weaknesses "backsliding" in time of crisis, it did give me the opportunity to acquire whatever ideals and principles I hold today. It exposed me to the teachings of Christ with all their social, economic and political implications—and I managed to get "implicated" to the extent that I am now in prison and glad to be there. It was a Southern Methodist Church that changed my attitude toward Negroes and taught me that to accept Christ was to recognize that all men were brothers, regardless of race, creed, or color.[23]

Other COs reported that their denominations did not particularly espouse pacifism, but they nevertheless feel that the church, by exposing them to Christianity, motivated them to become pacifists. An Episcopalian CO, James Lowerre, commented:

> While I slept through nearly all the sermons in my lifetime, I did hear lessons, and gospels, and epistles and stuff like that. Maybe it sort of soaked in, and I kind of believed the stuff. You're supposed to be good to your fellow man, et cetera. And I think that that has something to do with [my attitude] towards peace.[24]

Some COs in non-pacifist churches, such as Baptists and Lutherans, still became acquainted with pacifism through their churches, having come in contact with specific ministers who emphasized issues of peace and pacifism, and who worked ecumenically with more strongly pacifist denominations such as the Quakers and Methodists.[25]

Interwar Peace Movement

The interwar peace movement influenced a number of COs, although it is difficult to say to what degree, since COs frequently joined peace organizations because of a pre-existing commitment to pacifism. Many of the peace organizations were religious in nature, including the American Friends Service Committee (AFSC), the Catholic Worker, and the Fellowship of Reconciliation (FOR). Several COs said that Quaker workshops and summer camps formed their pacifist thinking;[26] others cited FOR publications and events.[27] On the non-religious side, some COs had involvements with the War Resisters League, and with political organizations such as the Keep America Out of War Congress and America First. Several COs also mentioned that the Oxford Pledge movement awakened or strengthened their pacifist convictions.[28]

In many ways, socialism was the closest non-religious counterpart to the pacifism of the peace churches. Though political rather than religious, a pattern of familial and organizational pacifism similar to that of the peace churches can be found in the socialism of the 1930s. In some areas of the country, the Socialist Party was a well-established social institution. Rudy Potochnik, a CO from Michigan, remembers his father's involvement with the Socialist Party USA and the Yugoslav Socialist Federation from his early childhood, and his own participation in the Young People's Socialist League. In addition to campaigning for socialist candidates, Potochnik remembers socialist singing choirs, debating teams, dramatic productions, and dances, and he refers to the Socialist Party as "a family affair."[29] The Socialist Party USA did not adhere to absolute pacifism, but its leadership in the 1920s and 1930s, particularly the duo of Eugene V. Debs and Norman Thomas, were outspokenly anti-war. Both had served prison terms for objecting to World War I, so that pacifism, while not a matter of doctrine, was widely accepted within the Socialist Party.[30] Also, like the peace churches, socialism had a marked effect on individuals who were not active members of the Socialist Party. Just as Quaker pacifism spread beyond peace church circles through the youth programs of the AFSC, so socialist pacifism gained a wider exposure through socialist seminars and rallies. The two worlds were not entirely separate: one CO, a General Conference Mennonite, felt that his pacifism developed during the time he spent at the Harlem ashram in the summer of 1940, a haven for both religious and socialist pacifists, and an American seedbed for Gandhian philosophy.[31]

College was also a source of pacifist inspiration for many COs. Those colleges affiliated with the peace churches were filled with formal and informal debate on the merits of a CO position, and the young men who attended these colleges remember discussing the proper role for pacifists in wartime late into the night.[32] Other college campuses were also filled with pacifist activity, much of it of the FOR/AFSC stripe discussed earlier. But there was also more generally political activity going on, especially in the mid-1930s, which one CO remembers as being similar to campus activity in the 1960s against the Vietnam War.[33] College was also influential in a purely academic sense, apart from religious and political organizing on campus; several COs felt that their pacifism grew under the tutelage of professors, who though not pacifist themselves, helped students to clarify their own thinking on issues of pacifism and conscientious objection.[34]

World War I

Most World War II-era COs had not been old enough to experience World War I first hand, but they were the primary recipients of its legacy. In a sense (as discussed in Chapter 2), the peace movement that won so many young men for pacifism in the 1930s was a direct reaction to World War I. Even peace church pacifism (which existed prior to World War I) was strongly reinforced by the American mood of post-war disillusionment. Aside from its role in the peace movement and the peace churches, the First World War influenced individual COs in idiosyncratic ways. One CO described newspapers from World War I that he saw at a friend's house: "They were Hearst papers, I guess. And they had pictures on them of the bodies strewn around. And they looked like sponges, they just were so full of holes, bullet holes. They had been raked with machine gun fire. And it all seemed utterly senseless to me."[35] Another CO blamed World War I for the Great Depression of the 1930s, which had a deep impact on his childhood years, which were spent moving all over Iowa doing itinerant farm work.[36]

A number of COs were deeply influenced by their father's experiences in World War I. Howard Ten Brink, a Methodist CO from Michigan, tells a fairly typical story about the effects of propaganda in World War I on his father:

> My dad had been opposed to our entry into the war [World War I]. And he was opposed to the war for the first few months after we were actually involved in it. But then the newspapers—and I don't know whether this was nationwide or whether it was just that part of Michigan—they had pictures of the Belgian kids who had their arms amputated by the Germans. And then he became as vociferous for the war as he had been against it before, and he volunteered to go as a doughboy. But our family doctor was on the draft board, and my father already had five kids, including a pair of twins just under me, and he told him that his place was at home. He urged him to raise all the produce he could on the farm and contribute his maximum to the war effort that way. And then after the war was over, they found out all these stories about amputating kids' arms had been fabricated, and the only amputation they ever did was on the negatives . . . on the photographs.[37]

Another CO, Gordon Nutson, describes his father's change of heart during World War I, the source of his own conviction that war depends on the deliberate deception of the public:

> My dad was a food administrator for Shiwasse County in Michigan. And the big job was to save sugar in the First World War for the soldier boys. And he was all out to kill the Kaiser. That was his whole philosophy, and he believed in it a hundred percent. My uncle, who was an old time socialist, Gene Debs and Norman Thomas socialist, kept telling my dad constantly, "Claude, you're way off base. This war business is a racket from beginning to end." And my dad got fed up listening to his brother, and one day he says, "I'm gonna go to Detroit and

prove that you're wrong." Well, the whole program was to save sugar, and that program was set up to get the people in the frame of mind to accept the philosophy of war, to get them to participate in the war program. And so one day my dad got his old tin Ford out, and drove all the way to Detroit, met these big wheels that were the head of this thing for the whole state of Michigan. He insisted he wanted to see where the sugar was stored. And there were just millions and millions of pounds of sugar that were stored, and all they were doing was selling it off the top on a black market and making all kinds of money. He quit the job for the whole county, the head job for the whole county for the war effort. Well, that's how the thing started. And from then on, he was gung ho against any kind of participation in war of any kind. And of course I grew up under that.[38]

This pattern was found in the peace churches as well. Paul Brunner, an Old Mennonite CO whose father volunteered for the army in World War I as a young man, remembers his father telling him: "Today they'd shoot me in front of my barn before I'd ever go into the military."[39]

Memories of World War I were further complicated for Mennonites and other people of German origin by the virulent anti-German sentiment in America during the First World War. Cal Edinger, a Methodist CO who later converted to the Society of Friends, tells of his father's deep bitterness over the treatment he received as a German-American during World War I, losing his job and being forced out of the church he helped to build. After returning to Iowa from California to sit out the war, Edinger's father said that he was so dejected that he almost put his four small children in a gunnysack and drowned them in the Mississippi River.[40]

A few peace church COs were carrying on a tradition of objection, their fathers having been objectors to World War I. Furthermore, World War I COs were adopted by many peace church pacifists as father figures or role models, even though they were not direct relations. A Brethren CO, Al Herbst, tells of a World War I CO who inspired his own pacifism:

One thing that sort of helped me to decide to go CO, one influence from my local church . . . one of the local church members in World War I had been a conscientious objector. And he was treated so badly that he died. Of course he was buried in a nearby cemetery, and I know somehow he was a hero in my mind. It was never talked about too much, and yet it did come up, and everyone thought he was very badly treated. Apparently he said he would do everything but take a gun. And the sergeant, or whoever the guy is up above said, well, he'd take a gun or else. And he apparently was very badly treated and died of exposure.[41]

Many COs cited specific books or authors that inspired or strengthened their pacifism. Among these were a series of revisionist histories of World War I, some specifically focusing on the arms trade, others speaking more generally about the political machinations behind the war. One novel in particular had an effect on many young men: *All Quiet on the Western Front* by Erich Maria

Remarque, the story of German draftees in World War I fighting a meaningless (to them) war. The novel was made into a movie in 1930, and the leading actor, Lew Ayres, was himself so moved by the story that he became a CO when he was drafted into World War II.[42] The foundations of Christian pacifism were explored at length by numerous theologians and ministers; especially influential were Kirby Page, A. J. Muste, and G. H. C. Macgregor. A more mystical version of pacifism was presented by Aldous Huxley and Gerald Heard.[43] The classical prophets of pacifism and civil disobedience—Tolstoy, Emerson, and Thoreau—were joined by its most recent prophet, Gandhi, and his Western popularizers, Richard Gregg and Krishnal Shridharani.[44] Additional literary influences that COs mentioned included general reading in Western history, which revealed the irrationality of war, and the reading of adventure stories that were filled with senseless violence.[45]

Independent Decisions

In spite of the vigor of 1930s pacifism, some COs felt that they came to their decision quite independently. Unaware of the peace organizations and pacifist literature that many others relied on to frame their pacifism, these COs considered the problem of war and drew their own conclusion, namely, that they could not participate. George Brumley, a Jehovah's Witness who spent most of the war in prison describes one such individualized experience:

> I did not receive any pacifist training as I was growing up. I did begin to develop an aversion to violence at an early age, I think. I was thinking about the cruel deaths and disappearances in Russia and Germany in the late '30s. I was nearing draft age. I was horrified at the modern (for those days) Italian aircraft bombing and strafing in Ethiopia. I did not know what I could do about it; I felt rather alone, really, but I knew I wanted no part of the war. I did not even know that some organizations existed to help those who did not want to participate in the draft or war. My parents did not know, I'm sure, that such organizations existed or they would have told me. My first feelings thus did not begin from listening to others, they were not based on intellectual teachings or philosophy but from a basic feeling that Jehovah does not approve of war between nations today, from a feeling of revulsion for war and violence and a realization of the futility of it.[46]

Some COs related early experiences with violence that led them in a pacifist direction, for example, through playground fights they participated in as children. Richard Brown, a CO from the state of Washington, tells of his gradual disillusionment with violence:

> The town I grew up in was a kind of post-frontier town, and there was a lot of normal violence, you know. The kids fought each other. And I was engaged in a lot of fights. I always hated to be in fights when I was in grade school, but I nevertheless got into a lot of them. Mainly because I didn't want to be in fights.

> If you don't want to be in fights, you tend to get into more fights. And I often won. Because I would fight so fiercely, and that made a great show. I didn't realize I was putting on such a good show, or I would have tempered it a bit. But when you win, that means that the next strongest boy is going to want to challenge you, he'll feel obliged to challenge you. So finally you get to a point where you can't win. Somebody's so big that there's no possibility of winning. And I got to that point after awhile, but it was a bloody kind of experience, and it isn't the sort of thing I'd want any kid to go through.[47]

Temperament and Identity

Quite a few COs indicated that they believed their pacifism to be native to their personalities, that whatever pacifist convictions they constructed in their conscious minds, it all really pointed back to a nonrational fact of individual temperament. As one CO says, "I was the guy that would always rather run around the block than get in a fight. . . . It's just that conscientious objection was made for people like me, I think."[48] Or as another puts it, "Some people are born to be baseball players and what not. And I think in my case it just seemed that that [conscientious objection] was the way I was going to go."[49]

For some, conscientious objection was central to their sense of identity. Ralph DiGia, a longtime staff member of the War Resisters League, commented: "I suppose I can even say that I could have joined the Army. I wasn't afraid of what they would do to me. They weren't going to beat me up unless, of course, I refused to cooperate. But I thought, if I went into the army, I probably would cooperate, and I would have destroyed who I was."[50] For others, it was not so much that war was immoral, but that participation in war did not conform to their plans for their lives. Simon Greco, interviewed for *Americans Remember: The Home Front* remarked: "I think it was the whole idea of who I was, what I was, what I was trying to do with my life. And somehow or other, killing people wasn't part of it."[51] Or even more briefly, as one CO said, "I had purposes of my life which were clear to me, and war was just not part of it."[52]

Sociological and Psychological Theories

Apart from COs' own views of their motivations, several researchers have devoted their energies to describing CO psychology. During the war, psychological tests were given to several small groups of COs. The results were fairly inconclusive; COs were found to be much like the general population. However, some general hypotheses were advanced about the CO samples: COs tended to think abstractly and theoretically (one psychologist read this as "idealism"), and are given to nonconformity and opposition.[53] Most other commentators did not try to analyze COs as a single class, but divided them into what can best be understood as good (or tolerable) and bad (or mentally ill) objectors. An example of this type of analysis can be found in *Stone Walls and Men* by Robert Lindner, a prison psychiatrist. He argues that one class of COs are perfectly healthy, but have been socialized differently from the norm. Included here are Mennonites and Jehovah's Witnesses, and Lindner describes their objection as "blind obedience" to habit and training, and not "a reasoned rejection." Another class of COs Lindner believes suffer from subconscious psychological difficulties. These COs are latently homosexual or sadistic, and are fighting these urges by overreacting against them. Thus the homosexual professes a desexualized love for all men and the sadist attacks political ideologies instead of human beings.[54]

A term that became popular for describing the more contentious COs was "constitutional objector," the suggestion being that these men object for the sake of objecting. As the wartime director of the U.S. Prison Bureau wrote in his 1943 annual report to the Attorney General: "His [the constitutional objector's] motivation frequently stems from an over-protective home or a mother fixation, or from a revolt against authority as typified in the home and transferred to society at large. He is a problem child—whether at home, at school, or in prison."[55] Another observer offers a similar theory to describe the behavior of radical COs: "They [constitutional objectors] are those who from early childhood have been resentful of discipline, those in whom 'that anti-feeling' is strongly developed and whose controlling motive has been to 'tell papa to go to hell.' "[56] One CO told me that he thought this might be a motive for his own objection:

> Now one thing that might enter into it is that when I was little, my dad used to be horribly brutal. And I remember one time he just totally lost his temper, and he kicked me until I was down in the mud, and then kept on kicking me. . . . I was talking to a fella who also went through CPS, and I mentioned this as a possibility, that we were rebelling against the government because we were rebelling against our parents. And he said, yeah, that occurred to him also. That we figured we'd taken enough crap from our parents and we weren't going to take any crap off the government.[57]

Making the Decision

Whatever motivated COs to choose their pacifist course, they all had to present themselves to their draft boards to be adjudged sufficiently religious and sincere to be awarded CO status (excepting those few nonregistrants who had to face a civil court instead). For some, the decision to step outside the American mainstream and request CO status was a difficult one to make. A Baptist CO, Bill Colburn, remarked: "It [the decision to be a CO] was difficult from the point of view that I did not like being different from my peers. I did not, at all. I just never enjoyed being outstanding in these ways. You know? That way, yes, it was difficult."[58] This reaction turned up repeatedly among peace church

COs (though it was by no means characteristic of all of them) who felt a certain yearning to fit in, to not stand out or be noticed, but who nevertheless felt compelled to follow their pacifist convictions.[59]

Such reluctance was virtually nonexistent among more politicized objectors, who seemed to thrive on the experience of being set apart from the crowd. Howard Ten Brink, who served in CPS though he originally refused to register, expressed this sentiment in describing the early days of his objection: "I felt tremendously buoyed up. Up until now my life had been humdrum and more or less meaningless in the larger picture, but I thought, now, by gosh, finally I'm going to amount to something. And my life is going to mean something."[60] Others recall no real sense of decision, but rather a feeling that their objection flowed naturally from their thinking and identity up to that point. Carl Paulson, a Catholic CO who was denied a CO classification and was eventually sent to prison for refusing induction into the army, described his decision like this: "I have no recollection of it being difficult, no. It just seemed . . . just natural, you know. Just like when you fall in love and you get married, it just seems natural."[61]

SERVING TIME AS A CO

All COs had their peacetime lives interrupted by the war, and found themselves in situations that provoked new thoughts and feelings. Thrust into a situation where one was never far from reminders of one's status as an objector, COs had ample opportunity to reflect on their position and the adequacy of the provisions made for COs. Their reflections on their wartime experiences help to show the tone of World War II pacifism and the issues which they react to even today.

Noncombatant Military Service

Noncombatant status was usually viewed as a compromise by the men who accepted it. Several COs said that they had applied for a IV-E classification, but were given I-A-O instead, and ultimately decided to settle for noncombatant status. Max Kleinbaum faced this situation, and remembers that "after a great deal of soul-searching, I decided to accept. The reasons I accepted are hard to pinpoint. I suppose I didn't have the courage to go to jail. I remember feeling that I wanted to experience what most others are experiencing."[62] Even the Seventh-Day Adventists, who encouraged noncombatancy, tended to speak of it as a compromise, a way of resolving conflicting duties between serving God and serving the state.

Yet noncombatant status was a powerful draw for many COs. For some, even though it was a compromise, it was an excellent one, a balance of the several demands they felt acting on them. In a July 21, 1942, letter to Harold

Guetzkow, then in CPS, John Ripley Forbes commented on his recent defection from CPS to noncombatant service:

> I only wish those most eager for this service would compromise and serve in noncombatant as some of us are doing. I do not feel it is too grave a compromise and I have certainly found as have many others especially the 7th Day Adventists that we can serve both our fellow man, our cause and God in a just and honorable way.[63]

The opportunity to be of real service, to be an integral part of the dramatic events that occupied everyone's minds in the early 1940s, was very attractive to some draftees. Noncombatancy was also an easier position to take in terms of governmental and social pressure. Selective Service encouraged pacifists to accept noncombatant status, both verbally and materially: after all, receiving wages, dependency allowances, and insurance was a real lure to men who wanted to minimize the impact of their pacifism on their lives and the lives of their families and loved ones.[64] Noncombatancy was also undeniably the service of choice for those who wanted to promote American victory, believed in the justness of the Allied cause, but felt constrained to nonviolence themselves.*

For the most part, noncombatants could serve in the military without divulging the fact that they were conscientious objectors if they chose to do so. There were of course many men in the army who were assigned to noncombatant tasks who had no conscientious scruples about serving in a combatant capacity. Thus, unless the issue of bearing arms came up, noncombatant COs were indistinguishable from other soldiers assigned to noncombatant duties. Even then, some COs were willing to be trained with weapons (though they were officially exempt from all training and use of firearms), apparently objecting only to actual battlefield use. One CO actually served as a rifle instructor for basic training units for a time.[65] Those COs unwilling to train with weapons were given KP duties while the other draftees received rifle instruction, but they were apparently not treated badly; for part of the war at least, there were separate basic training units for noncombatant COs. And once COs completed basic training and were transferred into the medical service, they could blend quite easily into the army.[66]

The distinction between noncombatant COs and regular draftees was most clearly seen with the Seventh-Day Adventist noncombatants, and this not because they refused weapons training, but because they would not work on the Sabbath—Saturday—which was a regular working day in the army. Delmar Stanley, a Brethren noncombatant, comments on the presence of Seventh-Day Adventists in his noncombatant training unit:

> Saturday morning we had to clean up the barracks and have drill. They [Seventh-Day Adventists] all got on their coats and went off to church, and they had the

*See Chapter 6 for further discussion of this point.

> day off, and the rest of us had to go out and drill. And then Sunday they would come back, but there was nothing doing on Sunday, so all they had to do was sit back. Yeah, we were very conscious of those Seventh-Day Adventists.[67]

Sabbath privileges rarely became an issue between the Adventists and the army, probably because the Adventists were willing to serve as medics in combat on Saturday—because Christ himself healed the sick on the Sabbath—but only objected to routine military activities (KP, drill, etc.) as a violation of the Sabbath.[68]

Conflicts did come up between noncombatant COs and the army over willingness to use weapons, though they were not continual or severe in most cases. Gil Bertochini, an Adventist objector, was asked to serve guard duty for his medical unit in a combat area in New Guinea, and gives this account of the confrontation:

> The commander asked me to be on guard duty. Well, you know, they don't ask, they command. He said, "You're on guard duty tonight." And I said, "Yes, sir." But I said, "Sir, I don't bear arms." And he got a little red in the face, you know, I think he was a little angry, but he said, "Go right ahead, and you're on guard duty regardless, whether you have a rifle or not," thinking that I would be frightened out. But I stood guard, from twelve to four, I think it was, in the morning. If the others knew that I was on guard without a rifle, I don't know how comfortable they'd feel. But that's the only time they asked me.[69]

Bertochini also experienced some harassment from soldiers in his unit. As he was being shipped overseas into a combat area, the first sergeant of his unit threatened to kill Bertochini during combat if he refused to carry a rifle.[70] In general, though, noncombatant COs were accepted as regular soldiers, and what bad feeling there was against them was eventually defused as a result of their conscientious service and willingness to share in the dangers of battle.[71] What noncombatants experienced in the military, both in combat and out, was little different than what was experienced by regular soldiers, the only exception being that noncombatant COs did not participate in trying to kill enemy soldiers. In combat, they suffered terror, shell-shock, and a sense of high purpose and adventure; away from the battle front they suffered from lack of freedom and uncertainty over their futures, but thrived on new challenges.[72]

Noncombatant COs had to struggle to maintain their religious and political views in a world foreign to their previous experience, and so strongly at odds with their pacifism. Several noncombatants mentioned difficulty in resisting the hate propaganda of the military. Yet Adventist COs, and perhaps other noncombatant COs as well, saw their religion strengthened during their time in the military. First, they took advantage of the opportunity to evangelize in the service, and they counted converts to Christianity as one of the triumphs of their experience in the military. And if nothing else, experience in battle brought several Adventists closer to their God. Tate Zytkoskee recalls his decision to become a minister:

> It was on patrol duty in the northern part of New Guinea, trying to determine the strength of the enemy way back in the jungles [when] I realized the dangerous situation we were in, that I made a promise to the Lord that if he spared my life during the war, that I would return and go to school and try to prepare myself for service for him. I could also mention if I were to take the time that there were occasions during my experience when I could directly see God's protecting hand. I've had knee mortars, shells, roll right beside me on the path as we were going over, a bayonet attack over the hill. I've had occasion to be in no man's land, so to speak, and feel my life was spared there. And had snipers shoot at me, and so forth. I felt the Lord's protecting hand on many occasions in combat.[73]

Civilian Public Service

In the minds of the men who designed Civilian Public Service, it was a witness of what pacifism could accomplish, a training ground for pacifist leaders of the future, and an experiment in Christian living. For some, CPS lived up to this ideal; for others it was a bitter disappointment. Selective Service, whom the churches had hoped would be a distant, inconsequential partner in CPS, persistently asserted its ultimate authority over the project. For those drafted into the alternative service program, CPS gradually deteriorated into a series of controversies, with some proudly defending both the concept of CPS and its execution, and others demanding its dissolution.

Pay and Other Financial Issues

The idea of laboring without pay in alternative service apparently originated with pacifist leaders who saw conscription as an opportunity to graphically demonstrate the dedication of pacifists to the welfare of humanity. The leadership never intended that all COs be required to make this sacrifice as a condition of their CO status; they wanted refusal of pay to be voluntary. Once the idea had been planted in the minds of government officials, however, it proved irresistible. By the time CPS finally shut down, the historic peace churches had paid seven million dollars for its operation, and COs had offered up eight million man-days of free work.[74] Had the United States government paid COs in CPS and maintained them, the cost to Selective Service would have been eighteen million dollars; as it was, Selective Service paid $4,731,000 for administration and technical supervision of the CPS program.[75] From this should be subtracted $1,225,000, the so-called "frozen fund." When COs worked in hospitals and as emergency farm laborers, Selective Service required that employers pay the COs at standard rates to avoid the charge that draftees were working for private profit. But since COs were not supposed to be paid, their wages were collected by the government. Lewis Hershey, the Director of Selective Service, agreed that this money would be given to the NSBRO to help maintain the CPS camps, but the Comptroller General vetoed this idea and put the money in the Treasury. The NSBRO objected, worried that the confiscated CO wages would be used to pay for the war, and so a compromise was worked out whereby the money was held in a special account known as the "frozen fund." Efforts were later made to use the fund to support the dependents of COs, but they were defeated, and the money "eventually disappeared into the Federal maw never to be seen again."[76] Aside from the question of receiving wages for work, there were other financial issues that created controversy in CPS. COs received no support for their dependents (one-third of COs had dependents), and they had no medical insurance or workman's compensation, in spite of the fact that thirty men died while in CPS, and fifteen hundred were discharged for physical disabilities.[77]

The government was happy to have COs laboring for free not only because of the money it saved them, but also because they felt it would prevent insincere objectors from seeking CO status. Colonel Kosch, head of Selective Service's Camp Operations division, testified to a Senate subcommittee on military affairs that "we have been against payment due to the fact that we feel that the very fact that a man does not get paid is one means of sorting the conscientious objector from the slacker or the fellow who is just trying to hide behind the skirts of the religious objectors."[78] Some COs supported the lack of pay because they felt it was good public relations, that civilians who learned that COs were unpaid would be impressed with pacifist sincerity and would redirect their righteous anger toward the government that was withholding pay. There seems to be some basis for this logic: Leo Crespi's study of public opinion towards COs revealed in 1945 that 75 percent of the public believed that COs should be paid.[79]

There were few COs I interviewed who would have refused pay if it had been offered to them, but most COs reported that they were reasonably reconciled to working for free. Many were not disturbed by the lack of pay because they had little need for money and were not used to having money anyway. As recent graduates of high school and marked by the Depression, no one expected to get rich, and there was not much on which to spend money when living out in the woods.[80] Some of these COs sympathized with those who had families to support, and recognized that from the standpoint of justice they should be paid, but nevertheless felt that the lack of pay was not worth getting excited about.[81] Others were frankly angry with the government, saying that if their work was worth something, the government should have paid for it. As one CO said, "If the government would give me the money that I'm entitled to according to their laws and regulations, I wouldn't have to do another lick of work."[82] Still, there remained COs who professed to be happy to make the sacrifice of unpaid labor as part of their witness. Lyle Krug, a Mennonite CO, stated, "We believed in our religious convictions and so we were willing to work and do it voluntarily."[83]

With such a variety of understandings, the controversy over pay in CPS raged on throughout the war, though no serious attempts were made to reverse the original administrative decision to forgo pay. However, in late 1943 the NSBRO went on public record as supporting pay for COs, partly in recognition of the fact that the original compromise with Selective Service was reached on the basis of one year's unpaid service, but had by then become labor without compensation for an indefinite period. By the end of the war, even General Hershey recommended to Congress that in the future COs be given some compensation.[84]

Church Administration

When the peace churches initiated the CPS program in early 1941, it was with a flourish of honorifics: CPS would be a "laboratory of Christian living," a "means to spread the gospel of Christ and glorify God." CPS would be a constructive enterprise in the midst of destruction, a chance to "serve in those enterprises which are removed in purpose as far as possible from war and bloodshed, and which are calculated to help the nations more easily forgive and forget the bitterness and hatred which war engenders." The rationale for working within the conscription system to develop an alternative service program finally boiled down to a statement by A. J. Muste to Evan Thomas, arguing that the responsibility of pacifism "is to say to the world in Christ's name not only 'War is not the way,' but 'This is the way, walk ye in it.' "[85] This philosophy came to be known as "walking the second mile" after Jesus' teaching in the Sermon on the Mount: "If any one forces you to go one mile, go with him two miles" (Matthew 5:41).

Though CPS rarely lived up to its early ideals, most COs were resigned to church administration.[86] They voiced occasional complaints, some of them worried that the church was selling its soul to the government for the "privilege" of administering CPS, but mostly they were reluctant to rock the boat. Of course, many COs were eighteen-year-old boys who followed their older brothers into CPS as eagerly as other young men followed their brothers into the army, and accepted CPS unquestioningly. But a significant minority developed a deep and principled objection to church administration, and their arguments pervaded the entire peace movement. To these COs, CPS was not an opportunity for Christian witness, but involuntary servitude, and the camps were not "schools for pacifist living," but concentration camps.

The COs who opposed church administration of CPS tended to find the second mile philosophy bankrupt without the crucial note of voluntarism. These critics felt the service ideal was fine, but could not thrive under conscription.[87] It is also important to stress that the idealized version of CPS belonged to the peace churches, and to a slightly lesser extent, to the FOR. The constituencies of these groups were inclined, at least in the beginning, to aspire to walk the second mile. But CPS included under its wing many COs who had no commitment to the ideal of constructive Christian service in wartime. Some COs interpreted Christianity quite differently, and others were not Christian at all, but Jewish, atheist, humanitarian, or political objectors. When these COs said "second mile," they did so pejoratively, and they suffered a painful alienation not only from wartime American society, but from CPS leadership as well.[88]

Eventually, the churches' eyes were forced open, to one degree or another. The early dreams of church control of CPS were quickly marred by the heavy hand of Selective Service authority. Albert Keim, in his article, "Service or Resistance? The Mennonite Response to Conscription in World War II," relates the experience of Tom Jones, director of Quaker CPS and one of the early enthusiasts of the CPS program. Jones was traveling with Colonel Lewis F. Kosch, a Selective Service official, to inspect one of the new CPS camps in 1941. Keim tells the story as follows:

> As Jones spoke enthusiastically about what he hoped could be accomplished through CPS, Colonel Kosch stopped him with "Who do you think you are? Don't you know I'm in charge of these camps under Selective Service?" Jones replied that he thought the Peace Churches had complete autonomy. Kosch replied, "My dear man, the draft is under United States government operation. Conscientious objectors are draftees just as soldiers are. Their activities are responsible to the government. The Peace Churches are only camp managers. Do you understand that?"[89]

The struggle for peace church control continued, until in 1942, the government made an unequivocal statement such that even the most idealistic CO in CPS could not mistake the power dynamic it revealed. Lt. Col. Franklin McLean, speaking for Selective Service, issued a memorandum to all camp directors (the peace church administrators) with the objective "to remove certain misunderstandings which seem to exist among assignees relative to the reason for their assignment and their status while in Civilian Public Service camps." The following three pages of text set out in the clearest possible terms a division of authority that flowed from Selective Service to the peace church administrators (who acted as representatives "of the church sponsoring the camp and also of Selective Service"), and that left no autonomy whatsoever in the hands of the draftee. The paragraph COs in CPS found most objectionable read:

> From the time an assignee reports to camp until he is finally released he is under control of the Director of Selective Service. He ceases to be a free agent and is accountable for all of his time, in camp and out, twenty-four hours a day. His movements, actions and conduct are subject to control and regulation. He ceases to have certain rights and is granted privileges instead. These privileges can be restricted or withdrawn without his approval or consent as punishment, during emergencies or as a matter of policy. He may be told when and how to work, what to wear and where to sleep. He can be required to submit to medical examinations and treatment and to practice rules of health and sanitation. He may be moved from place to place and from job to job, even to foreign countries, for the convenience of the government regardless of his personal feelings or desires.[90]

The McLean statement went on to inform COs in CPS that they were not slaves, or inmates of a concentration camp, because they freely chose CO classification, and could give it up at any time if the conditions of CPS no longer suited them.

As Selective Service staked out its turf ever more clearly, the NSBRO found it increasingly difficult to maintain its own unity. The FOR and WRL withdrew from the NSBRO in 1944, staying on only in a "consultative" capacity, because they felt the NSBRO had compromised itself in becoming an agent of Selective Service. The first group to withdraw from the administration of CPS units in protest against the CPS system was the Association of Catholic Conscientious Objectors (ACCO) in 1945. The CPS unit they had administered was turned over to governmental control. In spite of growing dissatisfaction, the peace churches continued their commitment to administering CPS until the end of the war. The AFSC, which had been flirting with withdrawal for some time, finally announced that it would cease administration and financial support of CPS in March 1946, the date when the draft law's required "duration plus six months" expired. Several other organizations—the Baptists and Methodists among them—followed suit, eager to disaffiliate themselves with peacetime conscription. The Brethren and Mennonites, in spite of some internal dissent, remained firm in their resolution to provide a non-government-directed alternative service program, and continued to administer CPS until the government halted conscription and the last of the COs was released.[91]

Significant Work

An integral part of the second mile philosophy of CPS was the concept of rendering healing service to a world torn by war. This was not a concept shared by Selective Service, and much of the frustration associated with CPS stemmed from the attempts of the churches to secure meaningful work projects for COs which could gain the approval of Selective Service. Early efforts to set up overseas medical and relief projects in the theatres of war were thwarted by the Starnes rider (see Chapter 2); later efforts to put COs in general hospitals and schools that were suffering acute labor shortages were vetoed by Selective Service because, as Colonel Kosch said, "We do not believe that the government should be a party to helping these men spread their pacifist propaganda."[92]

Many COs I spoke with complained that the government was purposely hiding COs away in the woods so that the public would not know they existed; Gordon Zahn called CPS "an experiment in the suppression of a dissident minority."[93] The basis of such complaints in fact is confirmed in this quote from General Hershey: "The conscientious objector, by my theory, is best handled if no one hears of him."[94] Those unafraid of harsh words referred to the CPS camps as "concentration camps."[95] Gordon Zahn elaborates on this theme in saying:

> It is almost too much to speak of these as concentration camps in a world and at a time when that term assumed dimensions of special horror. Yet that is what they

> were. More to the point, that is what the military officers of the Selective Service System intended them to be. No matter how liberal the regulations or how relaxed the discipline, the first priority was to gather these potentially troublesome conscientious objectors into isolated work camps, safely out of sight and mind. If the work project to which they were assigned produced something of lasting value, well and good. If not . . . that, too, was well and good.[96]

Independent of complaints about a *de facto* social quarantine, many COs described the work they did in CPS as insignificant. James Lowerre remembers some in CPS referring to it as "work of national impotence."[97] Interviews abounded with examples of unnecessary work undertaken only to keep COs busy: roads cleared and stumps dug out of frozen ground with picks and shovels while bulldozers sat idle within view; weeds raked up by hand until the men were needed for a more important task, at which time weed burners were brought out to finish the job in a hurry; chopping ice out of the tunnels of a road that was unused in the winter.[98]

In its salad days, the service philosophy of CPS inspired COs to spend their off-project hours learning first aid and relief skills, but once CPS was established, new inductees were quickly indoctrinated into the pointlessness of its endless cycle of work. Roy Mast, an Amish CO, remembers his first few days in CPS:

> I was out on project, and one of the things we did was cover little pine trees with wild grass that was mowed, and we'd cover these little pine trees about three or four inches high. About the second or third day, coming back, I realized we were gonna get finished by tomorrow noon or so on this field. And as I walked back to the truck, two of my friends—in fact one of my future brothers-in-law and another buddy—and I said, "We'll get finished by tomorrow noon. What are we gonna do then?" And of course they realized that I wasn't too enthused with this work. And they started laughing, they said, "Oh Roy, don't worry, we still got a couple hundred acres to cover. We never get finished 'til spring." And right there, I resigned. I resigned, I give up the intentions of getting anything accomplished. When I went out in the morning, I looked for nothing else 'til lunchtime. And after lunch, the same way 'til evening.[99]

Many COs became expert at looking like they were working while spending their time reading or talking. Gordon Zahn says that in the Catholic CPS camp in New Hampshire, cries of "Timber!" meant not that a tree was falling, but that the foreman was coming and everyone should look busy.[100]

However, not all COs experienced their work in CPS as meaningless. Some COs remember their work for the Forest Service with a sense of accomplishment.[101] Even more COs find the work meaningful in retrospect. Don Baker recalls referring at the time to his work in CPS as "raking leaves in the forest," but has seen his tree-planting efforts rewarded: "That little hillside is impressive after forty years."[102] Robert Cary suggested that CPS work seems more important from this vantage point because of the growth of the ecology movement in the last twenty years. Loris Habegger commented that he found his CPS work more important once he discovered how much meaningless work was being done by the army at the same time.[103]

Those in detached service frequently experienced more job fulfillment, and felt that they were more tangibly involved in service to humanity.[104] Dwight Hanawalt, a Brethren CO who served in a rural health clinic in Puerto Rico during most of the war, remembers it as a creative experience. He was so satisfied with the work he was doing that the controversies surrounding lack of pay and church administration never really touched him.[105]

A number of COs who had adopted the CPS ideal of Christian service and seen it frustrated throughout the war resolved their conflict in part by entering voluntary service immediately after the war. Finally discharged from CPS and free to do as they wished, these men embarked on missions of relief and rehabilitation to Europe, Asia, and Africa. A Mennonite CO, Peter Bartel, explains his motivations for volunteering for post-war relief work in saying: "I guess I felt when I was through with CPS, when I was discharged, I had really not done what I wanted to do, and this of course is why some of us volunteered for relief work. . . . I really felt that the fulfillment of my obligation came with my going into relief work."[106]

Life in CPS

If there was one salient feature of life in CPS, it was the variety of men who ended up there. Especially for COs who had grown up in rather narrow communities, the experience of meeting people of different religious groups, with different beliefs and opinions, had quite an impact. Gene Yoder, an Old Mennonite, comments:

> I think it [CPS] was real educational for me, being an Old Mennonite, because you wouldn't realize now how it was then, but you know back in those days—it was never taught that way, of course—but you kind of had the feeling that for instance GCs, General Conference [another branch of the Mennonites], were pretty far out. Back when I was in high school, if you dated a General Conference girl, you were really climbing out.[107]

Time and time again, those from the peace churches related their fascination with discovering points of view heretofore unimaginable. Many likened their years in CPS to college, saying that their interactions with other COs were an education in themselves. A Quaker CO, Seth Gifford, comments on this:

> In CPS there were a diverse group of people. And of course anyone who was not a Friend or a Quaker and brought up as a Quaker was diverse to me. And there were socialists, there were communists, there were atheists, there were humanists; and there were discussions. . . . Naturally, when you're working on a crew out in the woods, you were working chopping down trees, building a trail or whatever, you'd get into discussions. And it was a time that was really very educational for me. I think I did more reading, more studying in the time I was in CPS than I did

> probably in all the previous academic studies that I had undertaken from high school right through college.[108]

In a setting where college professors and high school students found themselves working as equals, the opportunity for intellectual growth and debate was enormous.[109]

The gathering of a great variety of men in a single camp was not only broadening, but also very difficult. A number of the more conservative Mennonites and Brethren questioned the motivations of their fellow COs in CPS, and resented the presence of men whose objections were mainly political and not religious. Some recommended giving the political objectors their own camp; others thought Selective Service should have had more rigorous standards for granting CO status in order to "weed out a lot of scum."[110] Differences in personal morality also disturbed the religiously conservative COs, and even some of the religiously liberal but personally conservative COs. "Political objectors," (a catch-all term which at times included Catholics and Russian Molokans) shocked their fellow campers by drinking, smoking, and swearing, and laying claim to certain bunkhouses which were known by names like "the opium den" or "the Casbah." There were even complaints about members of the peace churches who were not sincere objectors, but merely capitalizing on their church membership to avoid the army; one Mennonite CO mentioned that some of these Mennonites-in-name-only were dating the wives of servicemen who lived in nearby towns.[111]

The graceful art of living together in peace required endless camp meetings, where reportedly the most controversial question was when the lights should be turned off.[112] Having lived through some of this, Dwight Hanawalt commented:

> I think if ever it would come another war and they decided they were going to have CPS camps, and they decided I ought to administer one of those camps, I'd tell them, "Nothing doing." That was the worst job that any guy could have. Here were two hundred sharp people who had thought through something. And I suppose those who take that position are cantankerous enough. . . . You couldn't whip them intellectually.[113]

CPS was psychologically difficult for many COs, as no doubt the army was for many soldiers. Otto Dahlke, a sociologist who studied two CPS camps during the war concluded, "The CPS camps were characterized by social isolation, routine, and diminished cultural and social stimulation. Stultification easily followed."[114] Several COs found communal living and the all-male society of CPS very trying; for others the separation from wives, families, and church communities was a source of pain. Arthur Bryant remembers his resentment at being drafted:

> I was terribly lonely. I had been married a couple of years, and I resented bitterly the fact that regardless of whether it was CPS or the army, that I had to be torn away from my wife and forced to go to a place I had no desire to go, and to live a

> life that I had no desire to live. However, recognizing that there were literally millions and millions of other young men who had been forced to take those same actions, couldn't help but mitigate any personal affront at the situation.[115]

The greatest threat to morale, according to many COs, was that they had no idea how long they would be in CPS, or when they could return to their normal lives.[116]

CPS took its toll on the lives of COs: men in CPS showed a higher percentage of mental breakdowns than did men in the army. Some suggested this was due to the directionless nature of CPS, others thought family tensions over conscientious objection were to blame, still others assumed that COs were mentally unbalanced to begin with.[117] In *Another Part of the War*, Gordon Zahn suggests that much of the tension in CPS stemmed from being ignored:

> Perhaps a little overt persecution would have strengthened the morale of the men in the camps. At the very least, it would have lessened the sense of utter futility that haunted their days. . . . Harsh treatment at the hands of their keepers would have meant that someone thought enough of them and their witness to resent both.[118]

Partly as a reaction to the boredom and frustration of CPS, and partly as a principled protest against conditions, COs participated in a number of work strikes and slowdowns. These were especially common at the government camps, which had purposely gathered together all of the most serious CPS malcontents. At Germfask, a government CPS camp in Michigan, four thousand of the twenty thousand man-days of work were spent sick-in-quarters; one project superintendent recalls that the illnesses were planned so that all men whose last names began with the same letter of the alphabet would be sick the same day.[119] A CO newsletter from the time remarked on the Mancos, Colorado government camp, "Granted it takes all kinds of people to make up the world, but why do they all have to gather in Mancos?"[120]

Releases from CPS were decided on a point system, with those who had families or long records of service being released earliest. By January 31, 1946, 44.7 percent of the COs in CPS had been released, as compared with 60.6 percent of those in the armed forces. The NSBRO and General Hershey haggled over additional releases, but CO releases continued to lag behind, as Selective Service feared public opinion repercussions if COs were released while drafted soldiers continued to serve overseas. The last CO was released from CPS on March 30, 1947, the day before Selective Service was finally dismantled.[121]

Prison

The arrest and prosecution of COs was a routine matter in only a few areas where the population of COs was dense enough that the local authorities became accustomed to dealing with this curious brand of lawbreaker. Especially before Pearl Harbor, when COs were still an unknown quantity, the justice system was slow to rouse, but harsh when it acted. James Bristol, who registered, but then later refused to fill out his draft questionnaire, and Bill Colburn, who refused to register, were both visited by Selective Service officials who tried to persuade them to comply with the law, offering them various options that might satisfy their sensitive consciences. Bristol was told that he could sign a blank questionnaire, and they would give him either a ministerial exemption or a IV-E (CPS) classification, whichever he preferred. Colburn was told that he could register late without any penalty, and be virtually guaranteed IV-E classification. Yet when arrests were made, there were no signs of mercy: Colburn was held with fifty thousand dollars bail, while Bristol was handcuffed in his living room and taken away to jail.[122]

As conscientious objection became more commonplace, high bail sums and dramatic arrests became less common. Malcolm Parker recalls his arrest for refusing induction into CPS: "I received a phone call from the federal district attorney in San Francisco, and he said 'Well, we've got a warrant for your arrest here; would you like us to come out and pick you up or do you want to come down here?' "[123] Some COs were held only briefly before their trial and sentencing; Lawrence Templin recalls that he was in prison within a month of his refusal to register.[124] On the other hand, Fred Barnes, who became a Jehovah's Witness during World War II, spent a full year in jail in Kansas before he received a four-year sentence to federal prison.[125]

Trials were usually clipped and to the point; Tony Randles, interviewed for *Against the Tide*, recalls the following interchange between judge and CO as a typical trial: "'Were you classified by your local board?' 'Yes.' 'Did you do what they said?' 'No.' 'OK. Jail!' "[126] But trials occasionally became a forum for the intellectual defense of pacifism. Caleb Foote recalls his trial in San Francisco for refusing induction into CPS:

> I walked in there and I spent an hour, an hour and a quarter. We had this moral, intellectual discussion about anarchism, about putting yourself above the law, about civil disobedience. None of the sort of, what would you do if somebody tried to rape your mother type questions. Nothing of that sort. He [the judge] probed me on my family background, the fact that my father was a biblical scholar, and my own record at Harvard and Columbia and so forth, and he was obviously having a hard time. And at the end of a long time, he said, "Well, I'm going to revoke your bail and put you in jail. We'll let you sit there for two weeks while I have a pre-sentence report made. . . . [After two weeks] I came back to court and the judge made a little speech in which he said he felt like Pontius Pilate—a statement that was picked up by the AP, and I guess published all over the country—and ended up sentencing me to six months.[127]

During World War II, conscientious objectors accounted for one-sixth of all federal prisoners (COs comprised approximately one-third of all Selective Service violators). Their fellow prisoners were in for a variety of federal crimes: statutory rape, bootlegging, homosexuality in the army, check forgery, car theft, postal violations, and transporting a female across state lines for immoral purposes.[128] In contrast to World War I, when COs were treated harshly in military prisons, COs generally reported that prison conditions were acceptable, or at least as good as could be expected. George Brumley reported that the Jehovah's Witnesses were allowed a two-hour midweek Bible meeting, a Sunday morning religious meeting, and could receive subscriptions to *Watchtower* and *Awake!*. Political COs received news magazines and Dwight Macdonald's *Politics* and often had access to well-stocked libraries.[129] But prison was still prison; as James Bristol remembers:

> I just tried from the beginning to take it one day at a time. Every now and then you'd look ahead, especially when you first got in there, and your heart was down around your ankles. I don't mean it was all just a piece of cake, because it wasn't at all. I had one experience where I shook for about, I don't know how long, six or eight hours or something after something happened, which just was an indication of the tension and so on that's constant in a prison. It just never abates.[130]

Or as Neil Glixon sums up life in prison, "At its best, it's pretty damn bad."[131]

In 1944, prison reformer Harry Elmer Barnes described the inelegant fit of conscientious objectors into the penal system:

> The custodial personnel, routine, discipline and administration which are admirably suited to the ordinary and traditional prisoner, who is frequently pretty well institutionalized and adjusted to penal discipline, are at the same time exactly the type of attitude and procedure most likely to irritate a noncriminal, dissident and high-strung group such as the Conscientious Objectors.[132]

Though the COs themselves might choose different words, one cannot avoid the conclusion that many COs did not "adapt" to prison discipline. They continually came into conflict with prison authorities, sometimes as a result of planned cooperative actions, sometimes because an individual acted spontaneously against prison regulations. The most famous CO strike took place at Danbury Federal Prison in Connecticut in 1943. On August 11, 1943, nineteen COs declared a work strike to protest racial segregation in the prison dining room. The COs were moved to a separate cell block where they stayed for 134 days, until on December 23, 1943, the warden released them and integrated the dining hall.[133] In contrast, James Bristol's work strike was personal: he refused to work when he discovered that the prison farm was delivering food to the army. As he told the prison authorities, "I have no objection to people in the army eating, but if I'm gonna start to produce food for the army, I might as well sign those papers and get out of here." Bristol was demoted to the pick and shovel gang for his refusal to work.[134]

Gradually, protest in prison became less tied to specific abuses (e.g., racial segregation and defense work), and became more a matter of generalized noncooperation with the prison system. COs took a variety of absolutist positions: some refused to work, some refused to obey orders, some refused to eat. Absolutists had a tendency to escalate their protest the longer they were imprisoned as the logic of their position worked itself out. Malcolm Parker and John Hampton, already on work strike and in administrative segregation, went on a hunger strike to protest the continued imprisonment of Selective Service violators after the end of the war. Later, thirty-five to forty pounds lighter and routinely subjected to forced feedings, Parker and Hampton wanted to protest the treatment of Jehovah's Witnesses in prison, and could resort only to resisting the forced feedings as a form of protest. After announcing their intention to resist, the warden sent six burly prison guards in to hold Parker and Hampton down while they fed them by putting an enema tube up their noses.[135]

Wally Nelson, who also became an absolutist, tells the story of his conversion to a position of absolute noncooperation:

> By this time I was getting to know that prisons are very bad, that no one should be in prisons. I was very strongly against prisons by this time, and I began to get that by my feeding my body, I was helping them to keep my body there. And it came to me very clearly that if they were going to continue to keep me in prison, it was going to be their full responsibility to keep me there. They must keep me alive and everything, because I wasn't going to participate.[136]

Most COs drew the line at which they ceased to cooperate much farther along than this. In fact, the majority acceded to prison discipline without protest. This did not guarantee that they would be treated well, however. Fred Barnes remembers his lonely confinement in a Kansas jail, an annex off the courthouse, where he was the only prisoner for weeks at a time. In the middle of winter, the jailer turned the heat off at 5:00 P.M. and did not turn it on again until 6:00 A.M., leaving Barnes with only one blanket. When Barnes complained to the jailer of the cold, he responded, "Well, you know, there's a lot of boys out on the front tonight cold too."[137]

COs also took some abuse from patriotic fellow prisoners. There were incidents of verbal attacks and destruction of COs' property. Caleb Foote remembers overhearing prisoners making remarks such as, "Boy, if I had my way, I'd send them [COs] out and put them right in the front lines and let the Japanese shoot 'em all down."[138] But overt hostility against COs was rare (indeed many non-CO prisoners were delighted with the absolutist COs' assaults on prison authority), and did not view COs as wrong for opposing the war, but only foolish for announcing their intentions instead of avoiding being caught.[139]

Though COs in general were relatively well treated by the other prisoners, the same cannot be said for Jehovah's Witnesses, who were often the object of taunts and even violence. Fred Barnes relates his experiences in the El Reno Federal Reformatory in Oklahoma:

> We had some very rough times. I was in a reformatory. And I was in what was considered the most violent prison where the Jehovah's Witnesses spent time during the war. And the reason why, there were young people there who were easily agitated. They had their high emotions . . . and we had a good many mob acts against us. Very violent. As for myself, in one of these mob occasions, I walked outside the door of the building to attend one of our meetings, and I was knocked down and hit in the side of my head with a round point shovel and severely beaten. And I thought my head would never come back in shape.[140]

COs (other than the Jehovah's Witnesses) tended to receive better treatment from prison authorities than did other prisoners, partly because they had connections on the outside who would publicize any abuses the COs suffered in prison, bringing them promptly to the attention of the Attorney General and the director of the Bureau of Prisons. Also, COs were quick to reassure prison guards that they meant nothing personal by their disobedience, but, as John Hampton said, it "was strictly a matter between me and Selective Service."[141]

Most COs left jail on parole. Some were paroled into CPS after only a brief stay in prison. Others were paroled to hospital jobs, because hospitals were understaffed during the war and were thus forced to accept convicts as workers.[142] Prison tended to radicalize COs, however, and many who had formerly been willing to accept alternative service in CPS, but who had been denied CO status by their draft boards, later refused parole to CPS.[143] Some COs went a good deal further and refused parole altogether, arguing that they did not intend to abide by the restrictions of parole, and would not accept parole because it implied that they believed themselves to be criminals. By the time the war was over, these absolutist COs had proven to be intractable prisoners, and the prison authorities lived in fear that one of them would finally succeed in starving himself to death and thus create a public outcry. Seeing no other alternative, the prisons eventually released the absolutist COs, without making them complete their prison sentences or sign parole papers. As Malcolm Parker tells it, "They said, 'OK, here you go,' and just turned us loose, one by one."[144]

Changes of Status

The Selective Service System was quite flexible for COs who changed status during World War II, depending on the direction in which they wanted to move. CPS men could move anywhere: Selective Service was delighted to transfer COs in CPS to military service, noncombatant or combatant, and prison was theirs for the asking—all they had to do was to be "absent without leave" (AWOL) from CPS. COs in prison could leave for the army at any time, and for CPS if they were patient and impressed prison authorities with their sincerity. Those in military service faced a more difficult task: noncombatants could discard their CO status for full military service, but movement in the opposite direction was difficult, unless they were willing to risk court-martial; the same was true for regular soldiers who developed conscientious objections after induction.[145]

Approximately 2–5 percent of IV-E COs left CPS for full military service.[146] Most of the COs I spoke with who made this choice said that they did it in part out of disappointment with CPS. One Methodist CO began to lose faith in the effectiveness of pacifism as an alternative to the use of force when he observed the difficulty pacifists had in working together amicably in CPS camp. In a February 4, 1944 letter to his friends explaining his reasons for leaving CPS, he writes:

> Within the [CPS] camp there was a great deal of friction. A cooperative project was extremely difficult to obtain. Frequently petty matters were made questions of principle or personal desires a matter of conscience. There was more insistence on personal rights and liberty than upon personal duties or discipline. . . . If it is slow and difficult to work together in this country under rather favorable circumstances, how could we carry on any successful demonstration against an occupying Nazi force? Our talk of non-violent techniques of action as an alternative to war seems absurd in the light of our progress in their use in times of relative peace.[147]

Another strong motivation for entering the military was financial. George Brown, a Methodist CO, was primarily influenced to leave CPS by financial motives. He says, "I had a wife and child, and I was feeling very pressed at being unable to provide any support for them."[148]

Once in the army, ex-COs did well. They were not discriminated against by their fellow soldiers and generally felt comfortable in their new roles. George Brown remarked that "the army, rather than discriminating against me, was extremely fair and non-discriminatory. And I never figured out to this day whether it was ignorance, stupidity, or enlightenment."[149] Paul Ashby recalls being challenged once when the major he served under discovered he had been a CO. Ashby relates the incident:

> I can recall that he [the major] had to put something on paper. So he took out his .45, and he laid it on the desk. He said, "If I tell you there's a German spy outside this building and for you to go shoot him, will you do it?" I said, "Major, give me that gun." So he wrote down that I was a good fighter, I'd kill people if he told me to, and that was the end of it.[150]

Ashby had no further problems after this, and served as a flight instructor for most of the war.

About 5 percent of IV-E COs left CPS for noncombatant military service.[151] Their reasons for changing status were quite similar to those of the men who left CPS for full military duty, but they were not willing to give up their pacifism to the same degree. Delmar Stanley sees his switch to noncombatancy as a transitional phase. He became more aware of what was going on in the war, and it bothered him to be sitting at home while friends were facing crisis situations on the war front. Though he later came to favor full military service, at the time he felt unprepared to "accept the idea of actually doing the fighting."[152] Arthur Bryant, a Baptist CO, also felt uncomfortable with sitting on the sidelines during the most important years of his life, and ultimately decided that he could accept a noncombatant role in the military.[153]

Many COs in CPS debated walking out of CPS (and risking certain imprisonment if they stayed in the United States) as they came to adopt a more radical understanding of the ills of CPS. Those who never did walk out, but only considered it, frequently said that they stayed because they did not want to face prison, or because they were concerned about the reaction of family and friends.[154] Those who did walk out (approximately 3–5 percent of those in CPS)[155] referred to the same sort of restlessness and despair over sitting on the sidelines expressed by those who left for noncombatant military service.[156] Some felt that CPS failed to provide a real witness; others came to believe that it could never provide a witness because it rested on the rotten foundations of conscription. Men in the latter group viewed walking out of CPS as a way of becoming nonregistrants in spirit, though there was no way to undo the act of registration.[157]

To be a conscientious objector in World War II was perhaps not as difficult as one might assume from the vantage point of the 1990s, in a climate where people routinely hearken back to "the good war." Nevertheless, conscientious objection was an unpopular and marginal position, and it required real determination to hold to it. Having gained an understanding of who the COs were and how they experienced their outsider status during the war years, we can now turn to examining how they justify their unusual choice.

NOTES

1. Mulford Q. Sibley and Philip E. Jacob, *Conscription of Conscience: The American State and the Conscientious Objector, 1940–1947* (Ithaca, NY: Cornell University Press, 1952), 84.

2. U.S. Director of Selective Service, *Selective Service in Wartime,* Semiannual Report, vol. 2 (Washington DC: Government Printing Office, 1943), 259.

3. Lawrence S. Wittner, *Rebels Against War: The American Peace Movement, 1933–1983* (Philadelphia: Temple University Press, 1984), 41.

4. Theodore Rickard Wachs, "Conscription, Conscientious Objection, and the Context of American Pacifism, 1940–45" (Ph.D. dissertation, University of Illinois, Champaign-Urbana, 1976), 209.

5. My interviews provide some evidence that men who were nonreligious or primarily religious objectors stated their objection in religious language so as to qualify for CO status.

6. Mulford Q. Sibley and Ada Wardlaw, *Conscientious Objectors in Prison, 1940–45* (Philadelphia: Pacifist Research Bureau, 1945), 12, 14.

7. National Service Board for Religious Objectors (NSBRO), *A Directory of Civilian Public Service* (Washington DC: National Service Board for Religious Objectors, 1947), xviii–xix.

8. Lorell Weiss, "Socio-Psychological Factors in the Pacifism of the Church of the Brethren During the Second World War" (Ph.D. dissertation, University of Southern California, 1957), 164.

9. Wallace Nelson, interview by Deena Hurwitz for *Against the Tide,* privately held (hereafter abbreviated as "Hurwitz interview").

10. Sibley and Wardlaw, *COs in Prison,* 16. See also Roy Hoopes, *Americans Remember: The Home Front* (New York: Hawthorn Books, 1977), 232–33.

11. Gordon Zahn, *Another Part of the War* (Amherst, MA: University of Massachusetts Press, 1979), 14–15.

12. Adrian E. Gory and David C. McClellan, "Characteristics of Conscientious Objectors in World War II," *Journal of Consulting Psychology* 11 (September 1947): 247–50; Leslie Eisan, *Pathways of Peace: A History of the Civilian Public Service Program Administered by the Brethren Service Committee* (Elgin, IL: Brethren Publishing House, 1948), 50–57; Melvin Gingerich, *Service for Peace: A History of Mennonite Civilian Public Service* (Akron, PA: Mennonite Central Committee, 1949), 87; Wittner, *Rebels Against War,* 49.

13. Gordon C. Zahn, "A Study of the Social Backgrounds of Catholic COs in Civilian Public Service During World War II" (M.A. thesis, Catholic University of America, 1950), 86; Gordon C. Zahn, "A Descriptive Study of the Sociological Backgrounds of Conscientious Objectors in Civilian Public Service During World War II," in Catholic University of America, *Studies in Sociology,* Abstract Series, vol. VII (Washington DC: Catholic University of America, 1953), 24. Zahn's unpublished Ph.D. thesis, of which this is the abstract, examines a random sample of IV-E CO Selective Service files. The sample is representative and provides excellent sociological data on Civilian Public Service.

14. Wachs, "Conscription and American Pacifism," 222.

15. Harvey Deckert, interview for "Schowalter Oral History Collection—World War II Conscientious Objectors," Keith Sprunger and James Juhnke, coordinators, 122 cassette tapes, Mennonite Library and Archives, North Newton, Kansas (hereafter abbreviated as "SOH interview").

16. Wesley Prieb, SOH interview. Prieb is referring to a book of illustrated stories about Anabaptist martyrs: Thieleman J. van Braght, *Martyr's Mirror* (Scottdale, PA: Herald Press, 1938).

17. Fred Convers, interview with author, 2 October 1986, Berkeley, California.

18. Paul Goering, SOH interview; Peter Bartel, SOH interview; John Juhnke, SOH interview.

19. Lawrence Templin, SOH interview. For a description of Templin's father's objection, see R. Alfred Hassler, *Conscripts of Conscience: The Story of Sixteen Objectors to Conscription* (New York: Fellowship of Reconciliation, 1942), 40–42.

20. Roy Mast, self-interview answering author's questions, May 1987; see also Marvin Hein, SOH interview.

21. Charles Baker, interview with author, 24 September 1986, Modesto, California; Albert Herbst, interview with author, 6 September 1986, La Verne, California; Tate Zytkoskee, self-interview answering author's questions, May 1987.

22. Anonymous World War II conscientious objector, interview with author, 3 March 1987; Anonymous World War II conscientious objector, interview with author, 7 September 1986; Duane Windemiller, interview with author, 22 April 1987, Hampton Beach, New Hampshire; Harmon Wilkinson, interview with author, 23 February 1987, Whittier, California.

23. John E. Hampton, letters from prison, War Resisters League, Document Group 40, Swarthmore College Peace Collection, Swarthmore, Pennsylvania.

24. James Lowerre, interview with author, 3 March 1987, Orange, California.

25. James Bristol, interview with author, 27 May 1987, Philadelphia, Pennsylvania; Carl Paulson, interview with author, 23 April 1987, Upton, Massachusetts; Bill Colburn, interview with author, 5 May 1987, Concord, New Hampshire.

26. Caleb Foote, telephone interview with author, 28 February 1987; Rudy Potochnik, interview with author, 26 September 1986, Modesto, California; Gerald Rubin, interview with author, 2 October 1986, Corte Madera, California.

27. Paul Ashby, interview with author, 30 September 1986, San Francisco, California; Bob Stocksdale, interview with author, 1 October 1986, Berkeley, California; William Keeney, SOH interview.

28. James Bristol, interview with author, 27 May 1987, Philadelphia, Pennsylvania; George Brown, Jr., interview with author, 1 June 1987, Washington DC; Rudy Potochnik, interview with author, 26 September 1986, Modesto, California; Gerald Rubin, interview with author, 2 October 1986, Corte Madera, California; Richard Brown, interview with author, 2 October 1986, Berkeley, California; Gordon Zahn, interview with author, 29 April 1987, Charlestown, Massachusetts; Caleb Foote, telephone interview with author, 28 February 1987.

29. Rudy Potochnik, "Autobiography," privately held; Rudy Potochnik, interview with author, 26 September 1986, Modesto, California.

30. Gordon Nutson, interview with author, 25 September 1986, Modesto, California; Gerald Rubin, interview with author, 2 October 1986, Corte Madera, California.

31. Elmer Ediger, SOH interview.

32. Irvin Richert, SOH interview; J. Edwin Jones, interview with author, 6 September 1986, La Verne, California; Albert Herbst, interview with author, 6 September 1986, La Verne, California.

33. J. Lloyd Spaulding, SOH interview. See also George Brown, Jr., interview with author, 1 June 1987, Washington DC; Harmon Wilkinson, interview with author, 23 February 1987, Whittier, California; Walter Juhnke, SOH interview; Don Baker, interview with author, 1 October 1986, San Francisco, California.

34. James Bristol, interview with author, 27 May 1987, Philadelphia, Pennsylvania; Neil Glixon, interview for "An Oral History of American Jews who Chose to Become Conscientious Objectors or Resisted Serving in the Military from World War II—Korean War," Murray Polner, coordinator, ten cassette tapes, Swarthmore College Peace Collection, Swarthmore, Pennsylvania (hereafter abbreviated as "Polner interview"); George Fischer, interview with author, 22 April 1987, Danvers, Massachusetts.

35. James Lowerre, interview with author, 3 March 1987, Orange, California.

36. J. Lloyd Spaulding, SOH interview.

37. Howard Ten Brink, interview with author, 24 September 1986, Modesto, California.

38. Gordon W. Nutson, interview with author, 25 September 1986, Modesto, California. See also Gale O. Nutson, interview with author, 27 September 1986, Modesto, California.

39. Paul Brunner, SOH interview.

40. Cal Edinger, interview with author, 25 February 1987, San Gabriel, California.

41. Albert Herbst, interview with author, 6 September 1986, La Verne, California. See also Gilbert Grover, interview with author, 24 September 1986, Modesto, California; Russell Jarboe, interview with author, 25 February 1987, La Verne, California; Henry Blocher, interview with author, 10 September 1986, La Verne, California; Dwight Hanawalt, interview with author, 10 September 1986, La Verne, California; G. Hayes Reed, interview with author, 25 September 1986, Modesto, California; J. John J. Miller, SOH interview; Samuel Guhr, SOH interview.

42. Anonymous World War II conscientious objector, interview with author, 7 September 1986; Edward Brookmyer, SOH interview; Jim Peck, *We Who Would Not Kill* (New York: Lyle Stuart, 1958), 60. Ayres requested classification as a noncombatant, but was sent to CPS, where he again requested noncombatant status and was granted it.

43. Arthur Bryant, self-interview answering author's questions, May 1987; Paul Delp, interview with author, 3 March 1987, Orange, California; Harry Prochaska, interview with author, 1 October 1986, San Francisco, California.

44. Abraham Zwickel, Polner interview; Rudy Potochnik, interview with author, 26 September 1986; J. Lloyd Spaulding, SOH interview.

45. George Brown, Jr., interview with author, 1 June 1987, Washington DC; Gordon Zahn, interview with author, 29 April 1987, Charlestown, Massachusetts; Gordon Zahn, *Another Part of the War*, 4.

46. George Brumley, letter answering author's questions, 4 June 1987. See also Zahn, *Another Part of the War*, 4; Malcolm Parker, telephone interview with author, 28 February 1987; Mark Jonathan Harris, Franklin D. Mitchell, and Steven J. Schechter, *The Homefront: America During World War II* (New York: G. P. Putnam's Sons, 1984), 55; Lowell Naeve (in collaboration with David Wieck), *A Field of Broken Stones* (Denver: Alan Swallow, 1959), 6.

47. Richard Brown, interview with author, 2 October 1986, Berkeley, California. See also Roy Hoopes, *Americans Remember: The Home Front* (New York: Hawthorn Books, 1977), 232.

48. Duane Windemiller, interview with author, 22 April 1987, Hampton Beach, New Hampshire.

49. Sigmund Cohn, interview with author, 30 September 1986, Berkeley, California. See also, Arthur Bryant, self-interview answering author's questions, May 1987; John Juhnke, SOH interview; Lawrence Templin, SOH interview; Leland Sateren, interview with author, 9 February 1987, Edina, Minnesota.

50. Ralph DiGia, quoted in *Against the Tide: Pacifist Resistance in the Second World War, an Oral History*, Deena Hurwitz and Craig Simpson, eds. (New York: War Resisters League, 1984).

51. Hoopes, *Americans Remember*, 232.

52. Anonymous World War II conscientious objector, interview with author, 21 February 1987. See also Seth Gifford, interview with author, 30 April 1987, Providence, Rhode Island; Anonymous World War II conscientious objector, interview with author, 7 September 1986.

53. A. I. Rabin, "Rorschach Test Findings in a Group of Conscientious Objectors," *American Journal of Orthopsychiatry* 15 (October 1945) 515; Ray R. Kelley and Paul E. Johnson, "Emotional Traits in Pacifists," *Journal of Social Psychology* 28 (November 1948): 279.

54. Robert M. Lindner, *Stone Walls and Men* (New York: Odyssey Press, [1946]), 292–93, 304, 307.

55. Director of the Bureau of Prisons to the Attorney General, August 1944. Distributed as "The Official View of COs in Prison," by the AFSC Prison Service, Document Group 2, Swarthmore College Peace Collection, Swarthmore, Pennsylvania.

56. Anton T. Boisen, "Conscientious Objectors: Their Morale in Church-Operated Service Units," *Psychiatry* 7 (August 1944): 216–18.

57. Howard Ten Brink, interview with author, 24 September 1986, Modesto, California.

58. Bill Colburn, interview with author, 5 May 1987, Concord, New Hampshire.

59. John Y. Hostetler, SOH interview; Roy Mast, self-interview answering author's questions, May 1987; Loris Habegger, SOH interview.

60. Howard Ten Brink, interview with author, 24 September 1986, Modesto, California.

61. Carl Paulson, interview with author, 23 April 1987, Upton, Massachusetts. See also Gordon Kaufman, interview with author, 29 April 1987, Cambridge, Massachusetts.

62. Max Kleinbaum, Polner interview; Don Peretz, Polner interview.

63. Civilian Public Service Personal Papers, 1941–1950, Document Group 56, Swarthmore College Peace Collection, Swarthmore, Pennsylvania.

64. Sibley and Jacob, *Conscription of Conscience,* 89–90.

65. Duane Windemiller, interview with author, 22 April 1987, Hampton Beach, New Hampshire.

66. Delmar Stanley, interview with author, 24 February 1987, La Verne, California; Varden Loganbill, SOH interview.

67. Delmar Stanley, interview with author, 24 February 1987, La Verne, California.

68. Gil Bertochini, interview with author, 1 June 1987, Washington DC; Boonton Herndon, *The Unlikeliest Hero* (Mountain View, CA: Pacific Press Publishing Association, 1967), 22.

69. Gil Bertochini, interview with author, 1 June 1987, Washington DC.

70. Ibid.

71. Tate Zytkoskee, self-interview answering author's questions, May 1987; Gil Bertochini, interview with author, 1 June 1987, Washington DC.

72. Tate Zytkoskee, self-interview answering author's questions, May 1987; Varden Loganbill, SOH interview; Arthur Bryant, self-interview answering author's questions, May 1987.

73. Tate Zytkoskee, self-interview answering author's questions, May 1987. See also Gil Bertochini, interview with author, 1 June 1987, Washington DC; Herndon, *The Unlikeliest Hero,* 154.

74. Patricia McNeal, "Catholic Conscientious Objection During World War II," *Catholic Historical Review* 61 (April 1975): 234.

75. Sibley and Jacob, *Conscription of Conscience,* 124.

76. George Q. Flynn, "Lewis Hershey and the Conscientious Objector: The World War II Experience," *Military Affairs* 47 (February 1983): 3.

77. Heather T. Frazer and John O'Sullivan, "Forgotten Women of World War II: Wives of Conscientious Objectors in Civilian Public Service," *Peace and Change* 5 (Fall 1978): 47; Arthur Bryant, self-interview answering author's questions, May 1987; Cal Edinger, interview with author, 25 February 1987, San Gabriel, California.

78. NSBRO, *Congress Looks at the CO,* 38.

79. G. Hayes Reed, interview with author, 25 September 1986, Modesto, California. There seems to be some basis for this logic: Leo Crespi's study of public opinion toward COs revealed in 1945 that 75 percent of the public believed COs should be paid; Leo P. Crespi, "Public Opinion toward Conscientious Objectors: V. National Tolerance, Wartime Trends, and the Scapegoat Hypothesis," *Journal of Psychology* 20 (October 1945): 346.

80. Aretas Boone, interview with author, 24 September 1986, Modesto, California; Seth Gifford, interview with author, 30 April 1987, Providence, Rhode Island; Roy Mast, self-interview answering author's questions, May 1987; Rudy Potochnik, interview with author, 26 September 1986, Modesto, California; Delmar Stanley, interview with author, 24 February 1987, La Verne, California; Bob Stocksdale, interview with author, 1 October 1986, Berkeley, California; Sigmund Cohn, interview with author, 30 September 1986, Berkeley, California.

81. Harry Prochaska, interview with author, 1 October 1986, San Francisco, California; Charles Klaffke, interview with author, 23 February 1987, Duarte, California; Richard Brown, interview with author, 2 October 1986, Berkeley, California; Robert Cary, interview with author, 1 October 1986, San Francisco, California. Some COs mentioned that young men in the army were not well paid either, and that seemed to mollify them; see Howard Bogen, interview with author, 9 September 1986, Pasadena, California; Hubert Brubaker, interview with author, 25 September 1986, Modesto, California. Others were mostly disturbed by the fact that they were forced to live off of the peace churches' largess. Many non-peace church COs left base camps largely to lessen their feeling of financial obligation to the peace churches; in detached service the sponsoring agency paid room and board. See Paul Ashby, interview with author, 30 September 1986, San Francisco, California; Fred Convers, interview with author, 2 October 1986, Berkeley, California; Samuel Liskey, interview with author, 11 September 1986, Ontario, California; Howard Bogen, interview with author, 9 September 1986, Pasadena, California; Bill Colburn, interview with author, 5 May 1987, Concord, New Hampshire.

82. Samuel Liskey, interview with author, 11 September 1986, Ontario, California; Peter Bartel, SOH interview; J. John J. Miller, SOH interview.

83. Lyle Krug, interview with author, 28 August 1986, Mission Viejo, California; Eugene Carper, interview with author, 10 September 1986, La Verne, California; Robert Vogel, interview with author, 15 September 1986, Pasadena, California.

84. Wachs, "Conscription and American Pacifism," 168–69; Flynn, "Hershey and the Conscientious Objector," 3.

85. Wittner, *Rebels Against War,* 71; Eisan, *Pathways of Peace,* 40, 46; American Friends Service Committee, *The Experience of the American Friends Service Committee in Civilian Public Service under the Selective Training and Service Act of 1940: 1941–1945* (Philadelphia: American Friends Service Committee, n.d. [1946]), 7.

86. Harry Prochaska, interview with author, 1 October 1986, San Francisco, California; Samuel Liskey, interview with author, 11 September 1986, Ontario, California; Milton Goering, SOH interview; Gilbert Grover, interview with author, 24 September 1986, Modesto, California; Joe Dell, interview with author, 27 September 1986, Modesto, California; Wesley Doe, letter answering author's questions, 14 January 1987; Wesley Doe, letter to Private Berry (a soldier considering CPS), 16 October 1941, privately held; Sigmund Cohn, interview with author, 30 September 1986, Berkeley, California; Hobart Mitchell, *We Would Not Kill* (Richmond, IN: Friends United Press, 1983), 17; Saburo Mizutani, interview with author, 29 September 1986, Sacramento, California.

87. Peter Brock, *Twentieth-Century Pacifism* (New York: Van Nostrand Reinhold Company, 1970), 187. See also Wachs, "Conscription and American Pacifism," 175; Edward Orser, "Involuntary Community: Conscientious Objectors at Patapsco State Park During World War II," *Maryland Historical Magazine* 72 (Spring 1977): 146; Dave Dellinger, "Introduction," in *Against the Tide,* Hurwitz and Simpson, eds.

88. For Catholic perceptions of alienation in CPS, see Zahn, *Another Part of the War,* xi.

89. Albert N. Keim, "Service or Resistance? The Mennonite Response to Conscription in World War II," *Mennonite Quarterly Review* 52 (April 1978): 154.

90. Lt. Col. Franklin A. McLean, "Memorandum to the Executive Camp Directors," Camp Operations Division, Selective Service, 1942, privately held.

91. Wachs, "Conscription and American Pacifism," 188; Eisan, *Pathways of Peace,* 394; Sibley and Jacob, *Conscription of Conscience,* 322–23.

92. NSBRO, *Congress Looks at the CO,* 43. See also Bob Stocksdale, interview with author, 1 October 1986, Berkeley, California; American Friends Service Committee, *The Experience of the AFSC in CPS,* 40–51.

93. Gordon Zahn, interview with author, 29 April 1987, Charlestown, Massachusetts. See also Seth Gifford, interview with author, 30 April 1987, Providence, Rhode Island; Fred Convers, interview with author, 2 October 1986, Berkeley, California; Duane Windemiller, interview with author, 22 April 1987, Hampton Beach, New Hampshire; Eugene Carper, interview with author, 10 September 1986, La Verne, California; Donald Baker, interview with author, 1 October 1986, San Francisco, California.

94. Statement of Lewis Hershey, U.S. Senate, Committee on Military Affairs, "Conscientious Objectors' Benefits: Hearings on S. 351 and S. 675," 78th Congress, 1st session (Washington DC: Government Printing Office, 1943), 23.

95. In fact, a senator from North Carolina made casual reference to CPS in a debate on a compensation bill, saying, "At the present time there are about 7,000 conscientious objectors in concentration camps throughout the country"; NSBRO, *Congress Looks at the CO,* 62.

96. Gordon Zahn, *Another Part of the War,* 81. See also Paul Delp, interview with author, 3 March 1987, Orange, California.

97. James Lowerre, interview with author, 3 March 1987, Orange, California. See also Leland Sateren, interview with author, 9 February 1987, Edina, Minnesota.

98. Hoopes, *Americans Remember,* 235; Sanford Rothman, quoted in *Against the Tide,* Hurwitz and Simpson, eds.; Herman Nightengale, SOH interview; Albert Herbst, interview with author, 6 September 1986, La Verne, California; Eugene Carper, interview with author, 10 September 1986, La Verne, California.

99. Roy Mast, self-interview answering author's questions, May 1987. See also Adrian Wilson, quoted in *Against the Tide,* Hurwitz and Simpson, eds.; Duane Windemiller, interview with author, 22 April 1987, Hampton Beach, New Hampshire; George Fischer, interview with author, 22 April 1987, Danvers, Massachusetts.

100. Zahn, *Another Part of the War,* 73. See also Howard Ten Brink, interview with author, 24 September 1986, Modesto, California.

101. Delmar Stanley, interview with author, 24 February 1987, La Verne, California; Sigmund Cohn, interview with author, 30 September 1986, Berkeley, California; Fred Convers, interview with author, 2 October 1986, Berkeley, California; Irvin Richert, SOH interview; Lyle Krug, interview with author, 28 August 1986, Mission Viejo, California.

102. Donald Baker, interview with author, 1 October 1986, San Francisco, California.

103. Robert Cary, interview with author, 1 October 1986, San Francisco, California; Loris Habegger, SOH interview. See also David Jones, SOH interview.

104. Carl Paulson, interview with author, 23 April 1987, Upton, Massachusetts; Gordon Kaufman, interview with author, 29 April 1987, Cambridge, Massachusetts.

105. Dwight Hanawalt, interview with author, 10 September 1986, La Verne, California.

106. Peter Bartel, SOH interview. See also George Fischer, interview with author, 22 April 1987, Danvers, Massachusetts; Joe Dell, interview with author, 27 September 1986, Modesto, California.

107. Gene Yoder, SOH interview. See also Laban Peachey, SOH interview; Russell Jarboe, interview with author, 25 February 1987, La Verne, California.

108. Seth Gifford, interview with author, 30 April 1987, Providence, Rhode Island. See also Wesley Prieb, SOH interview; Gordon W. Nutson, interview with author, 25 September 1986, Modesto, California; Delmar Stanley, interview with author, 24 February 1987, La Verne, California.

109. Paul Ashby, interview with author, 30 September 1986, San Francisco, California; Richard Brown, interview with author, 2 October 1986, Berkeley, California; Zahn, *Another Part of the War,* 68–69.

110. Donald Beachler, interview with author, 26 September 1986, Modesto, California; Vernon Blosser, SOH interview; Hubert Brubaker, interview with author, 25 September 1986, Modesto, California; Justus Holsinger, SOH interview; Allen Grunau, SOH interview.

111. Vernon Blosser, SOH interview; Samuel Guhr, SOH interview; Zahn, *Another Part of the War,* 213; Lyle Krug, interview with author, 28 August 1986, Mission Viejo, California; Arthur Bryant, self-interview answering author's questions, May 1987.

112. Robert Cary, interview with author, 1 October 1986, San Francisco, California; James Lowerre, interview with author, 3 March 1987, Orange, California; Zahn, *Another Part of the War,* 64–66.

113. Dwight Hanawalt, interview with author, 10 September 1986, La Verne, California.

114. Otto Dahlke, "Values and Group Behavior in Two Camps for Conscientious Objectors," *American Journal of Sociology* 51 (July 1945): 27.

115. Arthur Bryant, self-interview answering author's questions, May 1987. See also anonymous World War II conscientious objector, interview with author, 21

February 1987; Eugene Carper, interview with author, 10 September 1986, La Verne, California; David Jones, SOH interview.

116. William E. Stafford, *Down in My Heart* (Elgin, IL: Brethren Publishing House, 1947), 76; Joe Dell, interview with author, 27 September 1986, Modesto, California; G. Hayes Reed, interview with author, 25 September 1986, Modesto, California; J. John J. Miller, SOH interview.

117. Robert Cary, interview with author, 1 October 1986, San Francisco, California. For further discussion of the tensions involved in CPS work, see James Lowerre, interview with author, 3 March 1987, Orange, California.

118. Zahn, *Another Part of the War,* 82.

119. Wittner, *Rebels Against War,* 78–79. For examples of work slowdowns and strikes in a Brethren camp, see Gerald Rubin, interview with author, 2 October 1986, Corte Madera, California.

120. Robert Cary, interview with author, 1 October 1986, San Francisco, California. The most serious strike to arise in CPS took place at the Glendora, California camp after the AFSC withdrew its administration. At this point, the war had been over for six months, and still COs were not being released because the government gave preference to soldiers, releasing them first so that they could have the chance to re-enter the economy without competition from COs. When Selective Service took over administration of the Glendora camp, approximately 150 COs called a work strike to protest their continued confinement. Eventually, all of the strikers were arrested, but most of them had the charges against them dropped and were released from prison and then CPS; only those the government adjudged to be "troublemakers" were charged for violation of the Selective Service Act. See Fred Convers, interview with author, 2 October 1986, Berkeley, California; Sibley and Jacob, *Conscription of Conscience,* 337–39.

121. Flynn, "Hershey and the Conscientious Objector," 4; U.S. Director of Selective Service, "Selective Service and Victory," Semiannual Report, vol. 4 (Washington DC: Government Printing Office, 1948), 183; Sibley and Jacob, *Conscription of Conscience,* 239; U.S. Selective Service System, *Conscientious Objection,* Special Monograph no. 11 (Washington DC: Government Printing Office, 1950), 89.

122. James Bristol, interview with author, 27 May 1987, Philadelphia, Pennsylvania; Bill Colburn, interview with author, 5 May 1987, Concord, New Hampshire.

123. Malcolm Parker, telephone interview with author, 28 February 1987. See also Caleb Foote, telephone interview with author, 28 February 1987.

124. Lawrence Templin, SOH interview.

125. Fred Barnes, telephone interview with author, 13 May 1987.

126. Tony Randles, quoted in *Against the Tide,* Hurwitz and Simpson, eds. See also Naeve, *A Field of Broken Stones,* 128.

127. Caleb Foote, telephone interview with author, 28 February 1987.

128. Julien Cornell, *Conscience and the State: Legal and Administrative Problems of Conscientious Objectors, 1943–1944* (New York: John Day, 1945), 16; Peter Brock, *Twentieth-Century Pacifism,* 199; Holley Cantine and Dachine Rainer, eds., *Prison Etiquette: The Convict's Compendium of Useful Information* (Bearsville, NY: Retort Press, 1950), 74.

129. Lawrence Templin, SOH interview; Neil Glixon, Polner interview; George Brumley, letter answering author's questions, 4 June 1987.

130. James Bristol, interview with author, 27 May 1987, Philadelphia, Pennsylvania. See also Naeve, *A Field of Broken Stones,* 201; Caleb Foote, telephone interview with author, 28 February 1987.

131. Neil Glixon, Polner interview.

132. Harry Elmer Barnes, "Conscientious Objectors as a Correctional Problem in the Second World War," *Prison World* 6 (July-August 1944): 29–30.

133. Sibley and Wardlaw, *COs in Prison,* 44–45; Wittner, *Rebels Against War,* 87–88; Peck, *We Who Would Not Kill,* 157.

134. James Bristol, interview with author, 27 May 1987, Philadelphia, Pennsylvania.

135. Malcolm Parker, *Prison Privilege* (Kaslo, British Columbia: KLC Publications, 1984), 81–86.

136. Wallace Nelson, Hurwitz interview.

137. Fred Barnes, telephone interview with author, 13 May 1987.

138. Peck, *We Who Would Not Kill,* 95–96; Caleb Foote, telephone interview with author, 28 February 1987.

139. Sibley and Wardlaw, *COs in Prison,* 35. See also Naeve, *A Field of Broken Stones,* 73.

140. Fred Barnes, telephone interview with author, 13 May 1987.

141. John E. Hampton, letter to his lawyer James Randles, 4 February 1945, letters from prison, War Resisters League, Document Group 40, Swarthmore College Peace Collection, Swarthmore, Pennsylvania. See also Parker, *Prison Privilege,* 73; Lawrence Templin, SOH interview.

142. Richard Brown, interview with author, 2 October 1986, Berkeley, California; Donald Baker, interview with author, 1 October 1986, San Francisco, California; Carl Paulson, interview with author, 23 April 1987, Upton, Massachusetts; Caleb Foote, telephone interview with author, 28 February 1987.

143. James Bristol, interview with author, 27 May 1987, Philadelphia, Pennsylvania.

144. Malcolm Parker, telephone interview with author, 28 February 1987; Wallace Nelson, Hurwitz interview; Bill Richards, statement to parole board, 13 January 1946, quoted in Edward C. M. Richards, *They Refuse to Be Criminals: Parole and the Conscientious Objector,* Nur Mahal Publication no. 1, 1946; Lawrence Templin, SOH interview.

145. Information on COs misclassified I-A and the problems they faced in the army can be found in Sibley and Jacob, *Conscription of Conscience,* 98–109, and American Civil Liberties Union, *Conscience and War* (New York: American Civil Liberties Union, 1943), 39.

146. Clarence E. Pickett, *For More than Bread: An Autobiographical Account of 22 Years' Work with the AFSC* (Boston: Little, Brown & Co., 1953), 334; U.S. Director of Selective Service, *Selective Service and Victory,* 179.

147. Anonymous World War II CO, letter to friends, 4 February 1944, privately held. See also Charles Klaffke, interview with author, 23 February 1987, Duarte, California; Paul Ashby, interview with author, 30 September 1986, San Francisco, California.

148. George Brown, Jr., interview with author, 1 June 1987, Washington DC. See also Albert Herbst, interview with author, 6 September 1986, La Verne, California; Richard Brown, interview with author, 2 October 1986, Berkeley, California.

149. George Brown, Jr., interview with author, 1 June 1987, Washington DC.

150. Paul Ashby, interview with author, 30 September 1986, San Francisco, California.

151. Pickett, *For More than Bread,* 334; U.S. Director of Selective Service, *Selective Service and Victory,* 179.

152. Delmar Stanley, interview with author, 24 February 1987, La Verne, California.

153. Arthur Bryant, self-interview answering author's questions, May 1987.

154. Henry Blocher, interview with author, 10 September 1986, La Verne, California; Charles Baker, interview with author, 24 September 1986, Modesto, California; Walter Juhnke, SOH interview.

155. Sibley and Wardlaw, *COs in Prison,* 5.

156. Richard Brown, interview with author, 2 October 1986, Berkeley, California.

157. Abraham Zwickel, Polner interview; Harris et al., *The Homefront,* 114; Wallace Nelson, Hurwitz interview; Arthur Wiser, statement to judge, quoted in Arthur and Lila Weinberg, *Instead of Violence* (New York: Grossman, 1963), 135.

4

Foundations of Pacifism

For many World War II conscientious objectors, religious concepts are foundational to the justification of their pacifism. This is no doubt traceable in part to sociological reasons: pacifism was vigorously promoted by the churches in the interwar years, and religion was not only the legal basis for conscientious objection, but also the most socially acceptable reason for being a CO during "the good war."[1] But in another sense, religion is an obvious choice for providing the groundwork of pacifism. A primary function of religion is to establish what is of ultimate value; any argument about morality, particularly one as basic yet unconventional as pacifism, profits from an appeal to ultimate value. In some cases, COs are careful to state that their position is not religious, but are nevertheless clear about expressing the ultimate, non-religious, values that inspire their pacifism.

Another major foundation for pacifism is not religious, but pragmatic. The political views of COs—their interpretation of the nature and causes of war—are often a crucial part of their objection to war. Without appeal to any underlying religious or quasi-religious motivation for pacifism, some COs are quite capable of providing an explanation for the phenomenon of war and a mandate for refusing to participate in it. More often, the religious and political views of COs are intermingled and offer mutual support to one another. Sometimes the religious rejection of war seems primary, and the CO's understanding of what war is and why it occurs is just a reflection of his pre-existing commitment to pacifism. Other times the reverse appears to be true: the CO finds that the idea of war offends him, and this prompts him to articulate the philosophical basis for his objection.

CHRISTIAN FOUNDATIONS FOR PACIFISM

God

The conceptions of God put forth by World War II COs cover the full range of Christian theology from the very liberal to the very conservative, having in common only their ability to produce an aversion to participation in war. At the more orthodox end of the spectrum, some COs speak of God as a powerful personality demanding praise and glory from humanity, and holding out the incentive of eternal life and the disincentive of eternal damnation. Though this view could be read as merciless, none of the COs I spoke with seemed to regard God as vindictive or unduly harsh. They spoke of God as deeply desiring the salvation of the entire world, at worst remaining indifferent to the fate of those who choose not to glorify him.* Paul Phillips, a Christadelphian CO, explained that humankind was created for the sole purpose of giving glory to God, and if individuals turn their backs on God, God bears no responsibility for them. The unregenerate are left to die without the resurrection and eternal life promised to those that glorify God.[2]

Obedience becomes a key virtue for the CO who sees God as a ruler to be pleased. Gil Bertochini expressed his doubts about civil disobedience by drawing a parallel between the laws of the state and God's laws: "I think it's an attitude and a spirit. We have many who are in rebellion against anything, any kind of law. I can't for the love of me see that these people who rebel against anything would be those who would obey and follow God's law."[3]

Believing as these COs do in a ruler God who can grant eternal life and who will ultimately triumph in heaven and earth, it is only sensible to accept God's authority and follow his directives. The only remaining link is to ensure that God commands non-participation in war; it is this conviction that determines the CO in his stand. Scriptural sources of God's commands will be discussed later; for the time being it is enough to note that the COs who believe in a personally powerful God believe that God forbids them to fight in war. As George Brumley, a Jehovah's Witness, recalls his gradual conversion to a CO position: "I became more and more convinced that war today is wrong because it is not Jehovah's will; that he does not approve of war today."[4] Or as Samuel Liskey, a member of the Associated Bible Students, remembers telling his draft board: "I told them that I wasn't put here to kill my fellow man and they could take me

*I have chosen to use pronouns for God that are consonant with the view of God I am describing. The "powerful personality" view of God was always described to me with masculine pronouns, and I felt that this was not an accident of the English language, but a theological statement. Other conceptions of God seem less tied to the generally masculine pronouns used to describe them, and in these cases I will refrain from using masculine pronouns in my analysis, and will leave interviewees' pronouns as they were given in the interview.

out and put me up in front of a firing squad before I'd go out and shoot somebody."[5]

It is important to note here that pacifism need not be intrinsic to God's character for the Christian to feel compelled to take a CO position. Indeed, several COs told me they would quite willingly kill people if God commanded it, and explained that God had approved killing for his followers in the past (the holy wars of Israel) and might do so in the future (Armageddon). For example, Paul Phillips describes the position of the Christadelphian denomination as follows:

> We feel that war between nations is morally wrong, but not all war is wrong. For instance, in the Old Testament, God commanded the children of Israel to fight. When God commands anything, it is right. Today, I think war is morally wrong because there is no nation that they call the kingdom of God. . . . And we feel that Christ is coming back to the earth to set up a kingdom here, and when he comes back, he will demand the subservience of the world. And that will be enforced. And I don't know if there will be a war then, and just how that enforcement will take place, but if it is something under the command of God, then it is right.[6]

COs who adopt this position feel bound to obey an individual will (God's), not a principle (killing is wrong), so their pacifism is wholly subordinate to their allegiance to God.

A second important conception of God is as creator. This is one source of the authority granted to the "powerful personality" version of God discussed above, but the concept of a creator God is broader, and produces additional justifications of pacifism. One such justification rests on the premise that as creator, God has the right to determine the question of life or death for creation, and that any attempt to kill another is a usurpation of God's rightful role. Hayes Reed, a Dunkard Brethren, gives this argument: "God has a right to do what he wants to, because human beings, he made us. But we're not to be the one to take a life ourselves."[7]

The concept of a creator God undergirds pacifism in another way as well: not only do humans not have the right to dispense with God's creation, they also have a responsibility to respect and protect creation, because it is good. God is revealed in creation, specifically in the human race, so to kill another is to destroy the beauty God has created. Gilbert Grover defends this position:

> I believe there is a personal God who is a creator of not only the world, but life, and especially man. And this gives inherent worth and dignity to man. . . . So obviously I just can't [believe] the current philosophies in the world, that chance plus enough time equals everything. I just can't believe that the order and harmony and beauty and intricacy of the whole universe, down to the little details of life, can be a matter of accident. There's so much design, there has to be creative intelligence behind it. And then if I think that creative intelligence has created man in his own image—which is not an anthropomorphic God, but making man with moral values built in him, capable of ethical decisions,

> intellect, and all of that—this gives tremendous importance to man. Tremendous dignity to man. And that I have to respect.[8]

Harmon Wilkinson of the Disciples of Christ denomination echoes this sentiment in saying, "International conflict in the twentieth century is not the solution to any problem. All it does is kill and maim lives, all it does is kill God's creature, all it does is kill God's creation, those made in his image."[9]

A third conception of God focuses not on the act of creation, but on the relation between God and humanity, that of divine parent and human children. In the World War II era, this was most commonly phrased "the fatherhood of God and the brotherhood of man," and its implication for pacifists was that brothers and sisters of the same parent should not be killing one another, regardless of the provocation. This family ideal is expressed by Robert Vogel, who was raised in the Evangelical and Reformed denomination, and later converted to Quakerism: "I try to take a world view, just the way I believe God would be looking at the world. If God has eyes to see, we're all his children, or her children. And that's the way I try to look at things."[10] The relationship between self, God, and others is seen as the forum for working out salvation; violence between self and others is seen as a breach in this process and a violation of the fundamental relationships humans share with each other and with God. Vogel continues: "I think salvation comes as one shows compassion, not through any miracle. And I think the grace of God comes in that way, that we see our fulfillment of our own spirits as we are compassionate towards others, and towards ourselves."[11] This principle is also defended by James Bristol, another convert to Quakerism, who says, "What we're called as religious people to do is to try to serve God freely and voluntarily by serving freely and voluntarily one another."[12]

A fourth, and more liberal conception of God is as a cosmic force, not necessarily personal, but certainly positive and beneficent. Under this conception, pacifism is a way of being in harmony with God, an alignment of self with God, and the principles on which God operates. Gordon Nutson describes this viewpoint:

> It [God] is a natural, positive, cosmic force in the universe. There are certain positive forces in the universe that are God's forces. It's just like the law of gravity. You get on a roof and you jump off, and certain things happen. What you sow, you also reap. You plant wheat, you get wheat, you don't get corn. . . . What you're trying to do with most prayer is you're trying to change God's mind. And it seems to me that what we should be doing is trying to find out what this positive force is, cosmic force is, so that we can live our lives rather than trying to change God's mind in terms of these things.[13]

The suggestion here is that violence is not in harmony with the laws of the universe (God's laws), and that it is a religious act to discern God's—and the universe's—preference for nonviolence, and to bend oneself to this law.

A final conception of God that is used by COs to support their pacifism is the Quaker idea of "that of God in each person." Under such a conception, to kill a human being is also to kill the spark of the divine that person harbors within him- or herself. This is condemned in two ways: first, killing fellow humans is elevated to the crime of deicide; second, to kill a person is to deny the power of the God within to redeem and transform that person. George Reeves comments on the first implication in an interview for *Against the Tide:* "After I became a Quaker, I developed more and more the feeling that there really is that of God in each person, that if you kill someone, you're killing the Spirit, the basis of human life."[14] The second theme is captured in a statement made by John Mecartney in an open letter to his friends in 1942 announcing his conscientious objection: "I believe that there is a bit of God in every normal person and that it is our responsibility in building a Christian world to encourage the development of that bit of goodness by love and not to destroy it by killing in war."[15]

Jesus

The dominant mood among COs in World War II was theologically liberal in terms of the role of Jesus in Christianity. Jesus was seen as a great moral teacher, and his divinity was either underplayed or denied. Bill Colburn, then a Baptist, recalls his wartime understanding of Jesus: "My view of Jesus at that time was that he was a very remarkable, exceptional man, a great teacher, but that he was not God-man."[16] Others were willing to accept the divinity of Jesus, but gave it a liberal interpretation. For example, Gordon Nutson favorably quoted Henry Hitt Crane, a World War II-era Methodist minister and pacifist, as saying, "We are all divine in the same respect as Jesus was divine, except he was more intensely divine."[17]

To this way of thinking, the significance of Jesus' life is that he was a human being among his own kind, sharing the same struggles, but bringing great ideas to bear on the problem of life. Dwight Hanawalt, a Brethren CO, expresses this view:

> To say that Jesus and God had this thing figured out from the beginning, and that he was never tempted . . . I mean, that was a fake, you see, and as far as I'm concerned, it wasn't a fake. Jesus, that's why he has real meaning to me is because he got tempted just like the next guy got tempted, and he came through it. And so when he says you can be perfect, he's saying you can.[18]

The theological warrant for Jesus' teachings came not from his identity with God—though in most cases a connection to God was assumed—but from the essential truths he proclaimed. Gale Nutson, along with many others, quoted the old cliché: "I think the things he [Jesus] said were true not because he said them, but because they were true."[19]

One of the things Jesus said, according to these liberal COs, was that we should all be nonviolent. Generally loathe to engage in proof texting, these COs base their belief that Jesus advocated pacifism on a broad understanding of what they called "the life and teachings of Jesus" (a phrase that came up in interviews with astonishing regularity). Robert Vogel traces the inspiration for his pacifism to this source:

> I don't think it was literalism so much as it was the life and spirit that Jesus was emphasizing in his life and in his ministry. You know, I was much taken by his parables, his magnanimity in forgiving people, in challenging people who wanted to stone the prostitute, saying, "You who is without sin cast the first stone." In the beatitudes, in the story of the second mile . . . it was these kinds of teachings and his willingness also to die, reluctantly, I'm sure, without resisting that kind of thing. These are very powerful elements that I guess determine my thinking. And when I joined the church, I made a commitment to follow Jesus.[20]

Imitation of Jesus was a strong theme among those who saw Jesus primarily as a moral teacher. George Fischer of the Advent Christian denomination saw his pacifism as a reflection of Jesus' nonviolence: "I felt that it was not the way Jesus would answer problems. To lethally kill someone else."[21] Or as Joe Dell, a Brethren CO, said: "It was hard for me to reconcile the overall teachings and the dominant style of Jesus' life with taking a gun, going out, and creating mayhem."[22]

Pacifism was seen as so central to Jesus' teachings that for many COs, it was unthinkable that they could be Christian without being pacifist. As Harmon Wilkinson remarked of his conscientious objection: "I just felt that as a Christian you couldn't take any other position."[23] Several COs described their Christianity as inseparable from their pacifism.* For example, James Bristol reported, "I felt back then that Christianity and war and the waging of war and so on were absolutely incompatible. If I ever felt it was necessary to go to war, that then I would renounce my Christian faith. I still feel that, believe that."[24] The sincerity of this commitment to following the teachings of Jesus can be seen perhaps most clearly in the fact that several COs I spoke with were reluctant to call themselves Christian though they believed in the gospel, raised their children in the faith, and attended church throughout their lives. For these COs, "Christian" was a standard so high that to lay claim to the title would be the ultimate in self-congratulation.[25]

Another style of relating Jesus to pacifism is to view Jesus not as the great moral teacher (though he may be that too) but as the atoning sacrifice. Under this interpretation, the primary significance of Jesus is that he paid the debt for human sin and re-established the possibility of human communion with God. This sacrifice is made the foundation for pacifism in a variety of ways: first, Jesus' crucifixion is conceived as a revelation of God's suffering love in which

*In fact, two COs I interviewed did dilute or renounce their Christianity when they broke with pacifism, one when he left CPS during World War II, and another when he had a change of heart after the Korean War and joined the National Guard. See Chapter 5 for details on these pacifist changes of heart.

Christians are called to participate. James Bristol remembers being deeply influenced by Henry Sloane Coffin's interpretation of the crucifixion, called *The Meaning of the Cross*, and concluding "if that kind of suffering love is at the heart of the universe, then that is reality, and nothing is further removed from that than war itself and all that goes into war."[26] Gilbert Grover of the Grace Brethren denomination also sees the crucifixion as an example that Christians are called to emulate by renouncing violence even in self-defense:

> I don't minimize the responsibility I have to try to afford protection to my family. But I think that even Christians place too much emphasis on the importance of their survival, and a very basic concept, the very life of Christ, demonstrated it. He didn't come to get his rights, he came to suffer his wrongs. And . . . the requirement of his disciples is the willingness to be expended in behalf of others.[27]

A second way of deriving a commitment to pacifism from the doctrine of Christ's atoning death is to argue that if one kills another person, one closes off that person's chance of accepting Christ and being saved. This argument surfaced repeatedly among fundamentalist COs, and provides an interesting (though inexact) parallel to the Quaker refusal to kill "that of God in each person." Where the Quaker view assumes a pre-existing spark of the divine in each individual which must not be destroyed, the fundamentalist view sees only fallen humanity, but humanity that nevertheless has the possibility of salvation so long as it remains alive. In *The Unlikeliest Soldier*, a biography of Desmond Doss, the Seventh-Day Adventist noncombatant who was awarded the Congressional Medal of Honor for bravery in battle, this conversation between Doss and another soldier is recorded:

> "It's not up to me to judge whether one of God's children should live or die," Desmond said. "That is a decision for the Lord to make, not me. I believe that I should do everything in my power to help all men hold on to life."
>
> "Suppose they aren't fit to live?"
>
> "Well, the way I look at it," Desmond said, "is that anybody who isn't fit to live surely isn't fit to die! What worse fate could possibly happen to any mortal than to die when he doesn't deserve to live? That would seal his doom forever. No matter how evil a person may be he deserves to live, for he may discover the teachings of Jesus and be saved!"[28]

This argument is taken one step further by a Catholic CO in his Form 47 to include not only refusal to kill, but also willingness to be killed: "If I permitted a bad man to kill me rather than I kill him, that he might later repent and receive pardon for his sins, this I believe would be a sacrifice pleasing to God and keeping the Fifth [Sixth] Commandment [thou shalt not kill]."[29]

A third interpretation of the atonement argues for pacifism as an appropriate response to the millennial hope of Jesus' return. Eunice Liskey, the wife of a World War II CO and herself a member of the Associated Bible Students, describes the connection between Jesus' crucifixion and his return:

> The economy of God is really demonstrated in that it only took one payment for the first man and all of his posterity and heritage, sin and death from him, so that they are guaranteed the opportunity to regain perfection because of the death of Christ. He also has a special offer that he made to those who would follow closely in his steps, lay down their lives as a sacrifice too. And as a result, be highly exalted to be with him.... But the death of Christ guarantees them a return from the grave in the resurrection time to a better condition when Satan will no longer be able to influence them. They will have to abide by the laws of God and be obedient to those laws in order to gain the right to live forever.[30]

Pacifism is drawn into the equation as one of the laws of God (found in scripture), and the motivation to follow the law is the hope of eternal life. As Roy Mast, an Amish CO, reasons:

> I have only one life to lose for my savior. He that loses his life finds it, and he that saves his life by force will lose it. So after all, eternity is a long, long time. And life here on earth is seventy, eighty years. So I'd rather have eternity with Christ than to have a couple years here on this earth with a just cause [just war].[31]

A final relationship between Jesus' crucifixion and Christian pacifism is that of enabling grace. Though the demand to follow Christ's nonresistant example is a difficult one, the ability to live up to this demand is given to the Christian through grace. (Again, the actual command to practice pacifism is found scripturally.) Gilbert Grover finds the strength to be pacifist through the redemptive death of Christ:

> I believe in the biblical concept that man is a rebel, a sinner, however you want to put it, and as such has pulled away from fellowship with the God that created him ... And I find that redemption is in the person of Christ, but was accomplished at Calvary settling the sin question. I believe in his death and his burial and his resurrection. And they're concepts that are even hard to fully grasp, much harder to define, but for those who accept him in a personal way, there is an identification with him. And that identification is not only that he settled the sin question for me, made possible fellowship with God again, but he has given his life, resurrection life and power to those who are identified with him. Which makes it possible to live by ethical principles in a harsh environment that sometimes might say do the opposite: kill. I just don't think that he could do that, or that I can. I have a feeling that he gives the power to meet a situation because of identification with him.[32]

Bible

A number of COs I spoke with rested their pacifism on a literal interpretation of the Bible. For example, Paul Phillips said of his denomination, the

Christadelphians, "We are a very fundamental group. Like the old story that if the Bible had said that Jonah swallowed the whale, we would believe it. So we're very fundamental, we stick very close to the Bible doctrine."[33] The most common scripture cited in support of pacifism by those who take the Bible literally was the sixth commandment given to Moses: "Thou shalt not kill." As Hubert Brubaker, a German Baptist Brethren CO, remarked: "I still feel that the Ten Commandments are as valid today as what they were when they were given to the twelve tribes of Israel."[34] Other common proof texts used by literalist COs included "Vengeance is mine, sayeth the Lord, I will repay," Christ's teaching to turn the other cheek, Christ's admonition to Peter to put up his sword, and especially "If my kingdom were of this world, then would my servants fight."[35]

For those who understand the Bible as the direct word of God, and who feel a responsibility to obey divine commands, these texts provide a strong justification for pacifism. However, some texts literally interpreted seem to suggest that there can be legitimate use of force. Fundamentalist pacifists deal with this difficulty in two ways. The first is to maintain that any interpretation leaves some unexplained residue, but that a pacifist interpretation leaves less than any other interpretation. Gilbert Grover takes this option:

> There are conflicts, particularly with the Old Testament, there are difficulties, but they're not as great as the difficulties of taking any other position. If I try to equate the teachings of Jesus or the whole tenor of the New Testament, redemptive love, loving your fellow man, vengeance belongs to God, whatever it is . . . I just run into a host of problems when I try to see any other position—certainly a militaristic one.[36]

A second method of dealing with problematic texts is to employ a historical motif: in certain eras and under certain circumstances, God approves of violence, but since Christ came, his followers are commanded to be pacifist. According to Paul Phillips, in the Hebrew scriptures God worked with the nation of Israel and approved warfare for them, but since Christ, God works with individuals and not the nation, and the true Christian should have no part of carnal warfare.[37] The position of the Russian Molokans, a small pacifist sect, is similar to this. As one Molokan stated on his Form 47: "Almighty God gave us His only begotten Son and through Him destroyed the ancient dynasty of the House of David and through Him gave us a new Divine Law by which the only weapon allowed was the Word of God and the Spirit of Wisdom."[38]

A somewhat different historical motif is employed by the Jehovah's Witnesses, who see a chronology in the Bible leading up to the year 1914. Fred Barnes describes this historical shift toward a Christian rejection of involvement in warfare:

> I understood that I wasn't to be involved in the affairs of this world because they were contrary to that kingdom under Christ Jesus that was to be set up in 1914. And I took my stand for that kingdom. Christ Jesus is the king of a literal

> government . . . I believe that God's kingdom was set up in 1914 in the time that the world turmoil started, and since that time, I can't be involved with things of the world politically. My allegiance is to God's kingdom, not to any government of this world.[39]

Pacifists who practice a more liberal interpretation of biblical texts do not face this problem of explaining the seeming contradictions between Old Testament wars and New Testament preaching to turn the other cheek. In fact, some pacifists are quite impatient with fundamentalist attempts to integrate the Hebrew scriptures and the New Testament. Gordon Nutson challenges:

> I'd like you to explain to me how come in the same book—not two books, not three books, the same book—that in one section God directed armies to go out in his name and dash the brains of the little children and the women up against the rocks and kill them. Now the same God, in the same book, there was a guy by the name of Jesus came along. And he was following this same God, and God apparently revealed to him that you overcome evil with good. That if somebody hits you on one cheek, you turn the other. And so on. Now try to get a fundamentalist to reasonably give you an answer to that. They can't.[40]

Liberal pacifists did not discard the Bible altogether, but they were willing to disregard large portions as historically conditioned. Wesley Doe, a Baptist CO, accepted a literalist interpretation of the Bible up until an experience in college in which he discovered a fossil lying on the ground and felt compelled to accept the doctrine of evolution and give up his former creationist beliefs. He now writes: "I believe that God inspired many of the writers but not all and not everything written by any of the writers of the Bible. Paul has given us some profound insights but also some very petty notions."[41]

Working with such a hermeneutic, liberal pacifists are free to place their emphasis on whatever portions of the Bible seem most significant to them. Given their interest in the life and teachings of Christ, it is only to be expected that they choose to emphasize the gospel portion of the New Testament. As Gene Carper, an Old Mennonite at the time of World War II, comments: "The teachings of Jesus to me is the essence of the New Testament."[42] Paul Delp, a Disciples of Christ CO, shares this attitude in saying that he does not believe in the Bible so much as in the Jefferson Bible (Jefferson cut out the words of Jesus and let them stand alone).[43] This emphasis on the gospel is narrowed down by many liberal pacifists to an almost exclusive emphasis on the Sermon on the Mount, which is read as a thoroughgoing pacifist text on the basis of verses such as "the meek shall inherit the earth," "turn the other cheek," and "love your enemies."[44] These COs feel free to sort the wheat from the chaff scripturally, but once having located the wheat, they feel bound to interpret it literally. Thus the Sermon on the Mount is viewed as a set of instructions that Christians are supposed to follow to the best of their abilities in all aspects of their lives. Again, these rules are to be followed not because the son of God revealed them, but because they are in fact correct, the best guide we have as to how we ought to live.[45]

A liberal interpretation of scripture led many COs to ignore the Hebrew scriptures in their entirety. Howard Bogen, an Evangelical and Reformed CO, said he focuses on the New Testament in his moral thinking and regards the Hebrew scriptures as historical documents and not much else. Saburo Mizutani, a Methodist CO, goes even farther to remark that "in the Old Testament they didn't say anything about pacifism."[46] However, there were some inspirations for pacifism from the Hebrew scriptures that appealed not only to literalists, but also to those who interpret the Bible more liberally. James Bristol, in a sermon written to explain his decision not to register for the 1940 draft, said:

> It is in the spirit of that prophetic tradition that I would make my witness. There has been far and above too much in our generation of the Church's protesting to the state only when the prerogatives of the institution were being challenged. How different was the protest which the Old Testament prophets presented to the rulers of their day! They did not stand before kings to complain about infringements upon their own personal liberties or upon the privileges of their institution. Rather was the burden of their message always that the policy of the king was damaging to the nation itself and to the Jewish people. I feel with all my being that it is more than high time for the Christian ministers of the world to take a stand against the increasingly powerful paganism of our day, not because the philosophy of force has begun to step on the toes of the Church or of her ministers, but solely and simply because the philosophy of force will prove ruinous to the nation and destroy the very people that it claims to protect.[47]

Church

Several arguments for pacifism are grounded in the idea that the church has a special mission on earth, and is responsible to a different standard than is the state. The strongest such view is the two kingdoms concept, found most prominently in the conservative wing of the peace churches. Aretas Boone of the German Baptist Brethren describes his understanding of the two kingdoms:

> They're two separate things. If you're going to be of the church, you can't be of the world, if you're going to be of the world, then your church takes second fiddle. And we feel like there's a complete separation. The world system rules the government, and we are subject to the government, but we don't take part in it.[48]

The existence of the church as a separate kingdom gives an added dimension to the demand to follow Christ's pacifist teachings, since the individual believer is also acting corporately to demonstrate a more excellent way of being to the world. In an unpublished article, "The Christian and the State," Gilbert Grover describes the Christian's duty to the world:

> Being delivered from Satan's dominion and translated into Christ's Kingdom, the Christian has been denaturalized and denationalized as far as the world system and its governments are concerned. He now has a heavenly citizenship (Phil. 3:20). By identification with Christ, Christians are a crucified, risen and ascended people. . . . While a citizen of heaven, the Christian remains in this world to be an ambassador for Christ (II Cor. 5:20). He has a heavenly commission to bear witness to the truth of the Gospel and is called upon to live consistently with the higher spiritual laws of Christ's Kingdom.[49]

The two kingdoms concept, strictly conceived, does not suggest that the church has any independent authority. It is only as the church is true to divine commands revealed through Christ that it has any rightful authority over the believer. It is thus best understood as a strengthening of pacifism, even a sociological cause of pacifism, but not a justification for it. Loyalty to the church is derivative. As Hayes Reed, a Dunkard Brethren CO, describes the relationship, "I would still go back to obedience to Christ and his teachings. . . . I made that promise when I came into the church, that I would back up the church, her position on peace, nonresistance and so on, because of what Christ said."[50] Nevertheless, for the members of denominations who disfellowship those who go to war, there is an additional justification for pacifism, and this is the baptismal vow made to be nonresistant, a vow made in the communal context of the church. The CO is thus bound not only to follow Christ, but to remain in the community of believers who support pacifism, a community that at times is allowed to stand in for the authority of God on which it rests.[51]

Less common is the appeal made directly to the authority of the church. Here again, authority ultimately rests with God, but the church is taken to be not just a community of believers (who could at any time go wrong), but a continuing revelation of God's will. Characteristic of this sort of justification of pacifism is the following statement by a Catholic CO on his Form 47: "The Catholic Church has always enjoined upon the Religious: i.e., upon those who have bound themselves to follow the best means to heaven, that they should not take part in war."[52] The Quaker church also holds a certain degree of authority for some COs because it is believed that by seeking the will of God together, a firmer truth is revealed to the church than to the individual believer. Thus though one individual may feel uncertain, he or she can rely with some confidence on the opinion of the church as a whole.[53]

The church also comes to the support of pacifism in that it is seen as a primary identity group for the Christian, one demanding a loyalty that can override the national loyalties upon which war relies. Thus Fred Barnes, a Jehovah's Witness who was imprisoned for insisting on neutrality toward World

War II, can now say:

> Just let me sum it up this way: Jehovah's Witnesses in Germany did not fight Jehovah's Witnesses in the United States, to be at peace. So how can a Catholic in Germany fight a Catholic in the United States? So that's what gives us peace of mind. . . . This is the Christian brotherhood that I've grown into that I started back there when I told you, back in 1942.[54]

Violence within a single religious group is anathema to those who see their church as a family of individuals united around common beliefs and practices, and who therefore have no conceivable reason to kill each other. George Brumley, also a Jehovah's Witness, remarks on this: "Isn't it amazing that both sides fighting in Nicaragua are Catholic; that Iran and Iraq are both Moslem, that most of the wars of history have been fought between sides claiming to worship the same God?"[55] This loyalty to co-religionists is sometimes extended to all people, bringing the argument back to the earlier discussed "fatherhood of God and brotherhood of man" justification of pacifism. Gil Bertochini, a Seventh-Day Adventist, illustrates this form of pacifist reasoning:

> Another guiding thing in this is that there were Christians in other nations. There were Christians in the German army, as well as in Japan. And if you didn't learn to love all people, at least you ought to love your brothers and sisters in Christ. But I believe very strongly, regardless of what their affiliations are, regardless of what their beliefs are, they're still your brother and sister. How can you go to battle against them and kill, if you love? I mean, that's inconsistent.[56]

For other COs, the Christian church provides quite a different justification for pacifism. Far from leading the believer down the true path, these COs see the church as having corrupted Jesus' teachings for inferior ends. Thus part of the justification for their pacifism is the belief that they must bring the church back to Jesus' teachings, that they must walk the true path so that the church can see where it lies. Gordon Nutson rails against the corruption of the Christian church when he says:

> If there was a war tomorrow morning, the Christian church as we know the Christian church today, they'd put a flag in their navel and get a man to start a drum and a bugle and they'd go down the street and support the war effort a hundred percent. And that's all in the name of Jesus Christ, to go out and murder in his name. And so frankly, you see, this whole thing is very difficult for me, to be in the church today, when this is the emphasis of the average person in the Christian church. For some crazy reason this message of the philosophy and teachings of Jesus Christ has never got through to the people that are sitting in the pews.[57]

NON-CHRISTIAN FOUNDATIONS FOR PACIFISM

Religious Foundations

Though the majority of World War II COs were Christian, and gave Christian justifications for their pacifism (at least to me and to their draft boards), a subset of COs cited other religious warrants for their pacifism. First there were those who came out of a Christian background, but have since come to believe that Christianity is only one of many world religions, and has no special claim to cosmic truth. These COs say that there are many paths to God, or as James Bristol puts it, "all religious faiths—and atheism too—are in communion with truth."[58] Though none of the COs I spoke with defended the proposition directly, they implied that pacifism is taught in all great religions, and it is this concept of religion-in-general on which they base their pacifism.[59] This is understood as a reinforcement of pacifism on the theory that people in different times and places, worshiping different gods, have come to the same (and correct) conclusion about the unrighteousness of war.

COs who were raised outside the Christian tradition were fairly rare in World War II. However, there were some who converted to non-Christian religious affiliations in adulthood and a few who were brought up in other traditions. There was a significant population of Jewish COs during World War II,[60] but those I spoke with justified their pacifism on philosophical and political grounds rather than religious ones. Still, they reflected that their Judaism affected their choice of conscientious objection, at least in terms of values which they had divorced from their religious roots. For example, Gerry Rubin remarked, "I understand more now than I did then . . . the part that Judaism had in forming my values system . . . the awareness in which the Jewish community as a whole was concerned about their fellow man, and about the future of man, and what man should do here and now about the world."[61] Max Kleinbaum takes a similar viewpoint:

> Religion played no part in motivating my position. What did play an important role was my understanding and appreciation of Jewish life as it was lived in the ghetto and as it was reflected by my parents, my father particularly. The emphasis on education, as against material things in life, the emphasis on social justice. . . . Everything I knew about Judaism emphasized values which were and which are completely inconsistent with the use of war, violence, in the solution of problems.[62]

Another non-Christian group represented among World War II COs were the Hopi Indians. The Hopi were never granted CO status by the government because Selective Service maintained that Hopi objection was not religious but political, grounded on the fact that Hopis considered themselves citizens of the Hopi nation and therefore owed nothing, and certainly not military service, to the

United States. This contention seems at least partially true. In the accounts I read of Hopi conscientious objection, resistance to federal government hegemony over the Hopi tribes was a prominent note.[63] Nevertheless, the Hopi COs also gave religious arguments for their pacifism. In an interview for *Against the Tide,* Thomas Banyacya, a Hopi CO, recalls his decision to refuse to register for the draft:

> We are all under one power of God or whatever you call him. In Hopi we call him Massau'u. I better leave and go the way of the Hopi belief and follow the Hopi to maintain the peaceful way, Hopi life of truth, honest and peaceful, kind. And so I want to follow that. . . . So that night when I hear the President of the United States talk about registration, I decided to wait awhile. And then I saw in my mind that I better not register. I think it best that I follow the law of the Great Spirit. . . . Then I just decided I must hold onto the Spiritual Way like the Elders say.[64]

Several COs in my sample professed belief in reincarnation, and saw this as a support for their pacifism. Concurrent with the idea of their souls continuing in future lives was a belief that continued spiritual growth was their primary responsibility and the responsibility of all other living beings. This concept of spiritual growth and reincarnation was used in two ways to justify pacifism. The first is offered by a theosophist CO when he argues: "Nobody has the right to interrupt the learning processes of somebody else by killing him. That just shouldn't be done. Period."[65] Reincarnation also works to fortify pacifism by making survival and self-defense seem far less important, and thus taking away a major impetus to violent resistance. Ian Thiermann, in an interview with Deena Hurwitz, stresses this point in saying, "Death is of very little meaning at this particular point. We are all going to die, and my own understanding of life and death has moved so dramatically that I don't even question it: I know that I'm going to move into another vibration, whether I like it or not, whether [I] have faith or not."[66]

Philosophical Foundations

Non-religious arguments for pacifism in World War II were most often based on humanistic principles. Phrases such as "respect for human dignity," "sanctity of individual personality," "preciousness of the human being," and "honoring all forms of life" were typical of this view.[67] This humanism is the non-religious correlate of the previously discussed Christian conception of a creator God whose good creation must be treated with kindness and respect. The only significant difference between the two is that in the case of humanism, respect for life is not contingent on its divine source, but can be directly perceived in nature as it presents itself to our minds and senses. Rudy Potochnik illustrates this lack of concern with the source of creation when he says: "I do think the human race is a marvelous experiment of something, of God or nature or something. And I'd like to see it progress."[68] Pacifism is derived from humanism through a respect for persons and a desire to protect and preserve humanity. Caleb Foote draws the limits of a classic pacifist humanism in saying: "I did not then and I don't now believe in any supreme being. I believe that life is a natural process, and that we live and that we die. The idea of eternal life has always seemed an absurdity to me. . . . But I believe very strongly that you try to live so that you don't harm people or things."[69]

Humanist pacifism also balances on the idea that violence is not a good or productive way of relating, that nature does not depend on the war of one against all for its survival, but rather thrives on mutual support. Interpersonal caring and service to one another is a way of getting along, of demonstrating one's respect for the humanity of others. This is stated succinctly by James Bristol, who says, "there is a power other than that of violence."[70] COs sometimes rationalized this as an ethic of "niceness," according to which violence is wrong because it is unkind.[71]

Another humanistic parallel to a religious argument for pacifism is the concept of the human family. It relies on the divine parent/human siblings model discussed earlier, except that the divine parent is removed as an unnecessary extra postulate. Ed Jones follows this model in stating, "As a human race we are one, we live on a planet with one interdependent, interrelated support system."[72] Wally Nelson, in an interview with Deena Hurwitz, elaborates on this theme and the pacifism he sees inherent in it:

> By the time the war came along, I was well enough on in my thoughts, thinking that when I was invited to go and kill the Germans and Japanese, I was being invited to go and kill my brothers and sisters. It was just as real to me to say, "OK, the Nelson family is a pretty bad lot, and we want you to take this gun and kill your family because we can't get along, so we need to have peace, take this gun and kill your siblings and your mother and father."[73]

Bayard Rustin, a World War II CO who later became a prominent civil rights activist, states the fraternal ideal and its pacifist implication as a basic ethical premise in a letter he wrote to his draft board in 1943: "That which separates man from his brother is evil and must be resisted."[74]

Another philosophical support for pacifism is the notion of a radical individualism. Decisions should be made by the thinking individual alone, and not turned over to the state, the church, or anyone else. The connection between individualism and pacifism is asserted by Richard Brown:

> When people give their assent to a government or to a military to do what they are ordered to do, without thinking the whole thing over and making the decision on their own, according to their own conscience, that's where the real difficulty lies. We must never turn over our consciences to any one else. And if people all over the world observed that, then there couldn't be any war.[75]

This insistence on individual conscience, on earnestly striving after moral truth, does not guarantee that one will reach the conclusion that violence or war is always wrong (though Brown, for example, believes that it will), but it does pave the way toward acceptance of the social nonconformity that is part of conscientious objection.

One final philosophical foundation for pacifism is a conception of aesthetics that sees the purpose of life to be one of creating and conserving beauty. War is rejected as destructive, and as a distraction from the higher purposes of art. There was a significant contingent of artists in CPS who saw participation in war as lying outside their mission in life. William Everson, a World War II CO and poet, gives a reasoned basis to this pacifism of aesthetics in an interview for *Against the Tide:*

> I pointed out that the only thing that survives in a culture is the aesthetic contribution. Everything else will go, but one thing lasts. . . . Because the final thing that humanity doesn't want to see perish is art. It's almost as if the art product is the secret unconscious reason for its cultural existence. It isn't validated in its material wealth, that's very temporary. Nor is it validated in its military victories, because those are transitory too. But it is validated in its art, because this is uplifting, both transcendental and permanent. Even in religion, it's the artwork that survives. I think it's universal in that the aesthetic principle in Thomistic thought specifies that everything created retains in some way the trace of the Creator. And it's the aesthetic factor in the secular mode which is the divinity principle.[76]

POLITICAL FOUNDATIONS FOR PACIFISM

COs analyze the causes of war in two basic ways that can be separated from their religious and philosophical reflections on war and violence: the first is an economic analysis which traces the evil of war to greed; the second is a social analysis which insists that the taproot of war is self-righteousness. These two approaches are not incompatible, and most COs appealed to both as they explained what was wrong with war as a feature of international politics. Finally, COs raise objections to the practice of war, to the particular kind of killing war involves.

The Economic Analysis

By far the most common pattern among World War II COs was to point an accusing finger at the profit motive, or less euphemistically, at human greed, when looking for the cause of war. In the context of World War II, the preferred title for the villain behind international war was "munitions maker"; this has since been changed to "the military-industrial complex." The concept is essentially the same though the individual malice and immorality of the munitions marketeer has been traded for the bureaucratic inertia of the military-industrial complex. The earlier "munitions maker" version of the role of greed in promoting war is illustrated in this statement given by James Lowerre:

> I had heard of *Merchants of Death* and I knew about Krupp [World War I German war manufacturer] and so forth. And that when they flew over the foreign territory, there were places they were not to drop bombs because munition makers on both sides knew enough to avoid the other one. After all, what's going to perpetuate it if they stop having armaments on one side? We're going to win, and then we won't need more guns.[77]

The argument against the greed of the munitions makers that was established in the aftermath of War World I carried over to the wars that followed. Howard Ten Brink remembers being eager to join the Abraham Lincoln Brigade to fight in the Spanish Civil War, but says he has since realized that that war was far less clear cut than he thought at the time, because "Russia was interested in trying out their weapons, and they were supporting the loyalists. And Nazi Germany was interested in trying out their weapons, and so they were supporting the fascists."[78]

A number of COs argued that the manufacture of weapons, and the greed that motivates it, is pointing us in the direction of war even today. Ed Jones gives the updated version of the role of the profit motive when he says:

> And just recently, with the star wars, for example, someone said—which sounded very true as far as I'm concerned—that if star wars isn't stopped right here at the very beginning, that there's no way to stop it, because there will be contracts out to different pieces in L.A., Seattle, Dallas, and so on, for building parts of this. And if there's any move in Congress to eliminate it, they'll be flooded with letters from these people saying, "Don't eliminate it, we need it," and so on.[79]

The conviction that the profit motive lies at the heart of international war is stated most simply by Gordon Nutson, in a slogan repeated by several COs I interviewed: "My dad would say, 'If you took all the profit out of war, there would be no war.' And he's exactly right."[80]

The obvious corollary of the belief that nations go to war because munitions makers want money and governments want power is that the ordinary soldier is ultimately fighting for others' gain and not his own. The catch-phrase given by COs for this argument was, "It's a rich man's war and a poor man's fight." The poor are drafted and killed, while the rich are "making all kinds of profit and eating three-inch steaks."[81]

While the profit motive as a source of war was typically attributed to nations and industrialists, and individuals viewed as their victims, some COs also cited the greed and selfishness of individuals as a cause of war. Reference was occasionally made to the increased standard of living for individual workers in the defense industries,[82] but more often COs argued that average Americans were willing to resort to war to hold onto the wealth we enjoy compared to the poverty of the rest of the world. As Carl Paulson reflects:

> If you are in a war, it's usually to defend our way of life, which is on top of the world, you know? We have a higher standard of living, and all that kind of stuff. I remember seeing an ad once, I think it was in the *Woman's Day* magazine. I don't know what company was making it, but there's a picture of a Japanese with a handful of rice. It said, "Is this what you'd like for your daily food?" I don't know what big company had that ad, but I said, well, that's kind of selfish, obviously.[83]

Another, and related, economic source of war is found in the rightful demand of the poor for a share of the world's wealth. The wealthy love war for its ability to produce financial gain, while the poor must resort to war out of desperation, but in either case, war is caused by an unjust division of money and other resources, and an unwillingness on the part of the wealthy to give up their lion's share. Arle Brooks, in a statement to a court trying him for refusal to register for the draft, cites economic injustice as the cause of war: "The present wars are the natural product of our economic system and our way of living. Preparation for war is easier than going through the painful process of reconstructing our social and economic system and improving our own way of living."[84] Arthur Bryant takes the same position: "We cannot have a world where 10 percent of the people have 60 percent of the wealth, and endure. At some point there has to be some give and take and some adjustment. And in one sense at least, that's part of what wars are."[85]

The economic analysis of war sometimes translated into the more general objection that war is a misuse of material resources. This argument was particularly prevalent in interwar pacifism, where the financial cost of World War I to the nations involved was reported routinely as a rhetorical device (one which was no doubt very effective in the midst of the Great Depression). A typical statement of the position that war is prohibitively expensive is given by Sigmund Cohn:

> When I think of all the human resources and financial resources that are spent on war or defense; if that were used to feed the world, to improve the world, God, what a difference it would make! You could destroy poverty. But half our budget goes for war. Just think of what could be done, on a world-wide basis, with just the money from our country.[86]

The Social Analysis

An alternative analysis of war focuses on self-righteousness as the fundamental cause and evil of war. COs traced the scandal of war to the false identification of the individual's well-being with the ascendancy of the nation where he or she lives, and to the self-righteousness this attitude engenders. COs were quick to argue against nationalism and individual self-righteousness by pointing out that the misdeeds of the enemy are matched or exceeded by our own.* For example, in a letter to friends in February of 1945, Gordon and Gale Nutson made this comment: "It is our belief that we will never have a peaceful world if we continually place the guilt on the other fellow's shoulders. Only when we admit with the others that we have been guilty too, will we be on the road to making this a lasting peace."[87] This impulse to share the guilt is pervasive among World War II COs and also in much of World War II pacifist literature. The reluctance to equate one's own failings with the perceived crimes of others is seen as a fundamental cause of war. Pacifist rhetoric frequently relies on the attempt to draw parallels between the behavior of opposing sides and shatter the comforting illusion that there are "good guys" and "bad guys."[88]

COs also cite religion as giving a further support to the self-righteousness of individuals and their nations. Several COs noted that wars are generally fought with high moral purpose and the conviction that God, truth, and justice demand war. Religion, a source of pacifism for many COs, was still occasionally seen as a cause of war-mongering among the masses. Saburo Mizutani takes this position:

> It's a very strange thing. Take, for instance, in World War I: the British and the French were fighting a war for democracy and God, and the Germans were saying the same thing. And I think that's all part of the deal of trying to make the war a little more moral, you know. And because you're fighting it because of God, it's right and proper to fight.[89]

Fred Convers agrees, arguing (along with Linus Pauling, whom he quotes) that when one sees the history of religious wars, continuing today in Lebanon and Ireland, one has to conclude that theism has been very harmful to the human race.[90]

The Nature of War

Regardless of the ends for which a war is fought, COs object to the means employed. At the most simple and basic level, war is objectionable because it

*One important exception (which will receive more attention in later chapters) must be made for those pacifists who do not oppose war as such, but still feel they must refrain from participating in it. On one level, these pacifists offer a diagnosis of the causes of war that explains their refusal to participate, but since they hold a different moral standard for people other than themselves, they are able to favor United States participation in war, and blame the enemies of the United States for causing war. Thus on the political level pacifists who oppose only their own participation in war can hold views about war that are virtually indistinguishable from those of the non-pacifist mainstream.

involves the killing of other human beings. Terms such as "atrocity" and "indiscriminate mass murder" were used to describe the practice of war, and some COs emphasized most strongly this feature of uncontrolled, indiscriminate, and mass killing of human beings.[91] Other COs focused more narrowly on an individual level, purposely setting aside the mass nature of war and concentrating instead on the fundamental one-to-one relationship between enemy soldiers. These COs found a warrant for pacifism in two aspects of this relationship: first, in the moral taint acquired by killing another human being, and second, in the untimely death of an enemy soldier. In this comment, Richard Brown picks up both strands of thought:

> I tried to think it over as carefully as I could, what it would really be like to be out there shooting at people and being shot at: the confusion, worrying about it afterwards. I think when you kill somebody, even if he's the enemy, you have squeamish feelings about it. Most people do. And I think probably a lot of soldiers, they do it, but they don't like it, and they don't want to think about it very much. As a matter of fact, we had in our neighborhood a man who'd been in the First World War. Nobody could get him to talk about it. And he'd done some pretty heroic things, but he didn't want to think about it. It's just very depressing to kill people. The dead body's lying out in front of you, and you think, I could have been that guy. And he probably has a family that's going to miss him badly. And what's the reason of it all? Is it a good enough reason for having shot him? And that's what you worry about.[92]

Here the concern is not only with killing (as was true in the religious arguments for pacifism) but with killing the innocent, and this concern ties back into the belief that wars are fought because of nationalism and self-righteousness. For it is key that if individuals do identify themselves and their interests with the state, they do so in error, because the state does not serve the people's true interests. The moral force comes in the conclusion that when the government's and the people's aims and interests do not intersect, the people should not be made to suffer for the misdeeds of the government. Paul Delp makes this argument when he says: "To say that because a country has a bad government, you should kill the people that are under that government, I just don't follow this kind of logic. I don't understand it. It's beyond me."[93]

Under this view, war is a battle between the innocent and the innocent, with the guilty hiding in their plush offices far from the battle front. Many pacifists saw this as the great offense of war, that violence is not directed toward a person who has harmed you, but toward a person who is a drafted representative of someone who has supposedly harmed someone you have been drafted to represent. Robert Vogel makes this point: "The German youth, the Japanese youth, the Italian youth . . . all the young people that participated in the war virtually, were drafted. They had no personal quarrels with what the government called the enemy."[94]

This was occasionally broadened to an argument that the problem with war is that it allows violence to escape a personal, immediate context. Thus war is objectionable not only because it is violent, but because it systematizes and depersonalizes violence. Alfred Hassler, a youth secretary for the FOR who refused induction into CPS, recalls meeting a Selective Service violator in prison who told him, "I had no reason to go to war. . . . I'm not mad at anybody, so why should I shoot them?"[95] Don Peretz explains this objection to war in a more principled way:

> I guess it's that being a soldier in war makes one an impersonal killer. A killer not necessarily in defense of one's values or rights, or even life, but killing becomes an end in itself. This of course is the way battles are planned, the way officers who plan attacks plan them. In depersonalizing the enemy into numbers and units, one is also depersonalized, and one also loses one's own humanity.[96]

THE NECESSITY OF RELIGION

Codified in the 1940 Selective Service Act was the belief that true conscientious objection must be based on religious principles. Whether it was cause or effect, most World War II COs did cite religious beliefs in defense of their pacifism. Yet there was no agreement on whether religion is in fact necessary for a consistent pacifism. Some COs defended the assumption of the draft law that pacifism must be religious or that religious pacifism is the only type of pacifism worthy of recognition. For example, Samuel Liskey argued: "Personally I don't believe there is such a thing as a conscientious objector unless he's religious. There's a lot of them that don't base nothing on religion whatsoever. But I don't think they're right. It strictly comes from the Bible."[97] Most COs who held this position did not wish to deny political COs the right to object, but were still dubious about the integrity of a non-religious position. Hubert Brubaker, a German Baptist Brethren, remarked: "You can be not spiritual and be a pacifist, but to have any meaning, I think the two would have to go together."[98]

Other COs saw non-religious pacifism as a definite alternative, but felt that religion put the backbone into pacifism, and that without religion the CO position would be difficult to maintain. Robert Vogel speaks for this viewpoint when he says:

> If it had not been for my strong religious feelings, and if I had to simply rely on intellectual arguments, I probably would not have qualified [as a CO] and furthermore, I doubt whether I would have come out at the same place. I don't know. I really don't know. I think as I observe my colleagues, there were a lot of people who were COs before December 7th, 1941, Pearl Harbor. But once the United States was attacked, they set aside their arguments. There was no further argument.[99]

Howard Ten Brink, a Methodist CO, takes a similar position: "I think religion had very little to do with my decision to be a pacifist, but it had quite a bit to do with the determination to stick out whatever happened."[100]

A number of COs drew on both religious and pragmatic principles in justifying their pacifism, and felt that the two were inseparable. While not holding that any true pacifism had to be based on religion, they believed that in their own experience it was impossible to say what stemmed from religion and what did not. Richard Brown elaborates:

> I think that religion is tied into our lives, it's a part of our lives in a way that we can't separate. And it's hard to say how much is due to this and how much is due to that. How much of whatever decision you make is out of your experience, and how much of it is caused by religious attitudes; you don't know.[101]

Robert Cary gives a slightly different interpretation: "I consider them [reasons for being a pacifist] religious, but then that's partly because they are humanitarian. I can't separate my experience of the commands of the gospel from being involved with the world and the community."[102] Others took a similar position, except instead of seeing their religious and political reasons inextricably twined, they saw them as evenly divided, both contributing their part to a well-rounded pacifism. This comment is fairly typical: "There is the intuitive side, which I call religious, and there is the historical side, which I call pragmatic. And they're about equal in determining my views."[103]

The most common position taken on the question of religious versus pragmatic justifications for pacifism was that while both gave support to a pacifist position, the reasons for pacifism are so compelling that it can be sustained on either one of these grounds alone. Leland Sateren, a Lutheran CO, gives the definitive statement of this viewpoint:

> Everything that happens merely confirms what I believe. I suppose you'd have to say biblical all right, but good night, I don't think you have to have the Bible to come to the conclusion that the great illusion is the good that you can achieve by fighting. There are many great thinkers who have been pacifists who were not Christians at all.[104]

Another common position was that while religious beliefs were not very significant in terms of a justification for pacifism, religious heritage was. For these COs, questions of theological doctrine were either not of interest or produced ambivalence, while ethical values associated with religion could be adopted with passion and commitment. Gordon Kaufman, a Mennonite CO, comments on the relationship between theology and ethics in his belief system:

> In fact, one could say I had lots of religious questions and problems. Questions about the existence of God and belief in God and all the rest of that. But I had

> very few questions about what is a morally proper human life. Which I thought of in terms of this Mennonite-Christian kind of teaching. So it [pacifism] was religious in the sense that it was very much connected with the religious tradition in which I was brought up. And religious in the broad sense which the Supreme Court later came to allow—but didn't at that time—of having to do with a whole overall view of human life and its meaning. But there's a question mark about belief in a Supreme Being that was certainly in my mind, and which I had been struggling with in high school, and have been struggling with all the rest of my life.[105]

Several COs made similar comments, but added that their religious beliefs had deteriorated over the years, while their ethical values originally derived from religion had blossomed. Joe Dell, a Brethren CO, expresses this feeling:

> It's increasingly difficult for me to talk about God in any personal way, because I just don't think we know that much about he/she/it or whatever it is. And I don't know . . . it isn't all that important to me, I guess. . . . But I believe probably even more strongly than I did years back that some of the basic beliefs of the Church of the Brethren . . . are more fundamental in my way of thinking in my life than any time previously. Such things as—it's oversimplified—but love is much better than hate, cooperation produces lots more than strife and competitiveness, and so on down the line.[106]

Though the majority of COs accepted the possibility and the integrity of non-religious pacifism, most gave some credit to religion for motivating, sustaining, or creating their pacifism. Even those COs who took an entirely non-religious position themselves acknowledged that their values were Judeo-Christian in the sense that religious values have permeated Western culture to such an extent that virtually everybody makes use of them, whether at a conscious or unconscious level.[107] Some COs, however, were more rejecting of religious value as such. Fred Convers, who describes himself as an "evangelical atheist," relates this story of his development of a CO position prior to the war:

> By the time the war came along and I had been involved in pacifist activities more, not because of religion, but because of the people I was associated with at Cornell University, my grandmother was horrified, and put a lot of pressure on me to see the Episcopal minister that she worked with closely. And so I agreed to do that, and I went and talked to him, and I really felt he was quite an ass. He listened to my reasoning and what I thought was going on at the time—which really wasn't very accurate, anyway, I have to admit—but the only thing he could come up with was that Christ wouldn't be a martyr. I went away feeling that that was the most stupid thing that anybody could possibly dream up to say in that situation. Talking to a young man who is facing problems resisting the draft. Jesus Christ wouldn't be a martyr. I don't know what he meant by martyr. It just seemed to me he was so far away from the religious traditions that involved any martyrs that he somehow thought of martyrdom as some kind of stupid psychopathic activity. I can't imagine that. No, I didn't come from a religious

> background in pacifism. Quite the contrary, my taking pacifism back to religion was fruitless.[108]

In spite of the great diversity of religious, philosophical, and political beliefs among World War II COs, there are several points of similarity. First, most COs feel it important that their behavior mirror the mind of God, or of the universe, however they conceive this ideal. They tend to see religious truth as immediately translatable into human action: if we know that God is beneficent, then we must be so as well; if God or the universe is peaceful, then we must be pacifist. Second, those who use the Bible as a source for their pacifism take the teachings they favor at face value, and assume they were meant literally. This is particularly interesting because it holds true for both fundamentalists, who take the entire Bible to be the literal word of God, and for liberal Christians who give credence only to the teachings of a Christ who is not necessarily divine. Third, COs hold a strong view of the human family, whether they see these family bonds as resulting from a connection to a father God, a creator God, the church, or as a result of our shared humanity alone.

There are also interesting parallels to be seen among COs on the question of the meaning and purpose of life. Across a variety of perspectives, COs view life as an opportunity for learning, especially learning about spiritual and moral matters. The fundamentalist who believes all people must be saved by God through Christ, the Quaker who desires that all should be open to the voice of God within, and the believer in reincarnation who sees every individual developing spiritual insight over many lifetimes share alike a horror of destroying this life process for another through the act of killing them. The process of spiritual and moral growth is valued above more tangible, material ends, and sometimes above survival itself. (This is clearly seen in the case where an individual professes a preference for being killed over killing another, which would pollute him or her with a moral contagion that would eventually corrode his or her own spiritual standing.)

COs of all types also hold strong self-images that are at odds with their perceptions of larger society. Some describe their identity as Christian, implying a primary loyalty to their reading of Christian belief and tradition. Others see themselves as first and foremost members of the kingdom of God, and are prepared from birth to dismiss competing views as "worldly." Still others find their identity in their art or in their commitment to following the dictates of their conscience without regard for the opinions of the mass of human beings. All these self-images create a steadfast attitude of nonconformity and set-apartness able to sustain conscientious objection.

But the individualism of conscientious objection has other roots as well. COs of all types tend to be preoccupied with their own behavior, and relatively less concerned with the behavior of others. The attempt to mirror the mind of God and to view life as a process of spiritual growth are both inward-looking, and these have their parallel in the political realm as well. As we have seen, COs ascribe sin to all parties in a conflict, refusing resolutely to see a significant imbalance of guilt; the absence of such an imbalance justifies an almost exclusive attention to one's own guilt. Another political example of CO individualism is that most COs do not have a positive view of the state, and see it as something quite apart from their lives and the lives of the other individuals the state claims to serve. Even those COs who speak of the state in more positive terms have a qualified view, since they typically see themselves as separate from the state, and judged by different standards. These COs value the democratic freedoms they enjoy in the United States, but have no love of the principle of democracy itself: they are non-participants in government, wanting only that government provide order and protection and leave them free to pursue their God. Again, the emphasis is on individual morality, and the state is either ignored or criticized.

This alienation between the individual and the state means that while problems can be diagnosed as corporate—it is as a nation, and because we are a nation, that we wage war—solutions are characteristically individual. The antithesis of war is not so much cooperation between traditional states, but a recognition by individuals of their own true interests, and a casting off of the political/national overlay. For some this means an alliance with God and a resignation that states will go their own way, for good or ill; for others the alliance is with like-minded individuals with the hope that states can be brought around to a spirit of tolerance and generosity.

NOTES

1. See Leo P. Crespi, "Attitudes Toward Conscientious Objectors and Some of Their Psychological Correlates," *Journal of Psychology* 18 (July 1944): 81–117; and Mervin D. Zook, "How U.S. Magazines Covered Objectors in World War II," *Journalism Quarterly* 48 (Autumn 1971): 550–54.

2. Paul Phillips, interview with author, 11 September 1986, Ontario, California. For another view on the purpose of humankind and the voluntary praise of God, see Don Beachler, interview with author, 26 September 1986, Modesto, California.

3. Gil Bertochini, interview with author, 1 June 1987, Washington D.C.

4. George Brumley, letter to author, 4 June 1987.

5. Samuel Liskey, interview with author, 11 September 1986, Ontario, California.

6. Paul Phillips, interview with author, 11 September 1986, Ontario, California. See also Charles Klaffke, interview with author, 23 February 1987, Duarte, California.

7. G. Hayes Reed, interview with author, 25 September 1986, Modesto, California. See also Gilbert Grover, interview with author, 24 September 1986, Modesto, California.

8. Gilbert Grover, interview with author, 24 September 1986, Modesto, California.

9. Harmon Wilkinson, interview with author, 23 February 1987, Whittier, California.

10. Robert Vogel, interview with author, 15 September 1986, Pasadena, California.

11. Ibid.

12. James Bristol, interview with author, 27 May 1987, Philadelphia, Pennsylvania.

13. Gordon Nutson, interview with author, 25 September 1986, Modesto, California.

14. George Reeves, quoted in *Against the Tide: Pacifist Resistance in the Second World War,* Deena Hurwitz and Craig Simpson, eds. (New York: War Resisters League, 1984).

15. John Mecartney, "A Statement to My Friends," July 1942, Civilian Public Service Personal Papers, Document Group 56, Swarthmore College Peace Collection, Swarthmore, Pennsylvania.

16. Bill Colburn, interview with author, 5 May 1987, Concord, New Hampshire.

17. Gordon Nutson, interview with author, 25 September 1986, Modesto, California. See also Howard Bogen, interview with author, 9 September 1986, Pasadena, California.

18. Dwight Hanawalt, interview with author, 10 September 1986, La Verne, California.

19. Gale Nutson, interview with author, 27 September 1986, Modesto, California.

20. Robert Vogel, interview with author, 15 September 1986, Pasadena, California. See also Lawrence Templin, interview for "Schowalter Oral History Collection—World War II Conscientious Objectors," Keith Sprunger and James Juhnke, coordinators, 122 cassette tapes, Mennonite Library and Archives, North Newton, Kansas (hereafter abbreviated as "SOH interview"); Harmon Wilkinson, interview with author, 23 February 1987, Whittier, California; Leland Sateren, interview with author, 9 February 1987, Edina, Minnesota; Dwight Hanawalt, interview with author, 10 September 1986, La Verne, California; Charles Baker, interview with author, 24 September 1986, Modesto, California; Gale Nutson, interview with author, 27 September 1986, Modesto, California; Howard Bogen, interview with author, 9 September 1986, Pasadena, California; Bill Colburn, interview with author, 5 May 1987, Concord, New Hampshire; Robert Cary, interview with author, 1 October 1986, San Francisco, California.

21. George Fischer, interview with author, 22 April 1987, Danvers, Massachusetts.

22. Joe Dell, interview with author, 27 September 1987, Modesto, California. See also George Fischer, interview with author, 22 April 1987, Danvers, Massachusetts; Gordon Nutson, interview with author, 25 September 1987, Modesto, California; G. Hayes Reed, interview with author, 25 September 1986, Modesto, California; Robert Vogel, interview with author, 15 September 1986, Pasadena, California; Carl Paulson, interview with author, 23 April 1987, Upton, Massachusetts.

23. Harmon Wilkinson, interview with author, 23 February 1987, Whittier, California. See also Gale Nutson, interview with author, 27 September 1986, Modesto, California; Herbert Hogan, interview with author, 11 September 1986, La Verne, California.

24. James Bristol, interview with author, 27 May 1987, Philadelphia, Pennsylvania.

25. Gale Nutson, interview with author, 27 September 1986, Modesto, California. See also Harmon Wilkinson, interview with author, 23 February 1987, Whittier, California.

26. James Bristol, interview with author, 27 May 1987, Philadelphia, Pennsylvania. Bristol is referring to Henry Sloane Coffin, *The Meaning of the Cross* (New York: C. Scribner's Sons, 1931).

27. Gilbert Grover, interview with author, 24 September 1987, Modesto, California.

28. Booton Herndon, *The Unlikeliest Soldier* (Mountain View, CA: Pacific Press Publishing Association, 1967), 61. See also G. Hayes Reed, interview with author, 25 September 1986, Modesto, California; Donald Beachler, interview with author, 26 September 1986, Modesto, California; Tate Zytkoskee, self-interview answering author's questions, May 1987.

29. Gordon C. Zahn, "A Study of the Social Backgrounds of Catholic Conscientious Objectors in Civilian Public Service During World War II" (M.A. thesis, Catholic University of America, 1950), 107.

30. Eunice Liskey, interview with author, 11 September 1986, Ontario, California (part of interview with Samuel Liskey, same date and place).

31. Roy Mast, self-interview answering author's questions, May 1987. See also Gil Bertochini, interview with author, 1 June 1987, Washington D.C.; Paul Phillips, letter to author, 19 December 1986.

32. Gilbert Grover, interview with author, 24 September 1986, Modesto, California.

33. R. Paul Phillips, interview with author, 11 September 1986, Ontario, California. See also Gil Bertochini, interview with author, 1 June 1987, Washington D.C.; Hubert Brubaker, interview with author, 25 September 1986, Modesto, California.

34. Hubert Brubaker, interview with author, 25 September 1986, Modesto, California. See also Gil Bertochini, interview with author, 1 June 1987, Washington D.C.; Lyle Krug, interview with author, 28 August 1986, Mission Viejo, California; Samuel Liskey, interview with author, 11 September 1986, Ontario, California.

35. Donald Beachler, interview with author, 26 September 1986, Modesto, California. Scriptural references are Exodus 20:13, Romans 12:19, Matthew 5:39, Matthew 26:52, and John 18:36.

36. Gilbert Grover, interview with author, 24 September 1986, Modesto, California.

37. R. Paul Phillips, interview with author, 11 September 1986, Ontario, California.

38. Gordon C. Zahn, "A Descriptive Study of the Sociological Backgrounds of Conscientious Objectors in Civilian Public Service During World War II" (Ph.D. dissertation, Catholic University of America, 1953), 126.

39. Fred Barnes, telephone interview with author, 13 May 1987.

40. Gordon Nutson, interview with author, 25 September 1986, Modesto, California.

41. Wesley Doe, letter to author, 14 January 1987.

42. Eugene Carper, interview with author, 10 September 1986, La Verne, California. See also Russell Jarboe, interview with author, 25 February 1987, La Verne, California; Loris Habegger, SOH interview; Howard Bogen, interview with author, 9 September 1986, Pasadena, California.

43. Paul Delp, interview with author, 3 March 1987, Orange, California.

44. Herbert Hogan, interview with author, 11 September 1986, La Verne, California; Delmar Stanley, interview with author, 24 February 1987, La Verne, California; James Bristol, interview with author, 27 May 1987, Philadelphia, Pennsylvania; G. Hayes Reed, interview with author, 25 September 1986, Modesto, California; Saburo Mizutani, interview with author, 29 September 1986, Sacramento, California; Anonymous World War II CO, interview with author, 3 March 1987.

45. See especially Dwight Hanawalt, interview with author, 10 September 1986; and Wallace Nelson, interview by Deena Hurwitz for *Against the Tide,* privately held (hereafter abbreviated as "Hurwitz interview").

46. Howard Bogen, interview with author, 9 September 1986, Pasadena, California; Saburo Mizutani, interview with author, 29 September 1986, Sacramento, California.

47. James Bristol, sermon written for 13 October 1940, privately held.

48. Aretas Boone, interview with author, 24 September 1986, Modesto, California. See also Donald Beachler, interview with author, 26 September 1986, Modesto, California; G. Hayes Reed, interview with author, 25 September 1986, Modesto, California; Gordon Kaufman, *Nonresistance and Responsibility* (Newton, KS: Faith and Life Press, 1979), 78–79.

49. Gilbert Grover, "The Christian and the State," privately held.

50. G. Hayes Reed, interview with author, 25 September 1986, Modesto, California.

51. R. Paul Phillips, interview with author, 11 September 1986, Ontario, California; Hubert Brubaker, interview with author, 25 September 1986, Modesto, California; Laban Peachey, SOH interview; Eugene Carper, interview with author, 10 September 1986, La Verne, California.

52. Zahn, "Catholic COs in World War II" (M.A. thesis), 102. See also Gordon Zahn, interview with author, 29 April 1987, Charlestown, Massachusetts.

53. Rudy Potochnik, "Autobiography," privately held; Seth Gifford, interview with author, 30 April 1987, Providence, Rhode Island.

54. Fred Barnes, telephone interview with author, 13 May 1987.

55. George Brumley, letter to author, 4 June 1987. See also Gordon Nutson, interview with author, 25 September 1986, Modesto, California; Donald Beachler, interview with author, 26 September 1986, Modesto, California.

56. Gil Bertochini, interview with author, 1 June 1987, Washington D.C. See also anonymous World War II CO, quoted in Zahn, "Catholic COs in World War II" (M.A. thesis), 108.

57. Gordon Nutson, interview with author, 25 September 1986, Modesto, California. See also John Hampton, letter from prison, 24 May 1945, War Resisters League, Document Group 40, Swarthmore College Peace Collection, Swarthmore, Pennsylvania.

58. James Bristol, interview with author, 27 May 1987, Philadelphia, Pennsylvania. See also Saburo Mizutani, interview with author, 29 September 1986, Sacramento, California.

59. Malcolm Parker, telephone interview with author, 28 February 1987; Henry Blocher, interview with author, 10 September 1986, La Verne, California.

60. The exact number of Jewish COs in World War II is unknown. Of the twelve thousand in CPS, sixty described themselves as Jewish, but undoubtedly there were others who were raised Jewish but described themselves as non-affiliated or non-religious (for example, two of the four Jewish interviewees included in this study who served in CPS described their religious affiliation as "none" to CPS authorities). There are no statistics available for the religious affiliations of noncombatants outside of Seventh-Day Adventists, and prison statistics are given in much broader categories (e.g., "large religious groups," "philosophical or political objectors"); see Mulford Sibley and Ada Wardlaw, *Conscientious Objectors in Prison 1940–1945* (Philadelphia: Pacifist Research Bureau, 1945), 12.

61. Gerald Rubin, interview with author, 2 October 1986, Corte Madera, California.

62. Max Kleinbaum, interview for "An Oral History of American Jews who Chose to Become Conscientious Objectors or Resisted Serving in the Military from World War II—Korean War," Murray Polner, coordinator, ten cassette tapes, Swarthmore College Peace Collection, Swarthmore, Pennsylvania (hereafter abbreviated as "Polner interview").

63. American Civil Liberties Union—National Committee on Conscientious Objectors, Document Group 22, Swarthmore College Peace Collection, Swarthmore, Pennsylvania.

64. Thomas Banyacya, quoted in *Against the Tide,* Hurwitz and Simpson, eds.

65. Anonymous World War II CO, interview with author, 21 February 1987.

66. Ian Thiermann, Hurwitz interview. See also anonymous World War II CO, interview with author, 21 February 1987; Harry Prochaska, interview with author, 1 October 1986, San Francisco, California.

67. Sigmund Cohn, interview with author, 30 September 1986, Berkeley, California; John Hampton, letter from prison, 4 February 1945, War Resisters League, Document Group 40, Swarthmore College Peace Collection, Swarthmore, Pennsylvania; Gerald Rubin, interview with author, 2 October 1986, Corte Madera, California; Cal Edinger, interview with author, 25 February 1987, San Gabriel, California.

68. Rudy Potochnik, interview with author, 26 September 1986, Modesto, California.

69. Caleb Foote, telephone interview with author, 28 February 1987.

70. James Bristol, interview with author, 27 May 1987, Philadelphia, Pennsylvania. See also Arthur Bryant, self-interview answering author's questions, May 1987.

71. Albert Herbst, interview with author, 6 September 1986, La Verne, California.

72. J. Edwin Jones, interview with author, 6 September 1986, La Verne, California.

73. Wallace Nelson, Hurwitz interview.

74. Bayard Rustin, letter to draft board, 16 November 1943, CPS Personal Papers, Document Group 56, Swarthmore College Peace Collection, Swarthmore, Pennsylvania.

75. Richard Brown, interview with author, 2 October 1986, Berkeley, California. See also Fred Convers, interview with author, 2 October 1986, Berkeley, California.

76. William Everson, quoted in *Against the Tide,* Hurwitz and Simpson, eds.

77. James Lowerre, interview with author, 3 March 1987, Orange, California. See also Russell Jarboe, interview with author, 25 February 1987, La Verne, California; Lowell Naeve (in collaboration with David Wieck), *A Field of Broken Stones* (Denver: Alan Swallow, 1959), 6.

78. Howard Ten Brink, interview with author, 24 September 1986, Modesto, California.

79. J. Edwin Jones, interview with author, 6 September 1986, La Verne, California. See also Max Kleinbaum, Polner interview; Paul Delp, interview with author, 3 March 1987, Orange, California.

80. Gordon Nutson, interview with author, 25 September 1986, Modesto, California. See also Robert Vogel, interview with author, 15 September 1986, Pasadena, California; Russell Jarboe, interview with author, 25 February 1987, La Verne, California.

81. Gordon Nutson, interview with author, 25 September 1986, Modesto, California. See also James Lowerre, interview with author, 3 March 1987, Orange, California; Dwight Hanawalt, interview with author, 10 September 1986, La Verne, California.

82. See, for example, George Brumley, letter to author, 4 June 1987.

83. Carl Paulson, interview with author, 23 April 1987, Upton, Massachusetts. See also G. Hayes Reed, interview with author, 25 September 1986, Modesto, California; Malcolm Parker, telephone interview with author, 28 February 1987; Arthur Bryant, self-interview answering author's questions, May 1987.

84. Arle Brooks, quoted in *War and the Christian Conscience: From Augustine to Martin Luther King, Jr.,* Albert Marrin, ed. (Chicago: Henry Regnery Company, 1971), 239.

85. Arthur Bryant, self-interview answering author's questions, May 1987. See also Dwight Hanawalt, interview with author, 10 September 1986, La Verne, California.

86. Sigmund Cohn, interview with author, 30 September 1986, Berkeley, California. See also Henry Blocher, interview with author, 10 September 1986, La Verne, California; Dwight Hanawalt, interview with author, 10 September 1986, La Verne, California; R. Paul Phillips, interview with author, 11 September 1986, Ontario, California; Rudy Potochnik, interview with author, 26 September 1986, Modesto, California.

87. Gordon and Gale Nutson, letter to friends, 5 February 1945, privately held. See also J. Edwin Jones, interview with author, 6 September 1986, La Verne, California.

88. See, for example, John Hampton, letter from prison, 24 May 1945, War Resisters League, Document Group 40, Swarthmore College Peace Collection, Swarthmore, Pennsylvania.

89. Saburo Mizutani, interview with author, 29 September 1986, Sacramento, California.

90. Fred Convers, interview with author, 2 October 1986, Berkeley, California.

91. Ian Thiermann, Hurwitz interview; Robert Cary, interview with author, 1 October 1986, San Francisco, Cailfornia; Hubert Brubaker, interview with author, 25 September 1986, Modesto, California; Charles Baker, interview with author, 24 September 1986, Modesto, California.

92. Richard Brown, interview with author, 2 October 1986, Berkeley, California. See also Donald Beachler, interview with author, 26 September 1986, Modesto, California; Aretas Boone, interview with author, 24 September 1986, Modesto, California.

93. Paul Delp, interview with author, 3 March 1987, Orange, California.

94. Robert Vogel, interview with author, 15 September 1986, Pasadena, California. See also Wallace Nelson, Hurwitz interview.

95. Alfred Hassler, *Diary of a Self-Made Convict* (Nyack, NY: Fellowship of Reconciliation, 1958), 108. See also John Abbott, quoted in Mark Jonathan Harris, Franklin D. Mitchell, and Steven J. Schechter, *The Homefront* (New York: G.P. Putnam's Sons, 1984), 56; Wallace Nelson, Hurwitz interview; Caleb Foote, telephone interview with author, 28 February 1987.

96. Don Peretz, Polner interview.

97. Samuel Liskey, interview with author, 11 September 1986, Ontario, California.

98. Hubert Brubaker, interview with author, 25 September 1986, Modesto, California.

99. Robert Vogel, interview with author, 15 September 1986, Pasadena, California.

100. Howard Ten Brink, interview with author, 24 September 1986, Modesto, California.

101. Richard Brown, interview with author, 2 October 1986, Berkeley, California. See also George Brown, interview with author, 1 June 1987, Washington DC.

102. Robert Cary, interview with author, 1 October 1986, San Francisco, California.

103. Anonymous World War II CO, interview with author, 21 February 1987. See also Charles Baker, interview with author, 24 September 1986, Modesto, California.

104. Leland Sateren, interview with author, 9 February 1987, Edina, Minnesota. See also Gil Bertochini, interview with author, 1 June 1987, Washington DC.; Eugene Carper, interview with author, 10 September 1986, La Verne, California.

105. Gordon Kaufman, interview with author, 29 April 1987, Cambridge, Massachusetts. See also Morris Davis, statement to court, *Concord* (newsletter of the Tolstoy Peace Group), No. 3, Summer 1943 (found in Collective Document Group A, Swarthmore College Peace Collection, Swarthmore, Pennsylvania); Henry Blocher, interview with author, 10 September 1986, La Verne, California.

106. Joe Dell, interview with author, 27 September 1986, Modesto, California.

107. Gerald Rubin, interview with author, 2 October 1986, Corte Madera, California.

108. Fred Convers, interview with author, 2 October 1986, Berkeley, California.

5

Consequences and Moral Rules

Traditionally, moral reasoning has been analyzed in terms of two major types: consequentialism and deontology. Consequentialist theories decide which action is right on the basis of the consequences the action produces. For example, I may decide that it is wrong to kill you—even though I am angry with you—because the consequences of the murder would be bad for both of us: you would meet an untimely end and I would be arrested and imprisoned. In addition, I would be setting a bad example, your children would have to grow up without a mother, and so forth. The most common form of consequentialism is utilitarianism. Utilitarianism is merely a way of defining what consequences are desirable, what consequences can morally justify an action. For utilitarians, valuable consequences are those that produce "the greatest good for the greatest number of people."*

Consequentialist theories may be of two types, depending on whether particular actions or general rules are justified by appeal to consequences. Consequentialist theories may decide what is right and wrong anew in every situation (such that killing may produce more good than evil in some circumstances, and thus be justified under these circumstances). This type of consequentialism is "act-utilitarian": each moral dilemma one faces is resolved in terms of the consequences various actions will produce. Consequentialism can also be "rule-utilitarian," meaning that actions must conform to moral rules, and are not subject to justification on a case-by-case basis. Nevertheless, rule-utilitarianism is consequentialist because the rules themselves are justified by the consequences they will produce. Thus there may be a rule against killing

*Consequentialist theories need not aim at the principle of utility; they can, for example, be directed toward one's personal happiness (ethical egoism). But because utilitarianism is the most widely accepted version of consequentialism, I will use it as shorthand to refer to consequentialist theories in general.

because the consequences of killing are *generally* bad, even if in particular circumstances it seems that killing will produce good consequences.[1]

Deontological theories, on the other hand, decide what is right on the basis of characteristics inherent in the action: an act may be wrong because it is unjust, or forbidden by God, or because it involves killing. In any case, an action is not right or wrong because it produces good or bad consequences, but because it is right or wrong in itself. Pacifism is generally understood to be a deontological form of moral reasoning. Killing is prohibited because it is intrinsically wrong. Whatever the consequences of refusing to kill may be, the pacifist is constrained to follow a rule of pacifism and let the laws of cause and effect take their own course, whether for good or ill. Those who criticize pacifists typically interpret pacifism this way, and argue that pacifists are indifferent to the consequences of their actions, that they are literally willing to see the world destroyed so long as they can maintain their own personal purity. This is held to be a morally irresponsible position since no care is taken to ensure that one's actions are productive of the social good, that is, of good consequences.

This criticism captures some of the truth about pacifist moral reasoning, but it misses the larger truth, and ultimately criticizes the form of pacifism when its real quarrel is with the substance. Non-pacifists criticize the behavior of pacifists in real or hypothetical situations, arguing that pacifist actions demonstrate their lack of concern for the welfare of others. In fact, pacifists are deeply concerned with securing good consequences, but differ with non-pacifists as to what good consequences are and how they can most effectively be reached. This chapter will describe how pacifists view the interaction between a moral rule of pacifism and the responsibility to produce good consequences and how their foundational religious, philosophical, and political beliefs work to convince pacifists that following moral rules and securing good consequences are not finally incompatible.

In learning how pacifists are viewed by non-pacifists, there is no better place to begin than with Reinhold Niebuhr. In his study of interwar pacifism, *For Peace and Justice,* Charles Chatfield notes: "No former pacifist was more influential in winning support for the Allies than was Reinhold Niebuhr."[2] Niebuhr had long been a pacifist sympathizer, but with the rise of fascism in Germany and Japan, Niebuhr became increasingly outspoken in his advocacy of support for the Allies and eventually of U.S. intervention in the war. He simultaneously turned his moral outrage against the Protestant peace movement and developed a critique of pacifism that rested on a division between "pure pacifists," of whom Niebuhr approved, and "political pacifists," of whom Niebuhr was very critical. Translated into the terms of ethical analysis, Niebuhr's pure pacifists are true deontologists: they insist on adherence to a moral rule of pacifism for the sole reason that it is inherently right, and they turn a blind eye to the consequences of following this rule. They abjure involvement with politics because political leaders must take responsibility for social consequences and the pacifist cannot do this. On the other hand, Niebuhr's political pacifists are confused deontologists: they too insist on adherence to a moral rule of pacifism, but they go on to profess a concern with consequences. Niebuhr argues that these pacifists are committed to two incompatible goals, that it is impossible to simultaneously take a responsible view toward one's neighbor and keep one's hands clean of the taint of immoral means. Thus Niebuhr's political pacifists can either be deontologists or consequentialists, but they cannot be both. The force of Niebuhr's anti-pacifist argument was devoted to convincing political pacifists of this and compelling them to opt for either social responsibility (consequentialism) or moral perfectionism (deontology).[3]

It is important to note first that Niebuhr's analysis of pacifism seems to be correct on a sociological level. It is possible to divide World War II pacifists quite neatly into two camps, with those who announce their disinterest in politics and social responsibility on one side, and those who strive for social and political relevance on the other. Yet pacifists of both types give evidence of concern for good consequences, and the vast majority reject Niebuhr's claim that pacifism conscientiously applied offers no control over the social order. Pacifists who did not believe they were building toward a better world were rare.

SEEKING GOOD CONSEQUENCES

The desire for good consequences among liberal COs, those Niebuhr calls "political pacifists," is self-evident. Pacifism is to lead to "a new social order," to rescue the world from "the powers of darkness" or from nuclear annihilation.[4] The goal of pacifism is not merely personal perfection, but the transformation of the world. As James Bristol argues: "The last thing I want to do is keep myself unspotted from the world. . . . What I want to do is to prevent everybody from killing and also to remove the causes that lead people to kill and so on, that's what I want to do."[5]

Less obvious is the desire for good consequences among fundamentalist COs, those Niebuhr would term "pure pacifists." But here the goals of pacifism are also high, for pacifists are working with God to prepare for Christ's return, when peace and prosperity will extend over all the earth. As Paul Phillips explains:

> We do firmly believe that Christ is coming back to earth to set up a kingdom which will be worldwide, which will be administered by him and his immortal followers. It says, "you shall be made kings and priests and you shall reign on the earth." . . . There'll be mortal nations on the earth, who will benefit then from the reign of Christ. Can you imagine a just and capable ruler on this earth instead of what we have today? It says they'll study war no more. There'll be no wars, because everything will be in complete control. . . . That's what it's gonna be like when Christ returns. And it says, "They shall turn their swords into plowshares and their spears into pruning hooks. Nation shall not lift up sword against nation, neither shall they learn war anymore."[6]

Most telling perhaps is that the most frequent complaint about war was not that it was morally offensive (though this may have been taken for granted) but that it was ineffective in producing good social ends. As Paul Ashby sums up his understanding of war, "Primarily it's utter waste accomplishing nothing."[7] Time and time again, COs argued that war simply does not work. One such statement was made by Arle Brooks, who told a federal district court in 1941: "Wars have failed to solve the basic problems of the world. Participation in war to settle international and national differences does not do justice to man's intelligence."[8]

Part of the reason COs feel that war does not accomplish good ends where pacifism might has to do with the way in which they evaluate consequences. Pacifists have characteristic ways of weighing consequences, of deciding whether they are good or bad. When non-pacifists accuse pacifists of being unconcerned with the consequences of their actions, they mistake disagreement over what constitutes good consequences for a lack of interest in consequences altogether. Because pacifists have their own way of evaluating consequences, what a non-pacifist might term a success, a pacifist will term a failure, and vice versa. There are two major emphases at work in pacifist evaluation of consequences: first, pacifists tend to prefer long-range consequences over short-term ones, and second, they value deep individual change above large-scale but shallow social change.

Long-Term Consequences

Pacifists seem generally willing to accept major sacrifices in the short run under the conviction that pacifism will triumph given enough time, and bring the good consequences that pacifists seek. If the military metaphor can be forgiven, pacifists believe they can lose battles and still win the war. In an October 1939 article in the *Saturday Evening Post*, Milton Mayer wrote:

> "What good can you do in jail," they [his friends] ask. "A [Eugene] Debs [Socialist Party leader], yes. But who ever heard of Mayer? Who cares if Mayer opposes the war?" And my answer is that Mayer is indeed inconsequential, but a thousand Mayers, a million Mayers, ten million Mayers, may prove to be too many to ignore. And if there are only a hundred Mayers this time, their example may produce a thousand Mayers next time. That will mean a lot of wars before the Mayers are heard, but I can wait.[9]

Repeatedly the theme of building for the future, strengthening the peace movement and keeping it alive, came up in interviews. While acknowledging that pacifists might not end the present conflict, COs expressed the belief that by objecting to the war they were working to secure the long-term goal of a peaceful world. A pre-war statement by Don Benedict and seven other draft resisters from the Union Theological Seminary illustrates this theme: "We do not expect to stem the war forces today; but we are helping to build the movement that will conquer in the future."[10] Just how long the time scale for reaping the benefits of a pacifist witness may be can be seen in this slogan which appeared regularly on the masthead of *The Catholic CO* during World War II: "We hope that war will be overcome through the Church, and even if, after two thousand years, this hope is still unfulfilled we still hope and go on knocking at the door like the importunate man in the Gospel."[11]

COs believe that war is not a viable method for securing positive long-term consequences because it only rearranges the imbalances of an unjust society and does not rectify them. Where the non-pacifist is impressed with the urgency of righting a particular wrong, even if the result will not be ideal, pacifists wish to suffer certain wrongs in the short run with the conviction that by so doing, the ideal can be reached in the long run. Pacifism is favored then simply because it works better than violence, though this may not be immediately apparent in the short run. In his Form 47, one CO justifies his pacifism on these grounds:

> Advanced study in International Relations has given me some comprehension of this field. The slow but more lasting results of good will as against the temporary and unsatisfactory results of violence as I see these two methods at work in family, community, and international life, together with meditation and prayer on these things have led me to my present position.[12]

Occasionally COs backed up the claim that pacifism is socially efficacious by historical example. Paul Delp was questioned by a member of his draft board who wanted to know what he would do if he were crossing the plains in a covered wagon and a band of Indians were about to rape his grandmother. As Delp tells it, he replied: "Well, the history of our treatment of the Indians leaves something to be desired. In New England they were abused and killed, and as a result, the Pilgrims and these people were massacred by Indians." Delp contrasted this to the situation in Pennsylvania where the Quakers "gave pacifist treatment" to the Indians and were well treated in return.[13] John Mecartney uses the historical example of the Christian religion to argue that pacifism may produce short-term disaster but will bring long-term success:

> I believe that the life of Christ exemplified a way of settling conflicts by love instead of violence. Jesus showed how loving them who hate you and praying for them who persecute you is the Christian way both personally and internationally to settle conflicts. The world situation at Christ's time was similar to that of today. Christ loved His enemies instead of killing them. The Roman empire died but Christianity has come down through the centuries.[14]

Changing Hearts and Minds

Pacifists also insist that individual change is of greater value than are changes in social institutions, an emphasis that one might expect given the pacifist valuation of personal spiritual and moral growth. COs most frequently expressed this by stressing the importance of changing "hearts and minds." This is tied into the preference for long-term consequences, for it is believed that lasting change is the result of many individual transformations. Good consequences are reached by changing the way people think and react, and not by changing the laws and leaders that govern them, for this can only yield short-term and temporary improvement. George Reeves, interviewed for *Against the Tide*, tells of his gradual conversion to pacifism and to a more individualized approach to evaluating consequences:

> I came to pacifism largely because of a complete disillusionment with force and violence as a way to change society. I had held the position that we would have to come finally to violence to change society in a socialist direction. . . . It was the Spanish Civil War that finally convinced me that if the people on the left, the socialists, communists, and anarchists could not work together, even shot each other, then there was little hope. In fact there was no hope whatsoever for a revolution coming out of that background. The only way you could change was to change individual people, and to work slowly for group change.[15]

Bill Colburn also considers individual change essential to producing good social consequences. He explains: "Only to the extent that there are changes internally in human beings, in terms of our attitude and how we deal with people—a change of nature, you might say—will there be any changes in how we get on with each other."[16]

This process of changing hearts and minds is not channeled through large institutions; the government (or even the church) bureaucracy is not the source of this change. Social change is the result of a series of individual changes, and these are triggered most often by the influence of another individual. This belief gives natural support to the position of conscientious objection, for if change is to be sincere and lasting, individuals must be converted by means of argument and example and not by coercion and violence. The CO sees his refusal to be drafted to fight a war as an example to others who may see the wisdom of this way and emulate it.[17]

It must be stressed that pacifists rely on the method of example not because they feel that public life is unimportant in itself or irrelevant to the life of the individual, but because public life must be changed from the ground up. Institutions are changed by changing their constituency. The majority of COs simply do not look to the state for social progress. They see the state as so large, distant, and entrenched, as so committed to its private gain, that it cannot be moved except by people individually moving underneath it until a critical mass has accumulated and the state is automatically transformed. In a curious twist on Reinhold Niebuhr's thought, Harry Prochaska tells of being influenced toward pacifism by reading *Moral Man and Immoral Society:*

> That contrast appealed to me very strongly. And the feeling that his argument existentially was true, it *is* moral man and immoral society, for the western world anyway. But if there's going to be any change, then somehow there has to be a

> transition where personal morality becomes a mode of behavior in a public and a collective situation.[18]

For the pacifist, institutional change comes as individuals come to demand that institutions be accountable to the more stringent morality that applies in the private sphere.

FOLLOWING MORAL RULES

Not only do pacifists evaluate consequences differently than do non-pacifists, they also believe that good consequences will be most readily achieved by following moral rules. That pacifism should be rule-oriented is no surprise: taking the position that war and violence are always wrong (as the pacifist generally does) puts the burden of proof on those who would argue for an exception to the rule. A fundamental fact about pacifism (at least the absolute pacifism sanctioned in World War II draft law) is that it is not a matter of deciding right and wrong on a case-by-case basis, but is a commitment to a single definition of right and wrong that must apply always, however difficult or counter-intuitive pacifism may sometimes be.

The COs I spoke with demonstrated a driving need to feel that ethical imperatives hold across the whole range of human activities. Moral rules must be consistently applied—thus if killing is wrong in daily life, it must also be wrong in war. Typical statements of this argument are: "Just because a war came along I didn't think that made it right for me to go out and kill another person"; and "It's still murder whether it's under the command of an army officer or whether you do it yourself, it's still murder."[19] Gordon Nutson relates a dispute with co-workers, and reveals his own insistence on a single moral standard:

> There are several Baptists; fundamentalists in our office, and they'll say, "Well, you know, Gordon, let's face it, in war you're defending yourself. That isn't murder." And I say, "You mean to say that when you stick a bayonet through somebody's inwards and they're spilling out on the doggone ground and you say, 'Jesus, please bless this man, and I love him'? That's pure murder just like you take and spill his guts out on the street. It's exactly the same thing."[20]

The ability of the government to wage war and at the same time to punish murderers is branded as hypocrisy by some COs. James Lowerre remarks: "It's actually legalized murder, during war. You do the same thing after the war, and they shoot you, or they gas you. Or at least confine you for seven years."[21] Simon Greco, interviewed for *The Home Front,* recalls applying for CO status:

> Finally, I sent the questionnaire, and I wrote them a letter. I had to give a reason for being a conscientious objector, and one of the reasons I gave was that I didn't

> really believe that I was put on earth to kill people. Then I offered a deal to the government, because I realized I had very flimsy grounds in their eyes. I offered to go to war and do whatever they wanted me to do, with the provision that they would allow me to carry a gun after the war. If I were being asked to do what I considered committing murder in order to protect myself, I felt that after the war, if my existence was threatened by any enemy, even if he was the guy next door, I should have the right to shoot him down.[22]

Here the claim is that one moral rule holds not only in war and in peace, but also for the government and for the citizen. Though the "deal" Greco offered the government was no doubt facetious, his appeal is for consistency in the application of a moral standard, even if this standard is not the one he favors.

The rule of pacifism also holds in spite of wrongs committed by another: Even if another person is doing evil, this does not give the moral agent the right to kill him or her. Howard Bogen states: "It [doesn't] really change my philosophy about killing someone. You know, it's still wrong whether that person does something wrong or not."[23] Or as Gordon Kaufman argues, "I still certainly don't think it is right to kill another human being in order to prevent them from killing someone."[24] Thus a righteous war can be condemned as easily as an aggressive war fought for self-gain. Even if the cause is just and the enemy has indeed transgressed moral bounds, the rule against killing is still in effect.[25]

Of course, the problem with relying on moral rules to produce good consequences is that situations may arise where it appears that to follow a rule of pacifism will produce very bad consequences. It is on these grounds that war is almost always justified by its apologists: if the choice is between war and good (or neutral) consequences, and pacifism and bad consequences, war seems the obvious choice. If pacifists are truly committed to securing good consequences, why do they refuse to abandon their pacifism in cases where the social order would be better served by war? The pacifist answer to this question is the crux of pacifist moral reasoning. It is here that we can discover the relationship between consequences and moral rules in pacifist ethics.

There are many reasons why pacifists adhere to a rule of pacifism in cases where pacifism seems counterproductive. One of these is that pacifists are inclined to distrust their ability to calculate what consequences will follow from any particular action. In the absence of accurate predictions of future consequences, they argue, the safest course is to act on rules that we know to be generally productive of good consequences. Pacifism is one such rule: more often than not, when the opportunity to kill someone with whom you have a conflict presents itself, better consequences will follow if you refrain from killing him or her. This may not always be true, but because you cannot know if you are in the midst of a real exception to the rule or only an imagined one, if you always follow the rule, you will be right in most cases.

An example of this reasoning can be found in Paul Delp's response to his draft board when he was asked what he would do if a "Jap" broke into his house and was about to rape his mother. He replied:

> "You want me to say that I'd kill the Japanese, and my mother and I lived happily ever after. But," I said, "that's not the only possibility. What if the Japanese killed me, and raped my mother anyhow? Maybe he's stronger than I am.... Wouldn't it be better ... after the situation's passed ... that my mother is alive and I'm alive and the Japanese is alive?"[26]

The same argument is given for the case of war. Gene Carper recalls how deeply Americans feared the communist takeover in Cuba, but notes that some good things are happening in Cuba now—better education, a lower rate of alcoholism—and how can we know if Cubans would be better off now if they were under a capitalist government or what it might have cost in money and lives to prevent the communist takeover?[27]

Further, COs distrust the human intellect not only because it cannot accurately calculate consequences, but also because it is capable of deceiving itself and rationalizing the use of violence when it is not truly justified. For example, George Fischer felt he could not kill another human being because he knows that he can be wrong about things, and if it later turned out that killing was not the appropriate response, the act could not be revoked.[28] Milton Mayer expresses this same fear that his intellect will lead him astray, inventing justifications for actions that are simply wrong. Writing in 1939, he says:

> I can make my decision now, to go or not to go, and, as in any prejudgment, take the chance of having decided wrong. Or I can postpone my decision as events move closer and closer. Today I have the prudence essential to making a choice. Will I have it tomorrow, a month from now, six months from now, as the war fever rises around me? I know, of course, that I can't really make a choice until I meet the problem face to face. But I know, too, that as the war fever rises, as the emotional sweep of events rolls up, there comes a time when I can no longer exercise the prudence that enables me to choose. When that time comes I may still think I am choosing, but my choice will be dictated by my hysteria.[29]

Because human beings are subject to so many irrational and self-serving impulses, some COs see pacifism as a necessary restraint upon an intellect that may mislead us. As Sigmund Cohn claims, we are fully capable of convincing ourselves that we are choosing the good when we are really fumbling in the dark. He reasons: "We need protection against our intelligence. And pacifism may be one of the things that we have to accept."[30] In *War, Conscience, and Dissent*, Gordon Zahn focuses on this ability of people to morally justify even war's greatest abominations:

> Auschwitz and Hiroshima are equally evidence of this [inhumanity], not so much in the fact that they were possible (which is bad enough) but that the human mind was able to develop justifications for them. I have quoted this elsewhere, but it is relevant here: "Any mind which can formulate justifications for the wholesale

liquidation of men, that mind is corrupt." And the man who wrote that went on to add: "This corruption is general."[31]

SECURING GOOD CONSEQUENCES THROUGH MORAL RULES

The interesting feature of all these pacifist arguments about consequences—that long-term consequences and deep individual change are relatively more important than short-term consequences and superficial social change, and that rules are an effective safeguard against our lack of omniscience and wisdom—is that they are wholly consequentialist. Here there is no independent valuation of the right; actions are chosen to produce the best, most long-lived consequences by means of the most trustworthy method. All these propositions could be held by a rule-utilitarian who had no concern whatsoever with personal moral purity or the inherent character of her or his actions, but who simply believed that the most effective way of reaching good ends is through pacifist means. The only premise necessary to sustain pacifism for a rule-utilitarian is that better consequences will be achieved overall by following a rule of pacifism than by deciding action on a case-by-case basis.

Yet pacifist moral reasoning is more complex than this. Pacifists almost always rely on additional premises to justify their belief that following a rule of pacifism will yield good consequences. Assumptions about God, the universe, and human nature undergird the pacifist conviction that following moral rules and achieving good ends are not competing claims, but complementary ones. And again, this reliance on foundational religious or quasi-religious beliefs is characteristic of all pacifists: the distinction between "pure" and "political" pacifists is one between the specific beliefs pacifists hold, and not the general style of argumentation they use. The most common reasons pacifists give for believing that moral rules will bring good consequences are: (1) that God will guarantee good consequences; (2) that the universe is inherently moral and will reward right action with good consequences; (3) that humans by their nature will respond to love and goodwill; and (4) that suffering and martyrdom will stir compassion and a sense of justice in others and lead to reconciliation.

God's Controlling Hand

For pacifists who believe in a personally powerful God who commands that his followers be pacifist, the problem of simultaneously practicing a moral rule and producing good consequences is easily resolved. If one is following the laws God commands, what happens after they are followed is naturally God's responsibility. Fortunately, God has promised a peaceful millennium under Christ's reign. This belief provides the strongest possible argument for standing aside from violence even in situations where it appears that the consequences of doing so will be bad, because the God who is in charge of the universe has guaranteed that whatever the appearances, the consequences of pacifism will ultimately be good.

Here the relationship of a moral rule of pacifism to good social consequences is not self-sufficient; it is always channeled through God. Interestingly enough, non-pacifists can also work to produce good consequences, but again, this is true only as their actions are used by God to work his will. The central point is that God is in charge of history and that God will produce good consequences. To be a pacifist is to align oneself with God, to be an active and consenting part of God's plan. If one is not a pacifist, God is still in charge and will still bring good things to pass, but he will do so in spite of one's non-pacifism and not because of it. Responsible Christians can then do their part to bring in Christ's kingdom (the ultimate in good social consequences) by being representatives of it. Roy Mast explains:

> We are his [Christ's] representatives. If we don't pick up the torch, who has God to really place for the future? It's a little bit like I heard historian Toynbee from England once say: "God is an invisible God. And the only way he can make himself visible to man is through man." So it is our responsibility to carry the torch as Christians, to go out and as it says, "Go ye into all the world, and preach the gospel to every creature." And that is our responsibility to teach, and not to fight.[32]

Or as Gilbert Grover describes his role in this world:

> I would have to say that as a Christian, accepting the Bible as the standard of belief, and accepting the teachings of Jesus Christ, I am theologically more of a non-participant in governmental affairs. I regard myself as a member of Christ's kingdom first and foremost, and as a member of his kingdom, more in the position of an ambassador for my kingdom in a foreign environment, a foreign land. . . . I think that for me I could describe my role more as a stranger and a pilgrim in the land, but not directly responsible for its affairs.[33]

Those who do bear a direct responsibility for the affairs of this world, namely governmental leaders, must be willing to go to war to secure good consequences.[34] Governments are a part of a different kingdom than Christ's kingdom (to which the Christian belongs), and they follow a different ethical standard. But it needs to be made clear that it is not God's will that the nations resort to war; it is only that God permits war and can redeem it in his plan for the human race. God is working through unregenerate individuals whose only attachment is to the kingdoms of this world to produce the consequences he desires.[35] The only reason nations must go to war to achieve good consequences is because they are not Christian and lack faith in God. The same ends could be served through obedience to God (including obedience to his command to be pacifist): though the world might still be a dangerous place, and though conflicts would still arise, the nation who followed God would be protected by God. Gil Bertochini explains:

> If the whole nation was Christian, strongly so, believed in God and had faith in him, I think he would protect us. Because the Bible bears that out. In Israel in the Old Testament times, of course, he protected his people many times. So if we as a nation were a Christian nation, completely, a dedicated people to God, we wouldn't have the problem of facing enemies. We may have the problems, but the Lord would protect us, because we are his.[36]

National sovereignty is therefore not endangered by a pacifist stance since God will answer true faith by intervening to protect that faith and the nation which upholds it.

Obviously, it is this two kingdoms ethic which creates the sense of unconcern with consequences that Niebuhr attaches to the pure pacifist.[37] COs who adopt the two kingdoms ethic do take a more indifferent stand toward the problems of this world and are less inclined to argue with individuals who feel called to use violence to bring good consequences than do other pacifists. But the only reason these COs are willing to ignore the need to produce good consequences is because they believe that the consequences of their actions are already in far more capable hands than their own, and that with God, eventual success is assured.

The Moral Universe

Other COs argue that following a moral rule of pacifism will produce good consequences because by its very nature the universe will return good consequences for good actions (i.e., it will reward morality). In some cases, the universe is believed to be moral because it was created by God; in other cases there is no appeal to religious value and the morality of the universe is accepted as a given. The concept of a moral universe is usually enunciated in terms of means and ends: good ends will spring from good means, and if the means one chooses to use are consistent with the ends one seeks, success is guaranteed (in the long run). Thus the way to peace is through pacifism. In a February 1945 letter to their friends, Gale and Gordon Nutson articulate this stand and its reliance on belief in an inherently moral universe:

> We firmly believe that the things that Jesus said are true not because he said them but that he said them because they are true. In other words, he knew that it was a law of the Universe, the same as the law of gravity, that we reap what we sow in human relations as well as in actual planting of seeds in the ground. He knew that the only way to overcome evil was with good and not with more evil. He knew that love never faileth. Jesus was interested in results and he knew what results these actions would bring about in the long run for humanity. After all, this Christianity is just plain common-sense living if we want a peaceful world.[38]

The converse of the argument that good means produce good ends is that bad means will produce bad ends, or at least not the good ends at which they supposedly aim. Sigmund Cohn reasons, "If the means itself are the problem, and are so bad, the end might be overwhelmed by the means."[39] Or as Bayard Rustin wrote to his draft board in November of 1943 when he refused induction into CPS: "The Conscription Act denies brotherhood. . . . Its design and purpose is to set men apart—German against American. American against Japanese. Its aim springs from a moral impossibility . . . that ends justify means, that from unfriendly acts a new and friendly world can emerge."[40]

The means/ends argument forms an important part of the pacifist diagnosis of war, because the most common reason given for the failure of war to produce good consequences is that war, by its very nature, propagates itself. Again, bad means produce not good ends, but bad ends, and the cycle continues. Comments typical of this view include: "No war is a just war, it only sets up the circumstances that lead to the next war," and "Wars never settle anything. Wars just beget wars."[41] This property of war—that it reproduces itself—is explained in two ways: first, that war "breeds hate in the loser and aggression in the winner,"[42] leaving everyone with fresh reasons to engage in future wars; and second, that nations involved in war come to accept the use of violence, so that merely ending the present war does not put an end to the increased willingness to resort to violence.

This brings up another component of the means/ends argument: not only do bad means reap bad ends in a moral universe, but bad means also corrupt the moral agent (indeed, this is one reason why bad means cannot succeed). Once having adopted evil means, they cannot be set aside at will, because they have become a part of the person or nation who uses them. James Bristol enunciates both components of the means/ends argument in this statement to a federal judge in October 1941: "This is a moral universe. God's laws govern it. Evil cannot cast out evil; instead we become the very evil we seek to destroy."[43] In a 1987 interview, Bristol expressed the same view, saying:

> The minute that I say, "Well, now, for the time being, I'll have to put my convictions and my whole outlook on life and belief as to the future of the human race, I've got to put that up on the shelf for awhile," when I come back to get it, it won't be there. Not the way I left it, it can't be. Because you know, I'll be different.[44]

The corrupting influence of the evil means of violence was often cited by COs as a reason for objecting to war. They recited a litany of vices which flourish in time of war: hatred, theft, rape, lying, and so forth—making war evil not only because of violence, but because of all the other evils that trail along behind it.[45] The argument against war on the basis of its attendant immoralities is an argument against the belief that war can be kept clean, that it can be fought within distinct boundaries and under definite rules: in short, that it can be civilized. As one CO comments: "That's one of the subtle, vicious evils of war, that so often we become what we oppose."[46] Once those who propose to use evil means to bring good ends have become evil themselves, the method of war has failed in pacifist eyes.

Because the means of pacifism are good (in fact are identical with pacifist ends), it is seen as the remedy for the vicious cycle of war. The individual who refuses to participate in war makes it more difficult for war to continue, and by incremental steps, and with the accumulation of more and more people who refuse to fight, the whole system of war is eventually brought down. As Bob Stocksdale remarks, "The best way to stop war is not to participate in it."[47] Gordon Zahn argues at greater length:

> Pacifism is visionary, and it does draw heavily upon man's emotional nature. It is also more realistic and certainly much more practical than the fatalism which would see "no alternative" but to ride with the course of events, never questioning how they came to be what they are or the consequences they are certain to bring. The chain must be broken at some point and, the pacifist insists, this can only be done through the total renunciation of war and the ways of violence.[48]

It is here that responsibility for consequences and for following moral rules intersect. War is perceived to be an ongoing chain of death and destruction; to stand apart from war is both to move toward a better way and to make a moral judgment on the method of violence. Pacifism works because it mirrors the mind of the universe. By employing a law-like mechanism through which the universe rewards right action, pacifists believe they can have both personal righteousness and good social consequences.

The Power of Love

Another reason COs gave for believing that a moral rule of pacifism will produce good consequences is because the power of love is finally greater than the power of evil and will triumph over it. This is similar to the argument that good means produce good ends, but is less inclined to see the universe in mechanistic terms of cause and effect and more inclined to focus on interpersonal relationships. Love comes to human beings as they are, and it works because it understands that people will behave well if treated well, that if they are shown a better way, they will respond in kind. As one CO says, "I trust implicitly in the power of self-giving, redemptive love to overcome evil."[49] COs who rely on the power of love to bring good consequences stress that it is effective not just in a utopia, but in the midst of societies filled with hate, division, and war. In a statement to the federal court trying him for refusal to register, Lawrence Templin claimed that "love and non-violence are not merely factors in an ideal world, but working principles in a world of hate. Through them hate can be conquered."[50]

One religious source of this faith in the power of love is the Quaker idea of "that of God" in each person. Love succeeds in overcoming evil because it appeals to the spark of the divine in each person. In fact, love is believed to work better than violence in reaching the same ends because it produces the sort of consequences COs value: long-term and individual change. The individual who turns from evil because he or she has experienced the power of love has been transformed. The desire to do evil is gone. Thus the individual is not refraining from evil only so long as he or she is being forced to do so, but will practice the good indefinitely.

COs who trust the power of love believe that pacifism will be efficacious not only on the interpersonal level, but in national and international politics. In a statement made to his friends in July 1942, John Mecartney wrote:

> Just as love draws out attitudes of friendship from other individuals, so it is with nations. I believe that Christian love practiced on an international scale would defeat Hitler, Mussolini, and Japan, stop wars and form an international fellowship of all races, nations, and creeds. A nation practicing Christian love would settle every conflict in a just and lasting way. Christ never gave us reason to believe that a person can love his enemies and then go to war and kill them.[51]

Somewhat less idealistic pronouncements of the same concept were given by the COs I interviewed. Robert Cary reflects that as a nation, "Our whole concept of witness seems to be to provide the strongest military force when probably the greatest force would be to involve ourselves in ways in which we show love and concern for people."[52] Other COs make the argument from the opposite side, that since war cannot work to produce good consequences, pacifism is the only alternative. As George Reeves says, "No good society can be built on the basis of killing. . . . We must have reverence for life and we must preserve life. Pacifism is the only way that a good society can come to birth."[53]

The Power of Sacrifice

Closely related to faith in the power of love is the belief that through willing sacrifice, pacifists can gain the sympathy and understanding of others who will voluntarily turn from their evil ways. Like the power of love, the power of sacrifice is immersed in the world of interpersonal relationships, and has its roots in both Christianity and Gandhism. The suffering love that COs saw exemplified in Jesus' crucifixion was believed to be capable of producing good consequences, again, as with the power of love, by exciting people's latent moral sensibilities. The willingness to suffer for pacifism was seen by COs as a way of calling attention to the integrity and value of pacifism and appealing to the best in others. In his *Diary of a Self-Made Convict,* Alfred Hassler comments: "It is only a Christianity whose adherents are willing to face that kind of suffering [dying for faith] . . . that can hope to make a dent in this very bad world."[54] James Bristol shares the same hope that suffering will bring results in this statement from a sermon written in 1940:

> Refusal to register is admittedly a negative act, but it is conceivable that it could serve as a dam to stop the waters that are rushing in one direction and give us an opportunity to start them flowing in another. Many of us have talked about peace. We have held meetings about peace. We have distributed literature about peace, but all of these activities are very easy ones in which to engage. A firm, "Here stand I, God help me, I cannot do otherwise," for the way of peace and reconciliation will be much more costly, indicative of much deeper conviction, and to that extent more effective in promoting peace and good will among men. Talk is cheap. Meetings protesting this and that are a dime a dozen, but the blood of the martyrs may yet be the seed of world peace.[55]

The principle of Gandhian nonviolence also relies on the power of sacrifice to bring good social consequences. Violence and animosity feed on themselves, and to break the cycle, one must be persistently loving and sacrificial, and absorb the violence oneself. As Wesley Doe argues in a World War II-era letter to his parents, "No one does violence unless he has himself been hurt. Most people pass violence along until it culminates in tragedy whereas we ought to absorb it so that the tension may be relieved."[56] Through active sacrifice, pacifism can break the chain of violence and provide the opportunity for a new beginning.

THE PLACE OF CONSEQUENCES IN PACIFIST MORAL REASONING

Whatever pacifists say about their desire for good consequences or their belief that pacifism will bring them, this tells us nothing about the place of consequences in their overall system of moral reasoning. For it is possible that in spite of their talk about the good consequences of pacifism, pacifists are pure deontologists who care not at all about consequences. They may argue consequences only in an effort to persuade consequentialists while being personally indifferent to whether pacifism is socially efficacious or not. On the other hand, pacifist beliefs in God, a moral universe, or the power of love and sacrifice may merely be helpful devices which are in no sense necessary to their position, which is justified solely on the grounds that a rule of pacifism will produce good consequences and is therefore desirable (i.e., pacifism could be rule-utilitarian).

The best way to discover what role consequences play in a pacifist moral system is to perform the thought experiment of removing good consequences and to then see what happens to the moral system as a whole. If you could convince a CO that whatever he may have thought before, pacifism will not produce good consequences, but very bad ones, what will be his reaction? If the CO is a pure deontologist, his reaction will be something like this: "That's really too bad, I'm very sorry, because I would sincerely like to see good consequences following my pacifism. Nevertheless, I must continue to do what's right, and nothing can persuade me that it's right to kill." If the CO is a rule-utilitarian, he will respond to the proof that pacifism does not bring good consequences by rejecting his pacifism. For the rule-utilitarian's first commitment is to good consequences—if these cannot be reached through pacifism, then pacifism is of no imaginable use, and will be discarded. The rule-utilitarian's goal remains the same: only the methods change, and the only reason for preferring pacifism to non-pacifism is if it is more effective in reaching his goal.

The reaction of most pacifists is neither of these, which suggests that pacifist moral reasoning is neither strictly deontological nor strictly consequentialist by the ordinary definitions of these terms, but some blending of the two. Pacifists do not shrug off bad consequences and doggedly pursue personal moral perfection, but neither do they dedicate themselves to producing good consequences by whatever means appear to work best. A standard pacifist reaction to convincing evidence that pacifism does not yield good consequences would sound something like this: "But wait a minute . . . what's wrong here? Did I misinterpret God's commands? What kind of a world am I living in? It's certainly not the one I thought I was in." Thus the desire for good consequences and the conviction that pacifism produces them are woven in at the ground level of pacifist justification. When threatened with the possibility that a moral rule of pacifism produces bad consequences, pacifists are shaken to their foundations and must seriously reconsider the appropriate method of dealing with issues of war and violence. If you could prove to their satisfaction that a rule of pacifism does not bring the anticipated good consequences, pacifists would be forced to choose, and would either maintain their pacifism in indifference to the consequences of so doing, or would sacrifice their pacifism to the greater good of producing positive social consequences. For those COs I spoke with who came to believe at some point that pacifism would not produce good consequences, these were precisely the directions their changes of heart took. First were those who abandoned their pacifism (many of whom joined the military during the war, others of whom believe they would do so if they had the chance to make the decision today); second were those who were resigned to the ineffectiveness of pacifism, but still found reasons for continuing to be pacifist. (Of course, most COs did not feel driven to give up either their pacifism or their hope for good consequences, and retain both to the present day.)

Whatever finally motivated COs to give up their pacifism—and the causes are surprisingly varied—they did not merely exchange nonviolent means for violent ones as a rule-utilitarian would; rather they gave up their fundamental beliefs about the nature of God, the universe, and/or human beings, those beliefs that made sense of the simultaneous commitment to following a rule of pacifism and producing good consequences. For example, one CO's pacifism developed in the interwar years and grew out of the conviction that Jesus taught and practiced pacifism, and that if Christians followed his example, good results would ensue. He applied for and was granted CO status and spent several years in CPS before coming to the conclusion that pacifism might not ultimately prevent bad consequences, at which point he left CPS for the military. In a 1944 letter to his friends, this CO described his new position as that of "reluctant supporter," and explained:

> He [the reluctant supporter] adopts this method [support of fighting] because he feels that Nazi domination is a greater threat to his moral values than all the evils he acquires or engenders through warring against the enemy. . . . He feels there is more opportunity to build world peace through a military defeat of fascism than surrender to the Nazis or the Japanese military and dependence on the techniques of non-violence. His position is even more difficult because it is less Christian than the pacifist, who has faith that good will triumph because it is essentially in balance with the moral nature of society, hence will survive violence and needs no resort to violence to defend it, preferring to die and be born again. The reluctant supporter admires this faith but does not feel that it meets the test of experience. Evil as well as good may be strong and may prevail.[57]

Here it is plain that it is not only the method of pacifism that is sacrificed when good consequences are not forthcoming, but also foundational beliefs that good means will produce good ends and that the power of love will finally emerge triumphant. While good means may still be preferable, and while they may generally yield good ends, exceptional circumstances may arise under which the evil means of war can be morally justified. This CO continued an affiliation with the Methodist church after the war, but he says that his personal religious faith never really recovered from the blow it took in World War II when he decided that applying Jesus' teachings would not necessarily bring good social ends. As he remarks, "It [pacifism] had been so tied into it [religion] that I suppose I really found it difficult to build up a new religious faith."[58]

This pattern of an entire system of moral justification being rocked to its foundations by the discovery that pacifism may not produce good consequences can also be seen in Max Kampelman's pacifist reversal. Kampelman served in CPS throughout the war, but gradually began to question whether pacifism could be effective in the international sphere. His pacifism was rooted in the principles of Gandhian nonviolence and a belief that the power of love could sway enemies from their evil ways. It was only as Kampelman saw the opportunity for drawing on the power of love disappearing in a world where wars are fought with little face-to-face contact that he felt driven to abandon his pacifism. He recalls his departure from pacifism as follows:

> With the explosion of the atom bomb it became clear to me that the very elements of personal interaction and the power of love became irrelevant in the

> international scene where slaughtering could take place with the pushing of a button without the human dimension being evident. The human response factor was therefore no longer present. And since I believed strongly in the need to resist evil effectively I could find no substitute for force and violence as a last resort for international politics. As the years evolved, my own pacifism completely disappeared as a reality. And I came to believe that the existence of military power by the United States was essential if there was to be a deterrent to the Soviet Union's aggressions.[59]

After the war, Kampelman joined the Marine Corps Reserve Unit to illustrate his support for the role the United States was taking internationally, and he says, "Were it necessary for me today to join the armed forces, I would do so."[60]

A particularly interesting example of a pacifist change of heart is that of Bill Colburn. After a brief period as a nonregistrant, Colburn was granted CO status and served in CPS. He faced the draft a second time during the Korean War and again applied for CO status, but several years after this, Colburn began to question his pacifism. He describes his World War II-era pacifism as liberal, based on a conception of Jesus as a moral teacher who should be imitated: "I did feel that he [Jesus] called us to follow him in our behavior in this way [pacifism], and that therefore it would also be effective if it was done on a national basis and not only on an individual basis."[61] The crisis in Colburn's pacifism came when he decided that very few people could live up to Christ's standard of pacifism and that he himself could not do so. If most people were incapable of true pacifism, Colburn reasoned, it could not be practical and could not guarantee good consequences. Since he believed that Christ taught pacifism, he felt compelled to give up his Christianity along with his pacifism, and he withdrew his membership from the church and joined the Massachusetts National Guard. Many years later, Colburn underwent yet another change of heart when he became involved with the Seventh-Day Adventist church and adopted a form of pacifism characteristic of fundamentalist COs: seeking personal obedience to Jesus' rule of pacifism, allowing the kingdoms of this world to go to war as they see fit, and trusting God to bring good things to pass in the long run.[62]

Colburn's transformations illustrate the real difference between Niebuhr's pure and political pacifists, and it is not so great as Niebuhr imagined. Both types of pacifists are committed to a rule of pacifism and to good consequences, and both rely on fundamental religious and quasi-religious beliefs that assure them that the relationship between moral rules and good consequences is reciprocal. The difference is that it is much more difficult to convince a "pure" pacifist that pacifism is not working to produce good than it is to convince a "political" pacifist. The pure pacifist who trusts God to usher in a better social order has explanations for the failure of pacifism to make a positive impact on society (e.g., human sinfulness), and faith that God will bring things to rights eventually. Thus "pure" pacifists may pass entire lifetimes watching the failures of pacifism accumulate around them and still believe that the ultimate good consequences of pacifism are assured. In contrast, if political pacifists are given evidence that love is not overcoming evil or that bad means are producing good ends, they will more readily re-evaluate their belief in the efficacy of pacifism.*

Yet some COs retained their pacifism even after deciding that it would not necessarily produce good consequences. They underwent some of the same trauma of seeing their most fundamental beliefs linking a rule of pacifism to good consequences challenged, but instead of discarding these beliefs and becoming non-pacifist, while preserving the quest for consequences, they relativized their fundamental beliefs and clung to a rule of pacifism in spite of consequences. These COs tended to take a fatalistic attitude toward the problem of war and the problem of large-scale social consequences generally. These COs viewed war as an inevitability. This was most common among COs in the conservative peace churches, who with centuries of a peace witness behind them were more keenly aware of the intractability of the problem of war. Irvin Richert remarks, "I think as a Mennonite I felt that there would always be wars and rumors of wars and that eventually belligerents would cause conflicts and there would be a major war."[63]

Liberal fatalists took a similar view, but were more inclined to despair and frustration. For these COs, war is irrational, a mystery, insanity. Loris Habegger describes wars as "cataclysmic events, paroxysms of madness."[64] In his memoir of CPS, *Down in My Heart,* William Stafford relates the comment of a fellow CO in CPS which illustrates the pacifist bewilderment in the face of war:

> It's as if the war is a game. . . . People retain the same qualities throughout big historical changes; a fad comes along, something like peewee golf, but with a slightly murderous effect, and people go along—with their same friendly feelings—murdering each other.[65]

Because war is such a peculiar phenomenon, and so seemingly impervious to human reason, a number of COs retreat to a concern with personal morality. COs who take this position argue that they cannot be held responsible for large-scale consequences that are out of their control, but only for their own behavior.

*A rule-utilitarian will re-evaluate the efficacy of a moral rule of pacifism more quickly still, and abandon the rule with much less provocation. This seems to be borne out in World War II pacifism, where a high percentage of pre-war pacifists of the "pure" type (for example, conservative peace church members) applied for CO status, while a lower percentage of "political" pre-war pacifists (for example, liberal Protestant church members) maintained their stand during the war. Socialist pacifists of the pre-war years had an even poorer record of retaining pacifism in the face of war, and this undoubtedly reflects the fact that their pacifism was defended almost solely on consequentialist—or rule-utilitarian—grounds. This offers some support to the pacifist contention that religion may not be necessary to establish the moral worth of pacifism, but that it may be necessary to sustain pacifism in times of crisis.

In 1941, before America's entrance into the war, James Bristol wrote to his draft board:

> I realize quite clearly that my refusal at this point to go further with the draft machinery will in no way retard America's plunge toward war. At the time of the writing of my sermon in October I did entertain the hope that refusal to register on the part of even a small number of men might check considerably our journey down the road to war. Now, however, I recognize the very apparent fact that no stand I take will in any way help to determine the future policy of my country.[66]

For these COs, faced with a world that will not yield to individual efforts to perfect it, the best individuals can do is to live their own lives well and rightly, and let the world go its own way. Al Herbst comments: "I can't keep somebody from shooting somebody else or from shooting me. You can't control anyone but yourself, and sometimes that's a hard enough job."[67] Seth Gifford makes the same point: "Really there isn't much that the individual can do except govern his own life by the principles that he feels are right."[68]

Yet a concern for good consequences remains, in that it is believed that pacifism is not producing *bad* consequences even if it is unable to produce good ones. Thus pacifism is at least neutral with respect to consequences, and the individual can choose to practice it without fear of being morally blameworthy from a consequentialist point of view. But the fact that pacifism continues to be valued after it is found to be morally neutral with respect to consequences indicates that there is some notion of deontological value operative here. This can be seen when COs assert the rule against killing as a sufficient explanation in itself for why they could not fight in a war. Examples include: "It's never permissible to use violence," "Killing people is not justified in any way," and "Killing is immoral, it's uncivilized, it is not human."[69]

Even more strongly deontological are arguments that place the focus on personal moral purity and make no reference to consequences at all. For example, Sam Guhr asserts: "I'd never be able to live with myself if I took somebody else's life, I'd rather have them take mine."[70] Milton Mayer takes this one step further when he concludes his 1939 article "I Think I'll Sit This One Out" by saying that he must do what he believes right not only in spite of consequences, but even in spite of God, if necessary:

> But he [Mayer himself] will have taken his stand, not because he thinks God or the big battalions are with him but because he can take no other. And he will have to say, with William the Silent, that it is not necessary to hope in order to undertake, nor to succeed in order to persevere.[71]

Still, it is not assumed that the consequences of this stand will be bad, only that they are unknown.

DEONTOLOGY AND CONSEQUENTIALISM

If pacifists were as unconcerned with consequences as their critics maintain, one would expect to find a majority of COs proclaiming that they would continue to be pacifist even if the world went to ruin as a direct result of their actions. Yet no pacifist to my knowledge has ever made such a proclamation. The central place of good consequences in pacifist moral reasoning seems secure, for when such good results are in doubt, a crisis is precipitated in the entire system of moral reasoning. Yet pacifism is not fully consequentialist. Recall that the debate between deontological and consequentialist styles of reasoning is taken to be the difference between evaluating actions only in reference to themselves versus evaluating them in terms of their consequences. Clearly pacifists evidence a concern with the inherent rightness of their moral choices, apparently independently of their concern for the consequences that follow in their wake.

It would seem, then, that pacifists are squarely in the middle of the deontology/consequentialist distinction, caring about consequences yet determined to follow moral rules that are in some sense inherently right. Yet if pacifists—with their determination to adhere to the morally right and leave the consequences to God (or some secular counterpart)—are not deontologists, then who is? Nobody, I would argue, and this because the traditional distinction between deontology and consequentialism finds a difference on grounds where one does not exist.* Pacifists *are* the mythical "deontologists," even with their commitment to producing good consequences.

Is there then no significant difference between the way pacifists and non-pacifists address moral issues? Do they merely make different substantive choices from within the same universe of moral discourse? I think this is not the case. I believe there *is* a significant difference between pacifist and non-pacifist moral reasoning, but that traditional moral theory has failed to locate it. In order to better see what this difference might be, let us take a second look at those facets of pacifist moral reasoning that conspire to place pacifists in the deontological camp. The first of these is the tendency to concentrate on personal behavior as the locus of morality and to be relatively less concerned with the morality of other people or groups. The second is the degree to which the right is valued for its own sake (i.e., not only because it produces good consequences,

*The pure deontologist is an ideal type, and it is extremely rare to encounter anyone in person or in print who even approximates the analytical description of a strict deontologist. Those who sound most like the classic definition of a deontologist are vague on the topic of consequences, but never take the position that the consequences of their moral choices could be eternally vile and they would not care. It is my belief that such persons are not yet persuaded that the consequences of pacifism will be bad, though they are also not certain that they will be good. I believe that if this doubt became certainty, they would discard their pacifism as others have done before them.

but because it is in some sense inherently right). Finally, the pacifist reliance on foundational beliefs (in God, the law of means and ends, the power of love and sacrifice) which act as intermediaries between moral rules and good consequences can show us where the defining difference between deontology and consequentialism actually lies.

Individual Responsibility and Social Change

When pacifists think about morality, they typically start with themselves, then move to groups with which they are identified—church, ethnic group, nation—and think only then, if at all, about the moral responsibility of whoever they define as other. Thus when faced with conflict, the pacifist believes it correct to ask first "What can I (my church/group/nation) do differently?" This basic tendency toward moral introspection expresses itself in a number of ways. One such way is the pacifist belief that good consequences are reached by changing hearts and minds rather than by manipulating blocks of social power. Social change is won through individual decisions to be faithful to a better way. Another expression of pacifist moral introspection is the way in which pacifists tend to look first at how the United States may be aggravating conflict rather than concerning themselves with the misdeeds of other nations. This takes the form of pointing to American imperialism, greed, and lack of international good will as a primary cause of war.

Most significantly though, pacifist moral introspection establishes a fundamental defense for the position of conscientious objection, for it is by laboring toward personal moral purity that the CO fulfills his moral responsibility. It is not considered necessary to persuade the other to desist from his or her wrongdoing, but only to ensure that oneself is behaving in an exemplary fashion. By taking a position of refusing to become personally involved in violence, the CO all but exhausts his moral responsibility: He is not harming others, he is not aggravating the conflict, and he is acquiring the moral strength and personal virtue necessary for successful conciliation.

Implied in the focus on individual moral behavior is an openness to social nonconformity. Morality is not decided in reference to the behavior of others, but in reference to moral standards. The goal is to live up to these standards, regardless of how badly others fail to attain them. What the state or one's peers choose to do does not influence the morality of the action in question. For many World War II COs, their nonconformity was tempered somewhat by the fact that they were conforming to the norms of some group with whom they felt a closer identification than with the state (for example, their church, their family, or their political organization). But for the majority, conformity was first and foremost to an ideal, and the demands of the state and others were relegated to a secondary position. Again, this neglect of the state's interests is illustrative of a generally negative view of the state among World War II COs.

The tendency toward moral introspection is a characteristic typically associated with deontological moral theories. Thomas Nagel discusses this feature of deontology in a series of lectures entitled "The Limits of Objectivity." Nagel distinguishes two types of values: agent-neutral and agent-relative. Agent-neutral values provide reasons to act for anyone, no matter who they are; these values are things that are good in themselves. Agent-relative values provide reasons only to specific individuals; they are things important to me, but perhaps not to you. Nagel argues that consequentialist moral theories are concerned only with agent-neutral value, with bringing about the best possible state of affairs for the whole world. If there is an agent-neutral reason for me to act to bring about certain ends, it is equally a reason for you to so act; it can even be interpreted as a reason for me compelling you to so act. On the other hand, deontological moral theories appeal to values that are agent-relative: I may have a reason not to harm other people, but this does not imply that you have the same reason, nor does it imply that I may compel you to recognize this reason. Furthermore, and most important for the consequentialist/deontological distinction, my agent-relative reason for not harming others is independent of agent-neutral reasons for bringing about certain ends. If the two are in competition, for example, I might choose not to harm you on the agent-relative grounds that harming you is not something that I do, while being aware that by so choosing I am offending against agent-neutral values, that is, I am bringing about (some) bad consequences. As Nagel explains, "Deontological reasons have their full force against *your doing* something—not just against its *happening*."[72]

It is in this sense that pacifist moral reasoning can rightly be termed deontological, for the emphasis in pacifist moral reasoning is on personal moral accountability. This also explains the rather curious frequency of appeals to moral pluralism among World War II COs. In some cases, this takes the form of an outright vocational pacifism: pacifism is right for Christians, but non-pacifism is right for non-Christians, who are also working to do God's will (though this may not be their intention). More often, COs argue that they choose pacifism for themselves, but they wish to allow others to choose their own course and to listen to their own consciences, even if these others ultimately choose to be non-pacifist. These COs hold that another's choice to be non-pacifist is worthy of respect. This is not simply liberal broadmindedness; with the exception of vocational pacifists, most COs deem pacifism to be right, and right for everybody. But an individual's responsibility is to act according to his or her best lights and give others the freedom to do likewise according to their conscience. Once this position is taken, it cannot be guaranteed that everyone will come to the conclusion that pacifism is morally correct.

From the point of view of consequentialism, this desire for personal adherence to a moral rule without apparent concern for others' adherence to the same rule seems puzzling. This is one feature of deontological moral reasoning that leads theorists to claim that deontologists are unconcerned with consequences. In fact, it is a question of emphasis. Both deontological and consequentialist theories care about both personal moral behavior and the good consequences this behavior brings. In the case of deontological theories (like pacifism), the focus is on personal behavior, and moral responsibility is responsibility for the moral quality of one's own behavior. Yet it is obvious that this behavior is expected to yield good consequences (over the long run); how else could it be justified? Consequences do not occupy the foreground, and in some cases are virtually never mentioned, but most often this is not because good consequences are unimportant, but because they are assumed to be the inevitable outcome of personal moral behavior.

Contrariwise, consequentialist theories focus on social outcomes as the seat of moral responsibility. One is constrained not so much to act rightly as to produce good ends. But good ends are produced by personal moral behavior; how else could they be produced? If the individual cannot produce good consequences alone, than his or her moral responsibility dictates persuading or compelling others to act in such a way as to produce good consequences. This too is a personal moral act. Personal moral behavior is not in the foreground of consequentialist theories because it is assumed. Consequentialism anticipates that personal moral behavior will emerge naturally from a preoccupation with social outcomes in the same way that deontology anticipates that good consequences will flow naturally from attention to personal moral behavior. Pacifists are deontological by this definition, but this must not be mistaken for an indifference to consequences.

Independent Valuation of the Right

Moral truth for pacifists is rarely understood as a changing quantity. Pacifists have a deep need for consistency in moral truth, for convictions that are true for all people and all groups, and in all circumstances.* This does not always imply a hidebound devotion to rules (though this is occasionally a feature of pacifism), but if a principle is deemed worthy, it is not to be violated. To admit too many exceptions and qualifications is to devalue a principle in pacifist eyes; generally speaking, the purer the rule, the more it deserves to be followed. This desire for consistency is at the heart of the concept of pacifism, of viewing war as wrong in itself, as an atrocity that no amount of extenuating circumstances can justify.

A corollary of this love of consistency is a kind of literalism. Wherever moral truth is grounded, whether in God, the universe, or humanity alone, pacifists are inclined to believe that there should be a one-to-one correspondence between

*This is in apparent conflict with the willingness of most pacifists to respect the non-pacifism of others. Yet when pacifists allow for differences of conscience, they do not allow for inconsistency in moral truth, only for imperfect and varying abilities to discern and live up to it.

moral truth and individual behavior. In some, this literalism is biblical literalism: as we have seen, both conservative and liberal COs who draw on scriptural authority tend to interpret it literally. Thus there are not separate standards for Christ and for fallen humanity, only a different ability to reach them. Other COs have no attachment to scripture, but still portray moral truth as exceptionless, as something that demands total adherence.

Again, this feature of pacifism is deontological. Such a passion for the purest and highest moral truth, and for behavior that gains its value through its expression of that truth, indicates that the morally right has intrinsic value that it is not dependent on the consequences it produces. According to most theorists, this is the hallmark of deontological moral reasoning. In *Ethics*, William Frankena distinguishes consequentialist and deontological theories by arguing that for consequentialists, "the basic or ultimate criterion or standard of what is morally right, wrong, obligatory, etc., is the nonmoral value that is brought into being."[73] In other words, the consequences that are desired are not in themselves moral, they are merely good. What *is* moral are those acts that are productive of good consequences, that create a better state of affairs, or in Frankena's words, that "produce a greater balance of good over evil than any available alternative."[74] In contrast, deontological theories do not make the right dependent on the good, but rather assert its primacy. The moral act is chosen not for the good it will bring about, but for the fact that it is right. (This rightness can be an irreducible fact or can be justified on the basis that the right is commanded by God, the state, or the rational will.)[75]

Whatever their attachment to the nonmoral good, it seems accurate to say that pacifists have a love for the morally right that cannot be subsumed under their desire for good consequences (interpreted as the realization of nonmoral good). God is not to be followed only because he guarantees good consequences, but because he is good and commands that which is ultimately right. If good means bring good ends, that speaks in their favor, but good means are also good in themselves: kindness is not preferable to violence simply because it works better, but because it *is* better. If it is possible to redeem others through love, to touch the hardened heart and bring change, it is also possible to refuse to kill out of love, to sacrifice for another with no promise of reward.

But pacifists are still seeking consequences through their moral choices: for example, the pacifist who is following God's commands is also anticipating the kingdom of God, which for the believer is the very epitome of good consequences. The difference between consequentialism and deontology here seems to be in the kind of consequences that are sought. For consequentialists, the good to be achieved is nonmoral; it is happiness, pleasantness, the absence of pain, the general health and well-being of all people. While these goals are highly valued, they are more appropriately described as "good" than as "right," so moral theory would term them nonmoral ends. For deontologists (including pacifists), the good to be achieved is moral: it is not just a happy world that is pursued, but a world where people do not tell lies or perpetuate injustice—

admittedly, a world that is "good," but also one that is morally "right." It is a world commensurate with the ideals and moral acts that bring it into existence.

Frankena believes that it is not theoretically possible to speak of the morality of an action being contingent on morally good consequences. He explains: "For the moral quality or value of something to depend on the moral value of whatever it promotes would be circular."[76] But for deontologists who are seeking good (moral) consequences, the relationship is not one of circularity, but of equivalence. Morality is both a means and an end, a tool for reaching ends that are desirable because they are moral—both means and ends participate in the quality of moral value. For deontologists, the consequences sought are not so much good as they are ideal. The good society of consequentialism is happy and healthy; the ideal society of deontology is virtuous. Frankena suggests that the nonmoral good sought by consequentialist theories need not be determined by the hedonistic standard of pleasure or happiness, but can be judged on the scales of power, knowledge, self-realization, or perfection. But once one starts seeking consequences like self-realization and perfection, it would seem that one has entered the realm of the moral. Again, the distinction between consequentialism and deontology is one of emphasis, of the kind of value sought somewhere along the moral/nonmoral spectrum. What one chooses to call "moral" and "nonmoral" is vital to the coherence of the consequentialist/deontological distinction, and as seen here, the definition is somewhat arbitrary.

Foundational Beliefs

It would thus seem that the differences between consequentialists and deontologists are primarily matters of emphasis. One focuses on social outcomes, the other on personal moral behavior; one seeks the nonmoral good, the other pursues the morally right. In either case the moral agent is choosing points along a spectrum with the same basic goal in mind: a society where people behave well so that human life can flourish. But there are reasons why one chooses the varying emphases of deontology and consequentialism, and it is here that the real differences between the two are revealed. Deontologists see a link between personal moral behavior and good consequences because they rely on the intermediaries of foundational beliefs in a powerful God, the unity of means and ends, or the power of love and sacrifice. These are beliefs in which consequentialists do not place much faith. In fact, much of consequentialism's appeal is that it can be sustained on very thin religious and philosophical underpinnings.

All of the pacifist's foundational beliefs assume some sort of benevolence, a basic goodness. God, the universe, or human nature is believed to be responsive to morality, to have a positive preference for the morally right, and to reward it with good consequences. I would argue that all pacifist moral reasoning can be derived from these foundational beliefs, and it is only in the context of these beliefs that pacifist moral reasoning makes sense. The problem with the traditional consequentialist/deontological distinction is that it does not take into account the dominant beliefs that make "deontological" moral reasoning explicable. Without its major premises, a deontological theory seems peculiar and perverse, fascinated by some intuitively grasped "moral right" and blind to social consequences. It is because moral theory insists on the most attenuated of religious and philosophical grounds that it finds consequentialism rational and deontology strange.

The inclusion of foundational beliefs in deontological moral reasoning also explains the primary attitudinal difference between deontologists and consequentialists. The goal of the consequentialist is to manipulate society to yield better ends—whatever works to achieve this is acceptable. Generally, those actions deemed right by ordinary bourgeois morality are believed to work best, but nevertheless, if actions that ordinary bourgeois morality condemned could be shown to be efficacious, they would be considered moral on consequentialist grounds. The basic attitude of consequentialism is a mechanistic one: by manipulating the correct levers, the desired product is created. The levers are not in themselves right or wrong, better or worse; they are just more or less effective. In contrast, deontological theories (such as pacifism) do not view the individual as the powerful force that can manipulate actions to produce good ends. The power of morality is external: it is the power of God, the power of moral truth, the power of love. It is only by aligning themselves with these more powerful forces that individual moral agents can hope to attain good ends.

It is here that deontology and consequentialism can be most fruitfully distinguished. It is not that deontologists are oblivious to the need for good social outcomes while consequentialists hold them central. Rather, it is that deontologists rely on a power of morality larger (and more reliable) than themselves, while consequentialists must wrest some moral sense from a universe which they perceive to be no better than neutral with respect to morality.

The distinction between consequentialism and deontology was developed and continues to retain its hold over moral theory because it attempts to articulate a difference in forms of moral reasoning that can be appreciated empirically. But theory has misunderstood practice and is no longer (if it ever was) an effective mirror for it. Moral theory has claimed that deontologists and consequentialists evaluate moral action differently, which, while true enough, misses the deeper truth that they do so because they believe themselves to be living in different moral worlds. The moral world occupied by pacifists postulates an unbreakable connection between right action and good result, while that of non-pacifists promises no such thing.

This is why World War II provides such a strong challenge to pacifism: it presents the possibility that great evil can obtain social power and produce terrible consequences, leaving pacifists helpless to hinder its progress without leaving their pacifism behind. If such is truly the case, pacifists are left without a mooring in their world where right equals good, and are cast adrift in the turbulent seas that consequentialists make their home, negotiating new and often precarious balances between the actions they deem right and the consequences they believe to be good.

NOTES

1. A discussion of consequentialism in general, and different forms of utilitarianism in particular, can be found in William K. Frankena, *Ethics*, 2d ed. (Englewood Cliffs, NJ: Prentice-Hall, Inc., 1973), 14–16, 35–43.

2. Charles Chatfield, *For Peace and Justice: Pacifism in America, 1914–1941* (Boston: Beacon Press, 1973), 312.

3. Reinhold Niebuhr, *Christianity and Power Politics* (New York: Archon Books, 1969 [originally 1940]). Niebuhr wrote numerous articles for *The Christian Century* and *Christianity and Crisis* in the pre-war years which presented his distinction between political and religious pacifists. In particular, see Reinhold Niebuhr, "Japan and the Christian Conscience," *The Christian Century* 54 (November 1937): 1390–91, and Reinhold Niebuhr, answer to editor's question, "If America is drawn into the war, can you as a Christian, participate in it or support it?" *The Christian Century* 57 (December 1940): 1578–80.

4. Paul Delp, interview with author, 3 March 1987, Orange, California; Richard Brown, interview with author, 2 October 1986, Berkeley, California; Wesley Doe, letter to author, 14 January 1987.

5. James Bristol, interview with author, 27 May 1987, Philadelphia, Pennsylvania.

6. R. Paul Phillips, interview with author, 11 September 1986, Ontario, California. See also Samuel Liskey, interview with author, 11 September 1986, Ontario, California; Booton Herndon, *The Unlikeliest Hero* (Mountain View, CA: Pacific Press Publishing Association, 1967), 37–38.

7. Paul Ashby, interview with author, 30 September 1986, San Francisco, California.

8. Arle Brooks, quoted in *War and the Christian Conscience: From Augustine to Martin Luther King, Jr.*, Albert Marrin, ed. (Chicago: Henry Regnery Company, 1971), pp. 239–40. Again, this sentiment is not restricted to liberal COs. For example, George Brumley, a Jehovah's Witness remarked, "Wars are foolish, harmful, stupid" (George Brumley, letter to author, 4 June 1987). See also Sigmund Cohn, interview with author, 30 September 1986, Berkeley, California; William Gerber, Polner interview; Bob Stocksdale, interview with author, 1 October 1986, Berkeley, California; Henry Blocher, interview with author, 10 September 1986, La Verne, California; Wesley Doe, letter to author answering author's questions, 14 January 1987; Howard Ten Brink, interview with author, 24 September 1986, Modesto, California; Bob Stocksdale, interview with author, 1 October 1986, Berkeley, California; Gerald Rubin, interview with author, 2 October 1986, Corte Madera, California; Harry Prochaska, interview with author, 1 October 1986, San Francisco, California; Dwight Hanawalt, interview with author, 10 September 1986, La Verne, California; Caleb Foote, telephone interview with author, 28 February 1987; Paul

Ashby, interview with author, 30 September 1986, San Francisco, California; Saburo Mizutani, interview with author, 29 September 1986, Sacramento, California; Harmon Wilkinson, interview with author, 23 February 1987, Whittier, California; Leland Sateren, interview with author, 9 February 1987, Edina, Minnesota; Malcolm Parker, telephone interview with author, 28 February 1987.

9. Milton S. Mayer, "I Think I'll Sit This One Out," *Saturday Evening Post* 212 (October 1939): 100.

10. Don Benedict, quoted in *Ten Fighters for Peace,* Don Lawson, ed. (New York: Lothrop, Lee, and Shepard, 1971), 97. See also the comments of another of the Union Theological Seminary group of draft resisters, Dave Dellinger, "Introduction," in *Against the Tide: Pacifist Resistance in the Second World War, an Oral History,* Deena Hurwitz and Craig Simpson, eds. (New York: War Resisters League, 1984); Jim Peck, *We Who Would Not Kill* (New York: Lyle Stuart, 1958), 12; Robert Vogel, interview with author, 15 September 1986, Pasadena, California.

11. *The Catholic CO,* quoted in Gordon Zahn, "A Study of the Social Backgrounds of Catholic Conscientious Objectors in Civilian Public Service During World War II" (M.A. thesis, Catholic University of America, Washington D.C., 1950), 97.

12. Anonymous World War II CO, "Special Form for Conscientious Objector" (form 47), privately held. See also George Fischer, interview with author, 22 April 1987, Danvers, Massachusetts.

13. Paul Delp, interview with author, 3 March 1987, Orange, California.

14. John Mecartney, "A Statement to My Friends," July 1942, CPS Personal Papers, Document Group 56, Swarthmore College Peace Collection, Swarthmore, Pennsylvania.

15. George Reeves, quoted in *Against the Tide,* Hurwitz and Simpson, eds.

16. Bill Colburn, interview with author, 5 May 1987, Concord, New Hampshire. See also George Brown, address at New Windsor, Maryland, On Earth Peace Assembly, 12 April 1986, privately held; Wallace Nelson, quoted in *Against the Tide,* Hurwitz and Simpson, eds.

17. Gordon Nutson, interview with author, 25 September 1986, Modesto, California; Richard Brown, interview with author, 2 October 1986, Berkeley, California; Howard Bogen, interview with author, 9 September 1986, Pasadena, California; Lowell Naeve (in collaboration with David Wieck), *A Field of Broken Stones* (Denver: Alan Swallow, 1959), 8–9; James Bristol, interview with author, 27 May 1987, Philadelphia, Pennsylvania; David Koven, quoted in *Against the Tide,* Hurwitz and Simpson, eds.

18. Harry Prochaska, interview with author, 1 October 1986, San Francisco, California.

19. Lyle Krug, interview with author, 28 August 1986, Mission Viejo, California; R. Paul Phillips, interview with author, 11 September 1986, Ontario, California.

20. Gordon Nutson, interview with author, 25 September 1986, Modesto, California.

21. James Lowerre, interview with author, 3 March 1987, Orange, California.

22. Simon Greco, quoted in Roy Hoopes, *Americans Remember: The Home Front* (New York: Hawthorn Books, 1977), 233.

23. Howard Bogen, interview with author, 9 September 1986, Pasadena, California.

24. Gordon Kaufman, interview with author, 29 April 1987, Cambridge, Massachusetts.

25. Another extension of the rule of pacifism is made by a very few vegetarian COs who believe that just as it is wrong to kill people, it is also wrong to kill animals. In the World War II era, vegetarian COs were organized as the Tolstoy Peace Group. They published a newsletter and gained an occasional convert from the general CO population. For further information, see Tolstoy Peace Group, Collective Document Groups A, Swarthmore College Peace Collection, Swarthmore, Pennsylvania.

26. Paul Delp, interview with author, 3 March 1987, Orange, California. See also James Bristol, interview with author, 27 May 1987, Philadelphia, Pennsylvania.

27. Eugene Carper, interview with author, 10 September 1986, La Verne, California.

28. George Fischer, interview with author, 22 April 1987, Danvers, Massachusetts.

29. Mayer, "I Think I'll Sit This One Out," 23.

30. Sigmund Cohn, interview with author, 30 September 1986, Berkeley, California.

31. Gordon Zahn, *War, Conscience, and Dissent* (New York: Hawthorn Books, 1967), 79–80.

32. Roy Mast, self-interview answering author's questions, May 1987.

33. Gilbert Grover, interview with author, 24 September 1986, Modesto, California.

34. See, for example, R. Paul Phillips, interview with author, 11 September 1986, Ontario, California; Gil Bertochini, interview with author, 1 June 1987, Washington DC; Gilbert Grover, "The Christian and the State," unpublished essay, privately held.

35. R. Paul Phillips, interview with author, 11 September 1986, Ontario, California; G. Hayes Reed, interview with author, 25 September 1986, Modesto, California; Donald Beachler, interview with author, 26 September 1986, Modesto, California.

36. Gil Bertochini, interview with author, 1 June 1987, Washington D.C.

37. Gilbert Grover, "The Christian and the State," privately held.

38. Gordon and Gale Nutson, letter to friends, 5 February 1945, privately held.

39. Sigmund Cohn, interview with author, 30 September 1986, Berkeley, California. See also Max Kleinbaum, interview for "An Oral History of American Jews who Chose to Become Conscientious Objectors or Resisted Serving in the Military from World War II—Korean War," Murray Polner, coordinator, ten cassette tapes, Swarthmore College Peace Collection, Swarthmore, Pennsylvania (hereafter abbreviated as "Polner interview"); Howard Ten Brink, interview with author, 24 September 1986, Modesto, California.

40. Bayard Rustin, letter to draft board, 16 November 1943, CPS Personal Papers, Document Group 56, Swarthmore College Peace Collection, Swarthmore, Pennsylvania.

41. J. Edwin Jones, interview with author, 6 September 1986, La Verne, California; John Abbott, quoted in Mark Jonathan Harris, Franklin D. Mitchell, and Steven J. Schechter, *The Homefront: America During World War II* (New York: G.P. Putnam's Sons, 1984), 90.

42. Lawrence Templin, statement to court, Lawrence Templin papers, Mennonite Library and Archives, North Newton, Kansas.

43. James Bristol, statement to federal judge, 31 October 1941, privately held.

44. James Bristol, interview with author, 27 May 1987, Philadelphia, Pennsylvania.

45. John Mecartney, "A Statement to My Friends," July 1942, CPS Personal Papers, Document Group 56, Swarthmore College Peace Collection, Swarthmore, Pennsylvania; Robert Vogel, interview with author, 15 September 1986, Pasadena, California; Anonymous World War II CO, quoted in Gordon C. Zahn, "Catholic COs in CPS," (M.A. thesis), 104.

46. James Bristol, interview with author, 27 May 1987, Philadelphia, Pennsylvania.

47. Bob Stocksdale, interview with author, 1 October 1986, Berkeley, California. See also J. Edwin Jones, interview with author, 6 September 1986, La Verne, California; Max Kleinbaum, Polner interview; James Bristol, interview with author, 27 May 1987, Philadelphia, Pennsylvania.

48. Zahn, *War, Conscience, and Dissent,* 306.

49. James Bristol, statement to federal judge, 31 October 1941, privately held. See also anonymous World War II CO, letter to friends, 4 February 1944, privately held.

50. Lawrence Templin, statement to court, Lawrence Templin papers, Mennonite Library and Archives, North Newton, Kansas.

51. John Mecartney, "A Statement to My Friends," July 1942, CPS Personal Papers, Document Group 56, Swarthmore College Peace Collection, Swarthmore, Pennsylvania.

52. Robert Cary, interview with author, 1 October 1986, San Francisco, California. See also Abraham Zwickel, Polner interview; Bill Colburn, interview with author, 5 May 1987, Concord, New Hampshire.

53. George Reeves, quoted in *Against the Tide,* Hurwitz and Simpson, eds. See also Max Kleinbaum, Polner interview.

54. Alfred Hassler, *Diary of a Self-Made Convict* (Nyack, NY: Fellowship of Reconciliation, 1958), 135.

55. James Bristol, sermon written for 13 October 1940, privately held.

56. Wesley Doe, letter to parents, n.d. [during World War II], privately held. See also Max Kleinbaum, Polner interview.

57. Anonymous World War II CO, letter to friends, 4 February 1944, privately held. See also anonymous World War II CO, interview with author, 3 March 1987.

58. Anonymous World War II CO, interview with author, 3 March 1987.

59. Max Kampelman, Polner interview.

60. Ibid.

61. Bill Colburn, interview with author, 5 May 1987, Concord, New Hampshire.

62. Ibid.

63. Irvin Richert, interview for "Schowalter Oral History Collection—World War II Conscientious Objectors," Keith Sprunger and James Juhnke, coordinators, 122 cassette tapes, Mennonite Library and Archives, North Newton, Kansas (hereafter abbreviated as "SOH interview"). See also Laban Peachey, SOH interview; Duane Windemiller, interview with author, 22 April 1987, Hampton Beach, New Hampshire; G. Hayes Reed, interview with author, 25 September 1986, Modesto, California.

64. Loris Habegger, SOH interview.

65. William Stafford, *Down in My Heart* (Elgin, IL: Brethren Publishing House, 1947), 72.

66. James Bristol, letter to draft board, 14 April 1941, privately held.

67. Albert Herbst, interview with author, 6 September 1986, La Verne, California.

68. Seth Gifford, interview with author, 30 April 1987, Providence, Rhode Island. See also John Abbott, quoted in Harris et al., *The Homefront,* 90; Vernon Blosser, SOH interview; David Koven, quoted in *Against the Tide,* Hurwitz and Simpson, eds.

69. Gordon Zahn, interview with author, 29 April 1987, Charlestown, Massachusetts; Paul Delp, interview with author, 3 March 1987, Orange, California; Max Kleinbaum, Polner interview.

70. Samuel Guhr, SOH interview. See also Fred Convers, interview with author, 2 October 1986, Berkeley, California.

71. Mayer, "I Think I'll Sit This One Out," 100.

72. Thomas Nagel, "The Limits of Objectivity. III. Ethics," The Tanner Lecture on Human Values, delivered at Brasenose College, Oxford University, 18 May 1979.

73. Frankena, *Ethics,* 14.

74. Ibid.

75. Ibid., 15.

76. Ibid., 14.

6

The Challenge of World War II

In gaining an adequate picture of World War II pacifism, it is imperative to know how COs understand the events that convince non-pacifists that war is the only answer, and to find out why COs feel these events are insufficient to justify war. The pertinent events in the World War II context can be reduced to three interlocking challenges to pacifism: the attack on Pearl Harbor (often seen by non-pacifists as an unprovoked foreign invasion of American soil), the threat of fascism to democratic freedoms (interpreted as the need to secure certain social values), and the Holocaust (understood as the obligation to protect innocents). Generally speaking, the greatest challenge to pacifism in the minds of non-pacifists during World War II was the attack on Pearl Harbor, since it was most effective at galvanizing American public opinion behind the war. Fascism was probably the greatest threat to pacifists from their own point of view, since pacifism was essentially a liberal democratic movement prior to the war. In retrospect, however, the Holocaust is unquestionably the prime threat to pacifism posed by World War II, in the minds of pacifists and non-pacifists alike. It is the Holocaust that puts the bite into the challenge "What about Hitler?"

When COs seek to interpret the events of World War II and determine the appropriate pacifist response to them, they give specific arguments very like those discussed earlier in general terms. First, they examine the roots of World War II, and find them in the same unsavory places as they do in all wars. Emphasis is placed on how the United States (or more generally, the Allies) bears responsibility for exacerbating the conflicts that led Germany and Japan to war, and on U.S. violations of the conventions of war. Atrocities on the enemy's side are interpreted as a feature of war rather than a reason to go to war. At any rate, COs argue, war is ill-suited to preventing atrocity. Next, COs maintain that World War II is an example of the general truth that "bad means produce bad ends," because World War II failed to achieve its goals; and on the other hand, that pacifism (and its good means) provide an opportunity for good ends, even in the difficult circumstances of World War II. Some more unusual arguments also surfaced, including those offered by COs who favored the Allies in World War II, although they felt unable to actively participate in the fighting, and also some that illustrate why particular COs may not have responded to the challenge of World War II as did most Americans. Finally, COs reflect on how and to what degree their pacifism was threatened by World War II, and how they have either answered or ignored this threat in the intervening years.

SHARING THE GUILT FOR WORLD WAR II

The conscientious objector's first line of defense against the challenge raised by World War II is to point out areas of U.S. complicity in the war. This corresponds to the tendency noted earlier among COs to insist that in any conflict there is guilt on both sides and to draw special attention to the guilt on one's own side. COs repeatedly made the argument that the conventional interpretation of the origins of World War II is a self-serving one invented by the winners of that war, and that in reality the Allies were not innocent parties roused to wrath by the abuses of the Axis powers, but equal partners with them in creating the crime of war.

Pearl Harbor

This revisionist history begins with the attack on Pearl Harbor. COs suggest that it was not the infamous sneak attack so beloved by the American press, but an attack that was provoked, even invited, by the United States. As Cal Edinger says, "Any serious student knew that things were coming to a head [with Japan]. All kinds of crazy things were happening. And there was a price to be paid for what we had done . . . for our world politics. They were not proving out."[1] A number of COs cited specific misdeeds of the United States in relation to Japan, particularly that the United States had been exploiting the war between Japan and China by selling scrap iron to Japan for their weaponry.[2] Others claimed that the United States had taken an aggressive posture toward Japan, that "the U.S. had been sinking Japanese ships in the Pacific, on sight and without warning, and firing on Japanese aircraft," and that the reason the United States naval fleet was stationed in Pearl Harbor was in preparation for an attack on Japan. As Paul Delp put it, "The Japanese just beat us to the punch . . . and bombed us before we bombed them."[3] In a letter to friends in 1945, Gordon and Gale Nutson took this form of reasoning a step further, giving this litany of American political and economic abuses of Japanese sovereignty dating back nearly a hundred years:

> Just when did the United States and Japan start fighting? Was it on December 7, 1941 when Japanese bombers attacked Pearl Harbor, or on December 5, 1941

> when newspapers headlined "U.S. TELLS JAPAN, 'BACK DOWN OR FIGHT' ?" Have we been at war since July 1941 when we finally shut off the supplies we were sending to Japan and completely froze all her assets in this country? Or did the war begin in 1924 when we passed the Oriental Exclusion Acts, refusing the yellow people the right to become U.S. citizens? Or did it begin when U.S. forced Japan to agree to free trade in China but did not force the British to give free trade in Hong Kong or Singapore, and did not give anyone free trade in the Philippines or the United States? Or did the war begin in 1931 when Japanese industrialists and army officers decided they wanted some closed-door colonies like the United States, British and Dutch already had, and attacked Manchuria? Or did it begin with our first official contact with Japan, when Admiral Perry sailed into Yedo Bay in 1853 with a navy that Japan couldn't match and demanded a port for America's use, and free trade in Japan?[4]

The pacifist reinterpretation of the attack on Pearl Harbor goes beyond the ways in which the United States provoked the attack to argue that the attack was actually welcomed by the Roosevelt administration as an excuse for breaking down American isolationist sentiment and persuading the United States to intervene in the war. A few COs suspected that the attack was actually invited by the United States as a propaganda device to promote American intervention. For example, Gordon Kaufman remembers being convinced at the time by pacifist literature that came out immediately after the attack that argued that "Roosevelt was making all kinds of moves to try to set up an episode that could be an excuse to get us into the war. . . . [This] was part of the American attempt to justify getting into a war that was unjustified."[5] Much more common was the view that Roosevelt did not purposely invite the attack, but he did know when and where it was coming several days in advance because the government had cracked the Japanese military code and intercepted its signals. According to this interpretation, Roosevelt did nothing to prevent the attack, but rather ensured that it would be as devastating as possible so that there would be no choice but for the United States to declare war. Several COs described Pearl Harbor as "the perfect excuse" or "a godsend" as far as Roosevelt was concerned, and one CO mentioned that his brother, who had been in the army at the time, knew about the attack on Pearl Harbor in advance, along with most of the rest of the military.[6] Other COs were more reluctant to accuse the government of malice and foreknowledge with regard to the attack on Pearl Harbor, but they retained a degree of suspicion, making comments such as, "I think the public at large never gets the explanation as to what's going on on the telephone and behind the scenes," and "I think that they [politicians] have a lot to cover up, and they do their best to do it."[7]

German Fascism

Pacifist revisionist history begins with Hitler in the same way that it began with Pearl Harbor: by telling a different story about the origin of the conflicts that led to war. Repeatedly, COs I interviewed stressed U.S. complicity in the rise of Hitler, insisting that Hitler never could have come to power if not for the Allies, and could have been stopped far earlier and without the expedient of war had the Allies chosen to make this their goal. COs constantly referred to the events that made the atmosphere ripe for Hitler's rise to power, particularly emphasizing the unjust settlement of World War I in the Treaty of Versailles, and the World War I food blockades that left Germany a shambles both economically and psychologically. One CO quoted Kirby Page favorably and expressed a sentiment many COs would echo: "Hitler caused the war, but the Allies caused Hitler."[8] Some COs referred specifically to provocative actions on the part of the United States when it was still technically neutral to the conflict in Europe (such as relaying position reports on German submarines to the Allies) and saw these as part of the continuing animosity that finally exploded into world war.[9]

COs offered a number of reasons for why and how the United States encouraged the rise of Hitler, and these were in keeping with the general pacifist diagnosis of the causes of war. First, the United States saw an economic advantage to be gained in the war, an advantage that was tremendously important in an era of economic depression. They financed the re-arming of Germany not only up to the start of hostilities, but even for some time afterward. As Gordon Nutson explains:

> Of course they [Germany] didn't have any money, so what had to happen is that you had to have investments from the United States and England. And so actually this is where the money came from to support the war machine in terms of the manufacturing to produce the equipment for war, to assist in the war effort as far as Germany was concerned. Well, as late as the Germans were coming into Paris, dividends were being paid to the British and to investors in England, and investors in the United States.[10]

The desire of the United States for economic advantages cut another way as well: not only did the United States see increased wealth as an effect of war, the United States also helped to cause the war through its economic imperialism. After World War I, the Allies relegated Germany (as well as Japan) to a position of second-class power, and kindled its desire for a larger piece of the economic pie, something Germany could only hope to gain through war since the Allies had no intention of magnanimously sharing the wealth.[11] In addition to economic advantage, COs argue that the United States (and the other Allies) saw a political advantage in encouraging Hitler. Concerned about the communist revolution in Russia, the Western powers hoped that Hitler's Germany would go to war against the Soviet Union and that in the process they would destroy each other and give all of Europe over to Allied hegemony.[12]

Evidence of Allied complicity in the rise of Hitler is the purported fact that the Allies made no attempt to stop Hitler in the early 1930s when it could still be done relatively easily. As Arthur Bryant argues, "If we were going to get concerned about Hitler, the time to get concerned about him really was when he was beginning to get a foothold, and there were many in this country who were supportive of his role."[13]

Propaganda for War

COs also accused the United States of falsely representing its reasons for fighting World War II. At the time of the war, the government justified its actions as part of a commitment to preserving democracy and preventing tyranny and oppression. This justification was challenged by COs who saw the United States undermining democracy and oppressing minorities within its own borders, or gladly tolerating tyranny in some countries while insisting on war to prevent it in others. Wally Nelson recalls the treatment of blacks in the 1930s and 1940s, and discounts the veracity of wartime propaganda which claimed to be fighting a war for freedom:

> If there ever was a holy war, a good war, World War II was supposed to have been that for people in this country and the Allies. However, the thing that I thought about immediately, the same government that were the good guys was the same government that was carrying on oppression all over the world. . . . So I could not be convinced that such a government was interested in and for freedom. Matter of fact, I knew this, that most of them was not interested in and for freedom, I knew this. They couldn't have been. Here I'm sitting on top of you, oppressing you, and I'm telling people I'm interested in freedom for people, and I'm sitting right on top of you. It doesn't make sense.[14]

Another CO, Roy Mast, asked why the United States made no attempt to stop the persecution of Russians by their own government, suggesting that if the United States really cared about protecting minorities, it would do so wherever there was oppression, and not just in Nazi Germany.[15]

Whatever the stated war aims of the United States were at the time of the war, in retrospect much of the popular justification of World War II has rested on interpreting the war as a mission to save the Jews. The CO objection to this argument is that this is a fanciful reconstruction of history (and a very convenient one for those who wish to proclaim Allied righteousness). As Dwight Hanawalt explains, "I don't think we went into the war because of what was happening to the Jews. I think that ended up to be a real neat package. . . . That's something that has given us a good rationale now, but I don't think it was a very good one at the time."[16] COs support this contention by pointing out how the United States turned away Jewish refugees before and during the war, and how the Allies as a group turned a blind eye to the Holocaust until it was far too late. Several COs related a story about a boatload of Jewish refugees who were not allowed ashore in the United States (and several other countries they tried) and who finally turned around to head back to Germany, only to be sunk by Nazi submarines in the middle of the ocean.[17] Some COs intimated that the Allies were as anti-Semitic as the Germans, and quite happy to let Hitler carry on his persecutions.[18] David Koven, interviewed for *Against the Tide* states the revisionist history argument most succinctly: "The truth is that the capitalist countries even at the height of the oppression of the Jews cared less about the Jews than they cared about using Jews for propagandistic purposes."[19]

Allied War Practices

Another way of implicating the United States in World War II was to draw attention to the ways in which the United States abused political power, used fascist methods, and fought a war that totally disregarded the rules of "clean" warfare. By condemning Allied war practices, pacifists sought to show that the United States had no right to stand in a position of moral judgment over Germany or Japan, or to use violence to enforce their moral judgments. In a wartime letter from prison, John Hampton stressed the similarities between wartime America and Nazi Germany: "Fascism and Communism have ample representation under American brands and labels, and there are lots of little would be Hitlers and Stalins running around over here trying to stir up a following, not to mention the imitators in Washington."[20]

COs pointed to the Allied use of terror bombing against civilians and to the atom bomb as evidence of the "equal sin" concept: Hitler may have attacked peaceful nations and murdered his political rivals, but the record of the United States was no better. In *A Field of Broken Stones,* Lowell Naeve recalls V-J day: "The papers talked enthusiastically and proudly of the bomb. We wondered—how could they? We felt sure the greatest crime ever committed had taken place. The U.S. had, it definitely appeared, done something far more terrible than terrorist Hitler had ever hoped to do."[21] Hobart Mitchell has similar memories of the atomic bombing of Hiroshima and Nagasaki. In his CPS memoir, *We Would Not Kill,* Mitchell comments:

> What an indictment of war! That it could cause this colossal plunge of our people from being horrified at the airplane strafing of poorly armed Ethiopians and the bombing of Madrid and Barcelona in the thirties to the self-righteous acceptance less than a decade later of a bomb that devastated two-thirds of a city and wiped out the people—men, women, children, aged, sick, everything. Had Japan or Germany perfected such a bomb and used it, our people would have been hysterical, shouting "savage," "inhuman," "barbarians," "devils" and worse. But since we were the ones who perfected and used it, the act was completely all right, the bomb was in the hands of the "right people." God was on our side.[22]

The argument against United States hypocrisy is stated even more strikingly by an American soldier, not a CO, who was in combat in the Pacific for most of the war. He writes:

> What kind of war do civilians suppose we fought, anyway? We shot prisoners in cold blood, wiped out hospitals, strafed lifeboats, killed or mistreated enemy civilians, finished off enemy wounded, tossed the dying into a hole with the dead, and in the Pacific boiled the flesh off enemy skulls to make table ornaments for sweethearts, or carved their bones into letter openers. We topped off our saturation bombing and burning of enemy civilians by dropping atomic bombs on two nearly defenseless cities, thereby setting an all-time record for instantaneous mass slaughter. . . . We publicized every inhuman act of our opponents and censored any recognition of our own moral frailty in moments of desperation.[23]

Don Peretz, who served as a noncombatant medic in Okinawa, also emphasized the horror of Allied war practices, telling of the torture of prisoners of war and the barbarous killing of enemy civilians. He again emphasizes the characteristic pacifist "equal sin" concept when he explains, "I saw incidents in which Americans behaved in ways which we are told the Japanese or the Nazis acted."[24]

Many COs cited the internment of Japanese citizens and Japanese-Americans as an American abuse of wartime power. Robert Vogel recalls, "I was opposed to Nazism. I was opposed to any form of racism. But . . . I was skeptical that we really meant it when we had these attitudes towards race in our own country. We had the attitudes toward the Japanese, which is another indication."[25] Caleb Foote, who was later imprisoned for refusing induction into CPS, was working for the FOR in San Francisco in the early 1940s, trying vainly to arouse public opposition to the "relocation" of the Japanese. Foote reports his amazement that such a drastic move could be so easily taken, and uses this to argue that the United States could claim no moral superiority over Nazi Germany:

> You've got a lesson in mass hysteria at a time like that. The total suspension of intelligence. It was just incredible. There was almost no opposition. We talk about the good Germans who kept their mouths and their eyes shut with what happened to the Jews. Well, there were plenty of good Californians, I'll tell you, who did the same thing. During the critical period of time when that atrocity could have been stopped.[26]

THE NATURE OF WAR

The sins of Germany and Japan in the World War II conflict, used by non-pacifists to justify war, are turned by COs to an attack on the practice of war itself. Rather than provoking their righteous anger, the atrocities of World War II merely convince COs that war is a suitable object for their moral outrage, that their diagnosis of war is proven correct in the case of World War II. From the most common, defining features of war, such as killing enemy soldiers, to the most horrific abuses, such as the Holocaust, COs argued quite simply that this is what war is, and why it should be condemned. They placed the blame for the horrors of war on the practice of war, and not on the individuals or nations who instigated these horrors.

For example, COs did not generally respond to the attack on Pearl Harbor with avenging anger toward the Japanese. For these COs, the attack was indeed devious, but deviousness is an ordinary part of war. As Paul Goering explains, "I looked on the Pearl Harbor attack as illustrative of what happened in war; that there are no really nice rules in war, that that's rather naive to think of war according to some rules."[27] One CO, Malcolm Parker, felt imperturbed by the attack on Pearl Harbor because it was not an unprovoked attack on civilians, but a calculated maneuver against a military target. And as he says, "When you've got a military installation, you're asking for it."[28]

More telling is that many COs accepted the Holocaust as being part of what war entails. These COs reversed the cause and effect relationship that is implicit in the challenge of the Holocaust: instead of saying that Hitler's murder of the Jews was a reason for going to war, pacifists said that the continuation of the war provided Hitler with additional motivation and, more importantly, the opportunity to murder the Jews. One link in this chain of reasoning is to connect atrocity with war; the Holocaust is exemplary of what happens in war. As Cal Edinger says, "A lot of atrocities went on, no doubt about it. That's the nature of war. And it's like a tremendous feeler, where it just spreads and wipes out everybody."[29] Efforts were made to show that the Holocaust was not unprecedented, but that similar exterminations had also been a part of other wars. Richard Brown argues:

> The tendency to use people, to use whole populations for very bad reasons and in a very violent way has always existed. The American treatment of the Indians, for one thing. The Turkish treatment of the Armenians, the war between the Catholics and the Protestants in the seventeenth century which reduced the population of Europe by one-third. There are plenty of examples. You can take almost any century and find holocausts.[30]

United States atrocities in World War II were also used to emphasize the idea that atrocity is part of war, and that since it is far less common in peacetime, the way to put an end to atrocity is to put an end to war.[31] The link between atrocity and war is the key to Max Kleinbaum's answer to the question posed by Murray Polner, "how can a Jew be a CO?" Kleinbaum gives a three-part answer: (1) because war produces the conditions that result in the massacre of Jews; (2) because Jews always do better in peacetime; and (3) because Hitler is produced by the conditions that result from war.[32]

Some COs suggested that the Holocaust would not have happened if the war had not begun. Though the Jews were being persecuted prior to the war, these COs noted that the death camps only came into being as Hitler realized that he would not win the war. Robert Vogel sees the Holocaust as resulting in part from Hitler's defeats in the war, noting that persecution of the Jews escalated as the tide of the war turned against Germany. He explains:

> The Germans I think took out a lot of their frustrations on the Jews. Just as the United States had to blame somebody in their own country for their plight: the Japanese-Americans were the fall guys this time; in World War I, the Germans were the fall guys. So you had to personify the enemy. And the Jews were the personification of the enemy by the Germans. And so as the war went against them, they had to find somebody to blame, and so the Jews became the scapegoats. Which wasn't the first time in history that that has happened.[33]

Following this line of reasoning, the best way to prevent a holocaust is to end the war, and this is precisely what a number of COs argued. As Vogel claims, "Some of us felt that as long as the war was going on, there was no way in which we could rescue Jews. And the problem was to stop the war so we could get these people out."[34]

This points to a more fundamental pacifist conviction, that war by its very nature does not allow one to right the wrongs of corrupt governments. Although the Holocaust was certainly wrong, the war did not end it until 6 million Jews had already been killed. The reason the war could not end the Holocaust is because the people who actually fought the war were not the same people who organized it, profited from it, and used it to meet their political and economic aims. Going to war to defeat the instigators of war was thus terribly inefficient, because it required the deaths of whole armies of innocents to get at the few guilty individuals. As Don Peretz says, "It's not those who plan the extermination of Jews or even those who carry out the extermination of Jews who are fighting in the front lines."[35] Or as Richard Brown characterizes it: "You have to kill innocent people. You never get to shoot at somebody like Hitler or Goering or Eichmann. You shoot at somebody who's very much like yourself."[36] And as Paul Delp points out, the real centers of Nazi power never were destroyed by American soldiers. He remarks, "There were thousands of German boys and thousands of American boys killed, and Hitler killed himself. I used to talk to kids before the war, and they'd say, 'I'm going over to kill Hitler.' Nobody killed Hitler."*[37] This is the familiar pacifist argument that

*It is interesting to note here that some COs would make an exception to the rule against killing if they actually could shoot at Hitler instead of German draftees. For example, Gordon Kaufman comments:

I wouldn't be able to say however . . . that given an opportunity to participate in a plot against Hitler's life, that I wouldn't do it; I couldn't say that now. I might do it. I don't know. It would depend on the circumstances. . . . If there was some kind of a center of terrible evil of that sort that one had a possibility of participating in the destruction of it violently, I might well do it. . . . Nonetheless, my basic stance I consider to be a pacifist stance.

(Gordon Kaufman, interview with author, 29 April 1987, Cambridge, Massachusetts)

war is objectionable because it is fought by draftees for others' gain. It is interesting to see that it is sustained even in the case where the war in question is not a corrupt imperialist struggle, but a relatively justified effort to destroy a brutal and evil power.

THE FAILURE OF BAD MEANS

However, war fails to destroy Hitler for much larger reasons than that an army of relatively innocent Germans stands between Hitler and his enemies. According to many pacifists, war fails because it is doomed to fail: the means of war are evil, and they will inevitably bring evil ends in their wake. This very general form of pacifist moral reasoning is applied by COs to the case of World War II, and it is found to be an adequate justification for standing apart from this particular war. Many COs even use World War II and its consequences to illustrate the truth of their conviction that bad means produce bad ends.

The argument that war and fascism are two sides of the same coin was a very popular one in World War II pacifist literature, and is still appealed to today when COs justify their pacifism. Because war and fascism are equally responsible for an evil state of affairs, they cannot be used to defeat each other. As Milton Mayer argues:

> It is not Hitler I must fight, but fascism. . . . If I want to beat fascism, I cannot beat it at its own game. War is at once the essence and the apotheosis, the beginning and the triumph, of fascism, and when I go to war I join "Hitler's" popular front against the man in men. I cannot fight animals their way without turning animal myself.[38]

Killing is the problem, and it cannot be corrected with more killing. Several COs used this argument to justify their objection in the face of the rampant evil of the Holocaust, saying, for example, "The slaughter of all those people was frightening, was horrible. But taking someone else's life, or four million more people, won't solve the problem."[39]

Again, part of the reason war cannot defeat fascism is that the practitioner of war is corrupted by war's evil means, and becomes fascistic in order to better prosecute the war. One CO made this argument in his Form 47 when applying for CO status, writing:

> Evil cannot be conquered by evil. Hitlerism cannot be conquered by violence. For in order to beat Hitler at his own game we must acquire the terrible skill of a devastating war machine. In so doing we will take unto ourselves the very things we loathe in the Nazi regime.[40]

Or as Wally Nelson remarks, "I hated the Nazis, but more than that I hated what they showed me I could become."[41]

Evidence that the evil means of war *did* fail to produce good ends is found by COs in several places. First, COs assert that while Hitler was defeated in World War II, Hitlerism was not. The problems of fascism, racism, militarism, and nationalism that Hitler represented are with us today and can emerge in equally virulent forms tomorrow. As Robert Vogel argues:

> We still have the Ku Klux Klan, we still have neo-Nazis, and we have a lot of subtle forms of racism. . . . I felt all along that we weren't going to defeat racism and militarism by war. And I think my predictions have come true. We still have racism, we still have war, and preparation for war, such as I have never seen before. So even the announced goals of World War II have not been achieved.[42]

These COs contend that if World War II was fought to preserve democratic freedoms and prevent tyranny and oppression, it simply did not succeed. Caleb Foote remarks, "You look around the world today, it would be very hard to make much of a case that World War II [has] had any beneficial results for humanity at all."[43] James Bristol notes that at the postwar settlements in Potsdam, the Allies agreed to the displacing of more people than Hitler displaced in his entire political career.[44] Other COs claimed that by stopping Hitler the Allies only put an end to one manifestation of the problem. As Harmon Wilkinson says, "Sure, we may have gotten rid of Hitler, but we didn't solve any of the underlying problem of what causes conflict in the twentieth century. And so we simply traded actors."[45]

A number of COs make the case that World War II failed not only to achieve its stated goals, but also to bring any improvement to the international situation, which as a whole is now claimed to be worse than it was before the war happened. Some COs cited the nuclear stand-off between the Soviet Union and the United States as the unfortunate consequence of World War II; others referred more generally to the expense of maintaining the military. For example, Harry Prochaska says, "One of the things that COs all the time during World War II were concerned about was the militarization of the United States. And it's perfectly clear that this has been one of the results [of the war]."[46] Or as Harmon Wilkinson explains, "Out of World War II came the confrontation between the United States and Russia. You can't say we've got a world at peace now; we don't. We've got a highly tense [situation], unlimited military budgets."[47] George Brumley argues that the losers of the war were the real winners, because they were not allowed to build up their military forces and were able to invest their resources in more profitable ways.[48] Finally, in true pacifist fashion, Richard Brown sees the winners of war as the real losers because they become corrupted by their reliance on evil means:

> Of course in the light of history, we can see that the difficulty with popular wars and good wars in which you're on the right side [is that they] always lead to bad wars. We get into the position where we think we can do no wrong, that we're

> the policemen of the world, that we're always on the right side. Then we get into a situation like Vietnam. And the nation passes through hell for many years, and emerges deciding that they had made a mistake, that they were wrong, and having to withdraw ignominiously.[49]

THE ALTERNATIVE OF PACIFISM

Pacifists have long been criticized for having no viable alternatives to offer for war, for refusing to use violence but refusing also to think about how the world can be kept safe, peaceful, and prosperous without resort to arms. This criticism, as most, rests on a half-truth. It is true that generally speaking—and there are some significant exceptions—most pacifists are not at all clear about how the needs of states can be met without war, and they frequently seem to throw up their hands, declare their ignorance about international relations, and retreat to a private witness against war. But this appearance is a result of the way pacifists reason about moral issues, and not an indication that they are unconcerned with world peace and freedom or feel that pacifism has nothing to contribute to that state of affairs. As discussed earlier, pacifists tend to focus on the means and trust that the ends desired will follow, unlike non-pacifists, who are more inclined to establish goals and then plan how to make progress toward them. Thus, challenges to pacifists about how social justice can be obtained without war yield responses that are generally unsatisfying to non-pacifists, that sound weak, simplistic, or naive to non-pacifist ears. Nevertheless, to the pacifist, who relies on certain assumptions about humanity, God, or the universe, the road to a warless future through pacifism seems clear and well marked.

Though COs do anticipate the success of pacifism in the long run, they frequently emphasize that they should not be held accountable for the problems produced by non-pacifists in the past: that it was unfair, for example, to ask pacifists how Hitler could be stopped without resort to war in January 1939, when non-pacifists had already done so much to fuel the coming conflict. As Harry Prochaska complains, "The problem is that pacifists are always asked what they would do at the time of the crisis, not what they would have done earlier to forestall such a crisis."[50] Or as Robert Vogel phrases the argument:

> Someone said to me one time, likened that whole question to sailing a ship on the Niagara River: it's perfectly safe to sail a ship up around Buffalo, but if you get caught in the stream, if you lose your oars and lose your power, it becomes more and more remote that you're gonna be saved from the cataract. And so it seems to me that it's unfair to ask a pacifist what he would do when he was without oars fifty yards from the cataract. The policies that the pacifist never supported—of condemning Germany for World War I, of maintaining a blockade of Germany after the armistice was signed, of depriving Germany of a lot of its territory . . . the Versailles treaty was not the kindest treaty that was ever written. All of these things laid the seeds for the rise of Hitler.[51]

Some COs argue that war may have been justified as the only option in World War II, but only because the international situation had reached a point of no return. War in this case is not truly justified, it is not chosen as a way of remedying injustice or stopping aggression, because the point of no return never would have been reached had pacifist methods been applied earlier. Dwight Hanawalt concedes that World War II may have presented circumstances in which the Allies had to fight, that by the time Poland and France had been occupied, war was the only option. But, he concludes, "the thing that I am not convinced of is that something cannot be done before a country gets that far."[52] Again, this is not a legitimation of war, but an acknowledgment that it may at times be inevitable, that pacifists cannot prevent it.

Others comment that had the Allies refused to fight Hitler, the results may not have been nearly as bad as people have suggested. These COs contend that the consequences of a fascist victory are, as all consequences, incalculable, so a war to stave off imagined evil consequences cannot be justified. For example, Robert Vogel makes the point that dictators eventually die, and governments eventually reform; perhaps suffering under the heel of a tyrant for decades does not equal the suffering of all those who die or are left homeless in war.[53] Another CO, Howard Bogen, speculates that if the United States had stayed out of the war, Germany and Russia might have "neutralized each other, and if that had happened, maybe more of Europe would be free now than it is."[54]

Pacifists occasionally mentioned specific ways war or its abuses might have been avoided. Foremost among these was economic aid to Germany. Several COs argued that had the United States sent food and other resources to Germany, helped to remedy unemployment, and supported the Weimar Republic, the citizens of Germany never would have been seduced by Hitler's rallying cry of war.[55] (This was basically a belief that the mistakes the Allies made in the Treaty of Versailles could still have been remedied even after Hitler came to power in the early 1930s.) Other suggestions were offered as to how Americans might have prevented the Holocaust without resort to war. Those who claimed that the Jews could not be saved until the war was ended (notably the organized peace movement) agitated for a negotiated peace, offering Germany economic incentives in return for the release of the Jews to Allied protection.[56] Dwight Hanawalt suggests that the Holocaust could have been prevented nonviolently, and goes back to assert that the Holocaust was not what the war was about, saying, "See, I think it [preventing the Holocaust] could have been done without killing twenty million people and flattening everything all over the world . . . but we didn't get into World War II because of the Holocaust."[57]

One way that COs defend the viability of pacifism in the case of the Holocaust is to call attention to the steps they and others in the peace movement took to help the European Jews, steps, they argue, which could have been more effective than the method of war adopted by the Allies. James Bristol recalls his efforts to combat anti-Semitism in the Young People's Interracial Fellowship in the late 1930s, while Cal Edinger tells of his participation in an AFSC program to go to

Germany and help Jews emigrate. Dave Dellinger tells of his concern over German fascism and anti-Semitism and what the program of the peace movement was regarding these developments:

> I came from a different kind of anti-war movement than the isolationists and, like those who were old enough at the time, from an earlier and more lasting kind of anti-fascism than that of the government and corporations. Besides having witnessed U.S. complicity in the rise of Nazism, I had studied abroad in 1936 and 1937, had had contact with the anti-Nazi underground and had stayed several times with Jews in the ghettoes of Germany. I had heard many Germans say that the worst thing that could happen would be for the Allies of World War I to overthrow Hitler militarily. "We have to do it ourselves," they would say, "and if the United States wants to help it should work now with the anti-Nazis instead of the Nazis."[58]

Though the steps COs took were small, they argued that they cared more for the victims of war, and had more genuine concern for the persecution of the Jews than did the U.S. government which was purportedly at war for these reasons.

Another defense of pacifism was to argue that even in a worst case scenario, Germany could not have taken over the world because its population was too small to control all the conquered peoples. Particularly, the argument runs, if people could have been taught to resist nonviolently, it simply would not have been in Hitler's own interests to capture more territory.[59] As Rudy Potochnik says, "We could resist fascism, if only the American people would be willing to accept with the same dedication a willingness to lose their lives in a nonviolent struggle as they are in a violent one."[60] This idea was also present at the time of the war. As Arle Brooks argued to a federal court in 1941, "The people of America are filled with fear of an invasion. Are we so morally weak that the power of one man could control one hundred and thirty million free people? Free people cannot be enslaved unless they will it."[61]

But many pacifists merely appealed back to the faith that pacifism conscientiously applied would eventually bring good results, either preventing future wars and holocausts or overwhelming them with the weight of the many triumphs of pacifism. This argument has both liberal and fundamentalist religious forms. An example of the liberal version of pacifist faith is this statement from Richard Brown: "In a way just being a CO, refusing to fight, even if it doesn't ever have any practical effect that is visible and tangible, it presents the idea that that thought is possible. And that goes out into the society in ways that you'll never know, and has its effect."[62] Here again is a standard pacifist theme: it is by sticking to one's principles and suffering the consequences that good ends are achieved. This is the essence of the method of nonviolent resistance as well. It should be no surprise then that the pacifist's favorite alternative to war is essentially the individual effort to be true to a rule of pacifism multiplied many times over.

The fundamentalist version of pacifist faith involved a trust in God to bring all things right and a firm resolution to be personally uncontaminated by the affairs of the kingdom of this world (to which Hitler belonged). Sam Guhr recalls his feelings about the war in saying, "As far as knowing what they did overseas and about Hitler and this thing, I never paid much attention. It just seemed to me it didn't bother me much and I guess we trusted the Lord that he'd take care of us."[63] One CO, Donald Beachler, found evidence that God was at work in history by noting that the Allies won the war because "he allowed America to win the war," specifically by letting the United States develop the atomic bomb before Germany did. Thus the pacifist need not worry about stopping Hitler; God would see to that.[64] George Brumley also called the war a victory for God, but for a different reason: he counts it a triumph that "Hitler is now gone, but Jehovah's people are stronger by the thousands, and they did not physically resist, but their spiritual resistance, their refusal to go along with him won."[65]

The need of these COs to see God's hand at work in World War II did not end with the assurance that Allied victory was God's will, but also demanded an explanation for why God allowed the Holocaust to be essentially accomplished before Germany's final surrender. Why did God not stop such an atrocity? Because, these COs explain, the destruction of the Jewish people was part of God's will, and Hitler was a tool in God's hands. COs suggested that God approved (or less definitely, permitted) the Holocaust for two reasons: first, to punish the Jews, and second, to return the Jews to Israel and thereby fulfill a prophecy that when the Jewish nation has been reinstated, Jesus will return.

The first school of thought believes that God was punishing the Jews through Hitler for their failure to accept Jesus as God's son, or more narrowly, for crucifying Jesus. Hayes Reed suggests that God allowed the Holocaust "to make the Jews more conscious of the fact that they killed a man [Jesus] too . . . and the Jews just had to go through the same thing."[66] Lest we conclude that the deaths of 6 million Jews have now atoned for the presumed Jewish involvement in the death of Jesus, these COs assure us that it has not. Roy Mast argues that God has had an ongoing problem with Israel, and has repeatedly used ungodly nations to punish Israel and bring it back to dependence on God. The Holocaust is just one more example of this pattern of God calling Israel to account. Mast concludes, "God has in years gone by, and to this very day, tried his best to have the Israel nation accept his son. He's bending over backwards to help the Israel nation, and they have completely forsaken him."[67]

The second school of thought is less blatantly anti-Semitic, stressing not punishment of the Jews, but relocation. As Donald Beachler describes it, "God has a plan for Israel in the latter days, setting up a millennial kingdom then and the judgment of the nations and the anti-Christ and the Armageddon battle and all that. . . . If it hadn't been for World War II, Israel would never have become a country."[68] Several of the COs who were overjoyed to see Israel become a nation—viewing it as a sign of the second coming of Christ—were genuinely disturbed that God achieved his purpose through such morally repugnant means. One way of confronting God's apparent use of Hitler's evil for good ends was to say that God did not arrange or morally sanction the Holocaust, but permitted it and provided that some good should come of it. Another way of dealing with this problem of theodicy was to emphasize that no one is lost to God forever unless he or she has chosen that path, and that anyone who died unjustly would eventually be raised at the second coming.[69]

What is interesting about this interpretation of the Holocaust is the way in which it frees the individual CO from the responsibility to react, with violence if necessary, to prevent atrocity. These COs' commitment to pacifism was not threatened by the Holocaust, because God was in control and actively arranging for good consequences to come out of the situation. There could be no need, then, for Christians to intervene and attempt to force a good resolution out of the conflict. In fact, pacifist resistance to the Holocaust or to Hitler would be pointless: as one CO remarks, "These things were prophesied, and man's not gonna change it."[70]

WORLD WAR II AS A JUST WAR

Not all COs felt it necessary to explain how pacifism could work in World War II (or how violence did not) because they were perfectly satisfied that World War II was a just war for the United States. Their interpretation of World War II was similar to that of the American populace in general, the only difference being that they felt they could not personally fight. For example, these COs described Pearl Harbor as an unprovoked attack on U.S. territory that fully justified the U.S. response of an immediate declaration of war. As Gil Bertochini says, "I thought that the Japanese empire was aggressive and we were threatened as a nation, as individuals."[71]

These COs (most of whom were noncombatants) advocated Allied resistance to Hitler as well as to Japan as an effort to stop aggression and prevent atrocity. Since it was imperative that Hitler be stopped by the powers that be, these COs felt they should help to stop him within the limits of their commitment not to use violence.[72] For example, John Ripley Forbes, who left CPS to be a noncombatant in the military, explains his decision in a 1942 letter to a friend who remained in CPS:

> I came to the conclusion that I would rather be guilty of taking part in war through noncombatant work of mercy and education then see something I consider far worse than war take over this nation. In other words I believe our enemies represent something far worse than total war with all that implies and I do not think I have fallen for propaganda. While I cannot kill or join this part of the service I can aid those doing a dirty job which I now believe must be done.[73]

Many of the COs I interviewed remembered wanting the Allies to win World War II. This identification with American interests was of two types. One group of COs favored the Allies, but not in their role as pacifists (i.e., they felt that pacifists should not take sides, yet they continued to hope that the United States would emerge from the war triumphant). For example, Bill Colburn recalls, "Even during the war, you'd be finding yourself kind of cheering for the Allies as they were making progress, you know? Even though you were a Christian, you had times when you almost wished you were there."[74] Another CO, Loris Habegger, remembers being disturbed by his feelings when Eisenhower's forces invaded Normandy, wanting to cheer the Allied advance but feeling that he shouldn't cheer for the Allies any more than he should cheer for Hitler.[75] Paradoxically, one of the reasons COs favored the United States and felt some desire to assist the war effort was because the United States guaranteed freedom of religion for its citizens and was kind enough to grant them CO exemption. Though unable to defend the United States violently, they were glad that others were willing to do so and thereby protect their religious freedom.[76]

A second group of COs identified with the American war effort as a matter of principle and not happenstance. They felt the United States was engaged in a just war and that all citizens should rally to the nation's aid. If, because of conscientious scruples, they could not do everything the government asked, they should zealously attend to whatever they could do. One CO who was in CPS remembers buying war bonds and saving scrap metal as his part of the war effort,[77] but the commitment to promoting the war effort was more commonly found in noncombatants, especially Seventh-Day Adventists. As Gil Bertochini argues, "I felt that it was proper and necessary to support your country. And I felt that it was also in the interest of our nation to have victory in battle. And so I felt the best thing to do was to be a conscientious cooperator."*[78] For these COs, the prohibition of killing was not an injunction to stand apart from war or to pass judgment on a war-making nation, so they tried to the best of their abilities to obey their government and help it in its mission to win the war.

ATYPICAL ATTITUDES TOWARD WORLD WAR II

Occasionally when COs were asked "What about Hitler?" they took unusual angles on the question that revealed at least part of the reason why they could feel comfortable with their conscientious objector convictions. One of these atypical positions was pro-German sentiment (to be distinguished from pro-Nazi or pro-Hitler sentiment, of which there was none among the COs in my research—though one could imagine that anyone who did feel this way would be disinclined to say so). The Mennonites particularly, having relatively recently

*The term "conscientious cooperator" was favored by the Seventh-Day Adventist denomination in an effort to emphasize its patriotism and willingness to serve the nation.

emigrated from Germany, and retaining much of their German cultural identity, did not have the same knee-jerk reaction of support for the Allies that most Americans did. Laban Peachey describes his attachment to German culture in these terms:

> I grew up as a child very conscious of the fact that we were German, had a German identity, and almost a German nationality. . . . You see, you have to understand a number of German and . . . Amish concepts [of the early 1900s]. For example, the Amish still talk about themselves versus the English. And language is something of a cultural vehicle: the people who talked your language were God's people, and the people who talked another language were English. OK, so as a child the German culture tended to be equated with being Christian, or being Amish or Amish-Mennonite. And now when the war comes, and you have that culture, over against what I call the English culture . . . those instincts don't ever go away. German is sort of a fireside language. And the rightness of German culture.[79]

This continued identification with the German people (including in some cases relatives in Germany) combined with Mennonite pacifist principles tended to make some Mennonites view the war in more neutral terms, seeing it as a tragedy for all concerned, including the Germans.[80] A few COs reported some anti-Semitism and pro-Nazi sentiment in their communities, though none indicated that this had played a part in their own objection to the war.[81]

Finally, there was an occasional CO who simply had no stake in a U.S. victory. For example, a Hopi leader wrote to General Hershey: "Now I want to know what these two nations, Germany and Japan, are doing. Why are they at war? Who are they after and who are they going to strike? Are they after me, a Hopi, who is still retaining his way of life or are they after you, a white man?"[82] Many black Americans were similarly unconcerned with U.S. victory, feeling that if Hitler conquered the United States they probably would be no worse off than they were under U.S. rule. A number of black Muslims refused to register largely on these grounds. However, the vast majority of blacks did not seek CO classification, and many served in the military in the hope that they would prove their loyalty and worth to white America in the process.[83]

Another atypical reaction was to articulate an identification with Hitler's victims rather than with Hitler's foes. The "What about Hitler?" question relies for its force on an identification with a hypothetical third party who observes Hitler's crimes against innocent parties and feels compelled to intervene on behalf of the oppressed. Yet some COs did not picture themselves in this role, and thought themselves more like the innocent and defenseless victims persecuted by Hitler. It is interesting to note that none of those who professed identification with Hitler's victims were Jews: all of the Jews I spoke with adopted the more usual identification with the avenging third party (though some still argued that the third party should be nonviolent). For some COs, it was their very identity as conscientious objectors that prompted their identification with Hitler's victims, for they realized that they would be shot in Germany for conscientious objection.[84] Those quickest to see an identification with Hitler's victims were Jehovah's Witnesses, whose German counterparts were persecuted under Hitler and confined to concentration camps during the war (when they were not summarily executed).[85] Other COs who identified with Hitler's victims included a Japanese-American who was sympathetic to the Jews because he experienced in America something similar to what the Jews experienced in Europe, and a homosexual who noted that the Nazis "were doing in the gays right along with the Jews."[86]

CO reaction to Hitler was complicated by the fact that most COs (and most Americans) had no idea that Hitler was systematically murdering European Jews until after the war was over and the concentration camp inmates were liberated. As one CO says, "[By the] time I knew about it, it was all over with."[87] Though a lack of awareness about the Holocaust was not unconventional, but quite common, what was unique to COs was a reluctance to believe what reports they did receive about Hitler's persecution of the Jews. Schooled in the interwar peace movement, won over to pacifism through exposés of the World War I propaganda machine (which attributed atrocities to the Germans that were later shown to be false), these pacifists heard reports of German atrocities in World War II and discounted them as propaganda. While they knew that the Nazi government was anti-Semitic, they had no idea that it was then carrying out the "final solution." As Richard Brown remembers:

> I figured this was just part of a campaign to alarm people and to get them to back the war. Then of course when the war was over and they discovered the concentration camps . . . it wasn't until the very last days of the war that the army overran these concentration camps. And it was not only discovered that what we had heard was true, but it was a lot worse than anybody thought it was. But that was a surprise to almost everybody, I think.[88]

Many COs I interviewed recall dismissing atrocity stories during the war as propaganda, and they were very dismayed to learn after the war that the stories were true. A few of these COs feel that the Holocaust gives sufficient reason for abandoning their pacifism, and that had they known what was going on in Germany during the war, they would have joined the military.[89]

LIMITING PACIFIST AIMS

World War II, both because it was popular and because in retrospect it seems so justified, provided a real threat to many COs' pacifist beliefs. Some felt their beliefs to be so undermined by the war that they gave up their pacifism. Perhaps a greater number backed off of their pre-war claim that pacifism could solve any problem better and more efficiently than war could, and sought to define their pacifism in ways less tied to its immediate success. Though most never abandoned their faith that pacifism would produce good consequences in the long run, they tended to regard World War II as one of pacifism's short-term failures, a situation filled with so much moral ambiguity that no one could be criticized for choosing the option of war.

Particularly in the case of the Holocaust, a typical CO response was one of discomfort and more or less feeble attempts to dispel a sense of guilt. One such means of rationalization was to accept that pacifism had no answer for the Holocaust, but to deny that pacifism was required to have an answer for everything. (This was sometimes accompanied by the claim that non-pacifists did not have an answer for the Holocaust either, that World War II did not save the Jews, but rather arrived on the scene only after 6 million had been killed, and few were left for the Allied armies to liberate.) As one CO says, "Frankly, I never tied the Holocaust into a pacifist theory."[90] Igal Roodenko, interviewed for *Against the Tide* explains at greater length:

> I felt helpless about the Jewish problem in Europe. I developed a certain cynicism that stayed with me until today. One way of expressing it is, "I am not obligated to have an answer for every problem in the world. I feel obligated to be concerned about these things, to try and find some answers. But I don't know the answer . . ." It is a very subtle and difficult situation to be in. Those who fought would say, by not having an answer, that was an answer too. And that's true. But that is one of the dilemmas of being a human being.[91]

Others appealed to their inability to make a difference anyway, not necessarily because no one could stop the Holocaust, but because one individual could not. Statements from this point of view include: "Even my participating in the war would not have changed the situation one iota," and "I suppose just as a single individual, I wouldn't make any difference."[92] A variant of this position is to argue that there is no pressing need to find a pacifist answer to the Holocaust because there are so few pacifists that the non-pacifist course will be taken regardless. These COs believe the responsible government is non-pacifist because its citizens are non-pacifist, and as a democracy, it must yield to the will of the majority.[93] This is not an acknowledgment that the non-pacifist course is right, but at least it is one kind of interim solution until such time as pacifists hold political sway and will be forced to develop nonviolent responses to atrocities like the Holocaust.[94]

Another way of limiting pacifist aims was to claim that even in the midst of a relatively justified war, it was important that at least some few people should remain pacifist. One CO refers to the CO position as a way to "stand up and be counted as not going along with what was happening," to present something different from the "hysterical unanimity" of a nation at war.[95] Another CO, Saburo Mizutani, saw his role in part as ensuring that pacifism be represented among the many responses to war. In his case, he felt this to be particularly important because he was a Japanese-American: "One of the thoughts that I had as a pacifist was that, heck, there's got to be some person of Japanese descent who is going the other way too. That we aren't all war-like, you know."[96] A final way of interpreting the assertion that some fragment of society should be pacifist is to suggest that a pacifist presence acts as a counterbalance to warmongering, and can thereby soften the overall attitude of a nation at war. Howard Bogen gives this argument:

> I'm not optimistic that everybody will become pacifist and the world suddenly will be a better place, but I still think that it's necessary for at least some people to follow the beliefs of pacifists. If nothing else, as a moderating influence, possibly, against some of the other ways.[97]

Generally speaking, these COs were not arguing that pacifists should remain a minority, leaving enough people behind to fight necessary wars; rather they were saying that pacifism could help to bring good consequences even within a world dominated by non-pacifists.

Others specifically referred to World War II as a lost battle for pacifists, but one that cast no doubt on the long-term worth of pacifism. Because these pacifists felt themselves impotent in wartime, unable to control the actions of their government, they felt it was reasonable to retreat into inactivity, to rest before entering the struggle again. In *We Would Not Kill,* Hobart Mitchell describes his feelings upon entering alternative service:

> I had hoped to find some solitude in CPS for thinking further about religious—or perhaps more exactly, spiritual—matters. I had done all the thinking that I wanted to do about the Government and the war. Since I could do nothing to stop the war, it seemed best to turn my back and try to keep my own psychological balance.[98]

One of the characters in William Stafford's *Down in My Heart* argues more explicitly that war is in effect a "time out" for pacifists. He says: "During a war is a time of rest for a pacifist; the war itself is an incident, a lost battle in itself; it is just a part of those cheatings, bluffings, maneuverings, which we have got to stay out of all the time."[99]

Many COs attempted to rationalize their unwillingness to participate in World War II on the grounds that their objection might not help, but could not hurt. Other COs asserted the rule of pacifism itself as a sufficient justification for being pacifist, without taking any stand on what the consequences of pacifism would be. Several Catholic COs took this approach, arguing that World War II was not a just war in the traditional Catholic sense, and thus not a war that responsible individuals could participate in regardless of what was at stake. Francis Bates gives an example of this kind of reasoning in an article from *The Catholic Worker:* "Since December 8, 1941, we have been engaged in a war which for us is unjust. . . . This war for us is unjust as we do not have a right intention, a just cause, and while the duly delegated authorities of our nation have declared it, I do not believe such was the will of the responsible citizens of our country."[100] Gordon Zahn specifically points out that the United States did not have just cause because it had been provoking the aggression of the Axis powers.[101] Zahn also argues against the means used in World War II as violations of just war morality. In *War, Conscience, and Dissent,* he writes:

> The bombing of Wurzburg [a German city destroyed by the British just before the end of the war in Europe] must be described, twelve years after the fact, as a work of calculated barbarism—and the slaughter of its inhabitants as a form of murder. . . . It is not a valid argument to say that all this may be true "but it was war." Such an argument represents a reversal of all logical processes. The fact that "it was war" justifies nothing. Instead, war and every act committed in war must themselves be justified, must be measured by the unchanging, objective standards of Christian morality. And these standards are quite clear in condemning the slaughter of noncombatants.[102]

This argument was not a strictly Catholic one; as Saburo Mizutani explains, "Even though Nazism was completely antithetical to my beliefs . . . my pacifism would [not] allow me to fight the Nazis."[103]

Many COs did not feel that World War II posed a serious challenge to their pacifism. They were prepared with explanations for why pacifism was an appropriate response to this war and how pacifism could still hope to produce good consequences. Some in fact saw World War II as a legitimate and necessary war for the kingdoms of this world, believed its consequences to be good, but had no trouble maintaining their own refusal to participate as combatants since as Christians this was their duty. Other COs also found it straightforward to maintain their pacifism in World War II, but for different reasons: these COs saw World War II as another war, like all wars, based on greed and self-righteousness. They pointed out the ways in which the United States aided and abetted Hitler, how the Allies added to the rising level of hostilities between themselves and the Axis powers, and how very many people were killed or left homeless by a war whose root conflicts could have been solved in more peaceful ways. In retrospect, they view World War II as a tragedy, but more than a tragedy, a real moral failure on the part of the United States. These COs see us living today with the consequences of that war, and they wonder aloud if we can survive.

But for some COs, World War II presented exceptional circumstances. For them, the issues at stake in World War II pressed hard against the limits of what could be contained within a pacifist analysis of morality and war. These COs equivocated when challenged by World War II, struggling to believe that they were not wrong in refusing to fight in this war, though they may not have been wholly right. They stressed their helplessness as individuals to determine large social phenomena, and sought to find some role they could play in wartime that would neither brand them as uncaring and irresponsible nor require them to flout their personal rule of pacifism. Sometimes these COs did abandon their pacifism, but more often they retreated to the high ground of a deontological ethic. Without giving up on consequences, they professed their inability to directly guarantee consequences and contented themselves with following the rule and hoping for the best.

NOTES

1. Cal Edinger, interview with author, 25 February 1987, San Gabriel, California. See also Henry Blocher, interview with author, 10 September 1986, La Verne, California; Gordon Zahn, interview with author, 29 April 1987, Charlestown, Massachusetts; Dwight Hanawalt, interview with author, 10 September 1986, La Verne, California; George Brown, interview with author, 1 June 1987, Washington D.C.; Arthur Bryant, self-interview answering author's questions, May 1987; Howard Bogen, interview with author, 9 September 1986, Pasadena, California.

2. Gordon Nutson, interview with author, 25 September 1986, Modesto, California; Carl Paulson, interview with author, 23 April 1987, Upton, Massachusetts.

3. Dave Dellinger, "Introduction," in *Against the Tide: Pacifist Resistance in the Second World War, an Oral History,* Deena Hurwitz and Craig Simpson, eds. (New York: War Resisters League, 1984); Paul Delp, interview with author, 3 March 1987, Orange, California. It would appear that Dellinger has the Pacific and Atlantic wars confused: the United States was involved prior to Pearl Harbor in attacks on the German fleet, but not on the Japanese fleet.

4. Gordon and Gale Nutson, letter to friends, 5 February 1945, privately held.

5. Gordon Kaufman, interview with author, 29 April 1987, Cambridge, Massachusetts. See also Henry Blocher, interview with author, 10 September 1986, La Verne, California; Walter Juhnke, interview for "Schowalter Oral History Collection—World War II Conscientious Objectors," Keith Sprunger and James Juhnke, coordinators, 122 cassette tapes, Mennonite Library and Archives, North Newton, Kansas (hereafter abbreviated as "SOH interview"); Joe Dell, interview with author, 27 September 1986, Modesto, California.

6. Harmon Wilkinson, interview with author, 23 February 1987, Whittier, California; Howard Ten Brink, interview with author, 24 September 1986, Modesto, California; Leland Sateren, interview with author, 9 February 1987, Edina, Minnesota; Samuel Liskey, interview with author, 11 September 1986, Ontario, California; Sigmund Cohn, interview with author, 30 September 1986, Berkeley, California.

7. Harry Prochaska, interview with author, 1 October 1986, San Francisco, California; Albert Herbst, interview with author, 6 September 1986, La Verne, California.

8. Joe Dell, interview with author, 27 September 1986, Modesto, California. See also Eugene Carper, interview with author, 10 September 1986, La Verne, California; Caleb Foote, telephone interview with author, 28 February 1987; Dwight Hanawalt, interview with author, 10 September 1986, La Verne, California; Gerald Rubin, interview with author, 2 October 1986, Corte Madera, California; George Brown, interview with author, 1 June 1987, Washington D.C.; Russell Jarboe,

interview with author, 25 February 1987, La Verne, California; Harmon Wilkinson, interview with author, 23 February 1987, Whittier, California; Peter Bartel, SOH interview; Loris Habegger, SOH interview.

9. Howard Bogen, interview with author, 9 September 1986, Pasadena, California; Irvin Richert, SOH interview; Carl Paulson, interview with author, 23 April 1987, Upton, Massachusetts.

10. Gordon Nutson, interview with author, 25 September 1986, Modesto, California. See also Robert Vogel, interview with author, 15 September 1986, Pasadena, California; James Bristol, interview with author, 27 May 1987, Philadelphia, Pennsylvania.

11. Howard Ten Brink, interview with author, 24 September 1986, Modesto, California; Jim Peck, *We Who Would Not Kill* (New York: Lyle Stuart, 1958), 64.

12. George Reeves, quoted in *Against the Tide,* Hurwitz and Simpson, eds.; Rudy Potochnik, interview with author, 26 September 1986, Modesto, California; James Bristol, interview with author, 27 May 1987, Philadelphia, Pennsylvania.

13. Arthur Bryant, self-interview answering author's questions, May 1987. See also Caleb Foote, telephone interview with author, 28 February 1987; Edward Brookmyer, SOH interview; Lyle Krug, interview with author, 28 August 1986, Mission Viejo, California; Bob Stocksdale, interview with author, 1 October 1986, Berkeley, California; James Lowerre, interview with author, 3 March 1987, Orange, California.

14. Wallace Nelson, interview by Deena Hurwitz for *Against the Tide,* privately held (hereafter abbreviated as "Hurwitz interview"). See also Gordon and Gale Nutson, letter to friends, 5 February 1945, privately held.

15. Roy Mast, self-interview answering author's questions, May 1987.

16. Dwight Hanawalt, interview with author, 10 September 1986, La Verne, California. See also Gale Nutson, interview with author, 27 September 1986, Modesto, California.

17. Dave Dellinger, "Introduction," in *Against the Tide,* Hurwitz and Simpson, eds.; Howard Ten Brink, interview with author, 24 September 1986, Modesto, California; Fred Convers, interview with author, 2 October 1986, Berkeley, California; Arthur Bryant, self-interview answering author's questions, May 1987; Robert Vogel, interview with author, 15 September 1986, Pasadena, California.

18. See, for example, Dwight Hanawalt, interview with author, 10 September 1986, La Verne, California; Caleb Foote, telephone interview with author, 28 February 1987.

19. David Koven, quoted in *Against the Tide,* Hurwitz and Simpson, eds.

20. John Hampton, letter from prison, 24 May 1945, War Resisters League, Document Group 40, Swarthmore College Peace Collection, Swarthmore, Pennsylvania.

21. Lowell Naeve (in collaboration with David Wieck), *A Field of Broken Stones* (Denver: Alan Swallow, 1959), 166. For the argument in terms of illegitimate warfare against civilians, see Caleb Foote, telephone interview with author, 28 February 1987.

22. Hobart Mitchell, *We Would Not Kill* (Richmond, IN: Friends United Press, 1983), 245.

23. Edgar L. Jones, quoted in Roland H. Bainton, *Christian Attitudes toward War and Peace: A Historical Survey and Critical Re-evaluation* (Nashville: Abingdon, 1960), 247.

24. Don Peretz, interview for "An Oral History of American Jews who Chose to Become Conscientious Objectors or Resisted Serving in the Military from World War II—Korea War," Murray Polner, coordinator, ten cassette tapes, Swarthmore College Peace Collection, Swarthmore, Pennsylvania (hereafter abbreviated as "Polner interview").

25. Robert Vogel, interview with author, 15 September 1986, Pasadena, California.

26. Caleb Foote, telephone interview with author, 28 February 1987.

27. Paul Goering, SOH interview. See also James Bristol, interview with author, 27 May 1987, Philadelphia, Pennsylvania; Gordon Kaufman, interview with author, 29 April 1987, Cambridge, Massachusetts; Richard Brown, interview with author, 2 October 1986, Berkeley, California.

28. Malcolm Parker, telephone interview with author, 28 February 1987.

29. Cal Edinger, interview with author, 25 February 1987, San Gabriel, California. See also Henry Blocher, interview with author, 10 September 1986, La Verne, California.

30. Richard Brown, interview with author, 2 October 1986, Berkeley, California. See also Gordon Nutson, interview with author, 25 September 1986, Modesto, California.

31. See, for example, Gordon Nutson, interview with author, 25 September 1986, Modesto, California.

32. Max Kleinbaum, Polner interview.

33. Robert Vogel, interview with author, 15 September 1986, Pasadena, California.

34. Ibid.

35. Don Peretz, Polner interview.

36. Richard Brown, interview with author, 2 October 1986, Berkeley, California.

37. Paul Delp, interview with author, 3 March 1987, Orange, California. See also Robert Vogel, interview with author, 15 September 1986, Pasadena, California; Carl Paulson, interview with author, 23 April 1987, Upton, Massachusetts. For an exception to pacifism in the case of assassination, see Gordon Kaufman, interview with author, 29 April 1987, Cambridge, Massachusetts; Harry Prochaska, interview with author, 2 October 1986, San Francisco, California.

38. Milton S. Mayer, "I Think I'll Sit This One Out," *Saturday Evening Post* 212 (October 1939): 97.

39. Charles Baker, interview with author, 24 September 1986, Modesto, California. See also Paul Delp, interview with author, 3 March 1987, Orange, California; Gordon Nutson, interview with author, 25 September 1986, Modesto, California.

40. Anonymous World War II CO, "Special Form for Conscientious Objector" (Form 47), privately held.

41. Wallace Nelson, Hurwitz interview.

42. Robert Vogel, interview with author, 15 September 1986, Pasadena, California.

43. Caleb Foote, telephone interview with author, 28 February 1987. See also Martin Ponch, quoted in *Against the Tide,* Hurwitz and Simpson, eds.

44. James Bristol, interview with author, 27 May 1987, Philadelphia, Pennsylvania.

45. Harmon Wilkinson, interview with author, 23 February 1987, Whittier, California; Paul Goering, SOH interview.

46. Harry Prochaska, interview with author, 1 October 1986, San Francisco, California.

47. Harmon Wilkinson, interview with author, 23 February 1987, Whittier, California.

48. George Brumley, letter to author, 4 June 1987.

49. Richard Brown, interview with author, 2 October 1986, Berkeley, California.

50. Harry Prochaska, interview with author, 1 October 1986, San Francisco, California.

51. Robert Vogel, interview with author, 15 September 1986, Pasadena, California. For an example of a similar argument applied to the case of Pearl Harbor, see William Stafford, *Down in My Heart* (Elgin, IL: Brethren Publishing House, 1947), 45.

52. Dwight Hanawalt, interview with author, 10 September 1986, La Verne, California.

53. Robert Vogel, interview with author, 15 September 1986, Pasadena, California.

54. Howard Bogen, interview with author, 9 September 1986, Pasadena, California.

55. Joe Dell, interview with author, 27 September 1986, Modesto, California; Rudy Potochnik, interview with author, 26 September 1986, Modesto, California; Martin Ponch, quoted in *Against the Tide*, Hurwitz and Simpson, eds.; Charles Klaffke, interview with author, 23 February 1987, Duarte, California; Sigmund Cohn, interview with author, 30 September 1986, Berkeley, California; Harry Prochaska, interview with author, 1 October 1986, San Francisco, California.

56. See, for example, Jessie Wallace Hughan, "What About the Jews in the Ghettoes?" *Pacifica Views*, 1 (September 1943): 1–2. Hughan was head of the War Resisters League during World War II.

57. Dwight Hanawalt, interview with author, 10 September 1986, La Verne, California.

58. Dave Dellinger, "Introduction," in *Against the Tide*, Hurwitz and Simpson, eds.; James Bristol, interview with author, 27 May 1987, Philadelphia, Pennsylvania; Elmer Ediger, SOH interview.

59. See, for example, Rudy Potochnik, interview with author, 26 September 1986, Modesto, California.

60. Rudy Potochnik, interview with author, 26 September 1986, Modesto, California. See also Saburo Mizutani, interview with author, 29 September 1986, Sacramento, California; Robert Vogel, interview with author, 15 September 1986, Pasadena, California.

61. Arle Brooks, quoted in *War and the Christian Conscience: From Augustine to Martin Luther King, Jr.*, Albert Marrin, ed. (Chicago: Henry Regnery Company, 1971), 240. See also Sigmund Cohn, interview with author, 30 September 1986, Berkeley, California; William Gerber, Polner interview; Saburo Mizutani, inteview with author, 29 September 1986, Sacramento, California.

62. Richard Brown, interview with author, 2 October 1986, Berkeley, California; Howard Bogen, interview with author, 9 September 1986, Pasadena, California; Lowell Naeve, *A Field of Broken Stones*, 8–9.

63. Samuel Guhr, SOH interview. See also anonymous World War II CO, interview with author, 27 September 1986; Hubert Brubaker, interview with author, 25 September 1986, Modesto, California.

64. Donald Beachler, interview with author, 26 September 1986, Modesto, California.

65. George Brumley, letter to author, 4 June 1987.

66. G.. Hayes Reed, interview with author, 25 September 1986, Modesto, California.

67. Roy Mast, self-interview answering author's questions, May 1987.

68. Donald Beachler, interview with author, 26 September 1986, Modesto, California. See also Paul Phillips, interview with author, 11 September 1986, Ontario, California; Samuel Liskey, interview with author, 11 September 1986, Ontario, California.

69. There were more COs who exhibited anti-Semitic attitudes than most pacifists would care to admit, but they were a distinct minority, and the majority of pacifists were appalled at anti-Semitism, and especially pacifist anti-Semitism. Perhaps the only consolation to them is that anti-Semitic pacifists are anti-Semites without teeth; that is, whatever their views, their pacifism prevents them from causing direct physical harm to those against whom they are prejudiced (though they will sit idly by and allow persecution if they believe it to be God's will).

70. Hubert Brubaker, interview with author, 25 September 1986, Modesto, California.

71. Gil Bertochini, interview with author, 1 June 1987, Washington D.C. See also Tate Zytkoskee, self-interview answering author's questions, May 1987.

72. Gil Bertochini, interview with author, 1 June 1987, Washington D.C. Qualified versions of this argument can be found in Dwight Hanawalt, interview with author, 10 September 1986, La Verne, California; and Bill Colburn, interview with author, 5 May 1987, Concord, New Hampshire.

73. John Ripley Forbes, letter to Harold Guetzkow, 21 July 1942, CPS Personal Papers, Document Group 56, Swarthmore College Peace Collection, Swarthmore, Pennsylvania. See also Duane Windemiller, interview with author, 22 April 1987, Hampton Beach, New Hampshire.

74. Bill Colburn, interview with author, 5 May 1987, Concord, New Hampshire.

75. Loris Habegger, SOH interview. See also Lloyd Rodgers, SOH interview; Paul Brunner, SOH interview; Marvin Hein, SOH interview.

76. Booton Herndon, *The Unlikeliest Hero* (Mountain View, CA: Pacific Press Publishing Association, 1967), 116; R. Paul Phillips, interview with author, 11 September 1986, Ontario, California.

77. Hubert Brubaker, interview with author, 25 September 1986, Modesto, California.

78. Gil Bertochini, interview with author, 1 June 1987, Washington D.C. See also Tate Zytkoskee, self-interview answering author's questions, May 1987.

79. Laban Peachey, SOH interview. See also Wesley Prieb, SOH interview.

80. Paul Goering, SOH interview; J. John J. Miller, SOH interview; Loris Habegger, SOH interview; John Y. Hostetler, SOH interview; Joseph Weaver, SOH interview; Lloyd Rodgers, SOH interview.

81. John Juhnke, SOH interview; Milton Goering, SOH interview.

82. Anonymous Hopi leader, letter to General Hershey, n.d., American Civil Liberties Union—National Committee on Conscientious Objectors, Document Group 22, Swarthmore College Peace Collection, Swarthmore, Pennsylvania.

83. Lawrence S. Wittner, *Rebels Against War: The American Peace Movement, 1933–1983* (Philadelphia: Temple University Press, 1984), 46–47.

84. See, for example, Ian Thiermann, quoted in *Against the Tide,* Hurwitz and Simpson, eds.

85. George Brumley, letter to author, 4 June 1987; Fred Barnes, telephone interview with author, 13 May 1987.

86. Saburo Mizutani, interview with author, 29 September 1986, Sacramento, California; Robert Cary, interview with author, 1 October 1986, San Francisco, California.

87. G. Hayes Reed, interview with author, 25 September 1986, Modesto, California.

88. Richard Brown, interview with author, 2 October 1986, Berkeley, California. See also anonymous World War II CO, interview with author, 3 March 1987; Fred Convers, interview with author, 2 October 1986, Berkeley, California; Sigmund Cohn, interview with author, 30 September 1986, Berkeley, California; Gale Nutson, interview with author, 27 September 1986, Modesto, California; Robert Vogel, interview with author, 15 September 1986, Pasadena, California; Gordon Zahn, interview with author, 29 April 1987, Charlestown, Massachusetts; Paul Ashby, interview with author, 30 September 1986, San Francisco, California.

89. Fred Convers, interview with author, 2 October 1986, Berkeley, California; Walter Juhnke, SOH interview; Gale Nutson, interview with author, 27 September 1986, Modesto, California.

90. Seth Gifford, interview with author, 30 April 1987, Providence, Rhode Island.

91. Igal Roodenko, quoted in *Against the Tide,* Hurwitz and Simpson, eds. See also Albert Herbst, interview with author, 6 September 1986, La Verne, California; Leland Sateren, interview with author, 9 February 1987, Edina, Minnesota.

92. Howard Ten Brink, interview with author, 24 September 1986, Modesto, California; Don Baker, interview with author, 1 October 1986, San Francisco, California.

93. Herbert Hogan, interview with author, 11 September 1986, La Verne, California; Gil Bertochini, interview with author, 1 June 1987, Washington DC.

94. Henry Blocher, interview with author, 10 September 1986, La Verne, California. See also Sigmund Cohn, interview with author, 30 September 1986, Berkeley, California.

95. Anonymous World War II CO, interview with author, 7 September 1986.

96. Saburo Mizutani, interview with author, 29 September 1986, Sacramento, California.

97. Howard Bogen, interview with author, 9 September 1986, Pasadena, California. See also Bill Colburn, interview with author, 5 May 1987, Concord, New Hampshire.

98. Mitchell, *We Would Not Kill,* 24, 40.

99. Stafford, *Down in My Heart,* 81–82.

100. Francis Bates, "Bates Leaves C.O. Camp to Protest War Conscription," *The Catholic Worker* 9 (May 1942), 6.

101. Gordon Zahn, interview with author, 29 April 1987, Charlestown, Massachusetts. Zahn goes on to declare that even had World War II been a just war according to Catholic definition, he would have maintained his pacifism by going beyond justice to love for the unjust enemy. See also Paul Goering, SOH interview; Robert Vogel, interview with author, 15 September 1986, Pasadena, California.

102. Gordon Zahn, *War, Conscience, and Dissent* (New York: Hawthorn Books, 1967), 56.

103. Saburo Mizutani, interview with author, 29 September 1986, Sacramento, California.

7

Epilogue: The Legacy of World War II Conscientious Objection

The pacifist moral reasoning of World War II conscientious objectors is a story of vast differentiation and striking similarity. Though there are certain cohorts of objectors who share the same basic beliefs, the right and left margins of World War II conscientious objection would seem as far separated from one another as the radical right and left are in society generally. Both politically and religiously, COs cover the entire spectrum from fundamentalist and conservative to atheist and liberal. It is interesting that these sometimes diametrically opposed religious views can yield identical ethical imperatives, that men who arrive at the same position *vis-à-vis* the draft law can disagree with each other so strongly on why they should arrive there. For example, many liberal pacifists are frankly scornful of the vocational pacifism and social withdrawal of conservative peace church COs, and there is a corresponding contempt of some religiously conservative COs for those whose pacifism has political roots.

Variation between COs occurs along several axes. Religiously, as we have seen, World War II COs can be biblical literalists or have no interest in scripture whatsoever; can believe in a God who creates and controls history or in no God at all; can believe the soul is reincarnated repeatedly or that it dies once and for all with the body. Politically, COs are arch-conservatives and anarchists, free-market Republicans and welfare-state Democrats. Even in the area of foreign policy where one might anticipate some agreement between pacifists there is none: there are pacifists who would advocate isolationism and a nuclear defense along with those who favor economic aid and unilateral disarmament. The picture becomes even more complicated when it is noted that not all COs believe the realm of politics to be an important one. Some COs see their life's mission to be working for political change, while others are apolitical on principle. The differences are so great and the mixture of alignments so varied that it would seem foolhardy to speak of a pacifist ideal type or even a typology of kinds of pacifism.

Yet beyond the variation in belief and practice lies a certain unanimity of thought and feeling, characteristic ways of viewing the individual, the state, moral truth, and moral responsibility. Though not all individual pacifisms exhibit all these features (and though none of these features are exclusive to pacifists), these broad patterns of moral reasoning give pacifism its identifiable structure, and provide the theme for which individual pacifisms are the variations.

Reviewing the moral reasoning of World War II conscientious objectors gives us empirical information about how people morally justify acts that are deemed questionable by normative society's standards. This is important not only theoretically, but actually, for moral reasoning counts in the real world. It is the means by which we live together, defend our choices to one another, and work toward moral consensus. More than that, it is not unreasonable to believe that how people talk about moral decisions is an important factor in what decisions they actually make. As C. Wright Mills argues in his article, "Situated Actions and Vocabularies of Motive:"

> To term them [motives] justification is *not* to deny their efficacy. Often anticipations of acceptable justifications will control conduct. ("If I did this, what could I say? What would they say?") Decisions may be, wholly or in part, delimited by answers to such queries.[1]

It is partly by imagining how we will respond to challenges about the (moral) appropriateness of our behavior that we choose how to act. T. M. Scanlon makes this desire to justify one's actions basic to his moral theory of contractualism. In "Contractualism and Utilitarianism," he writes:

> In fact, it seems to me that the desire to be able to justify one's actions (and institutions) on grounds one takes to be acceptable is quite strong in most people. People are willing to go to considerable lengths, involving quite heavy sacrifices, in order to avoid admitting the unjustifiability of their actions and institutions.[2]

Finally, if we are to proceed in the business of assessing the morality of war, it is imperative that we return to World War II and carefully consider the factors that do or do not make that war just. So long as World War II is unreflectively remembered as "the good war" or "the righteous war," we will be haunted by the specter that compelling reasons to go to war could again arise, this time—in a nuclear age—with more dire consequences. Whether one ultimately decides that World War II needed to be fought or not, the arguments of World War II conscientious objectors provide a different and perhaps important angle on the question. COs as a class have ample reason to remember a war that most Americans have forgotten, if indeed they experienced it at all. The vast majority of American citizens simply have no motivation to remember the war as anything other than "the good war." Those who were not alive at the time of

World War II have been told that the United States entered a war against nations that were the very personification of evil just in time to save the free world through a combination of heroic action and scientific genius. Given the outcome of that war and the current political climate, they are unlikely to hear anything else. On the other hand, those who experienced the war in their own lives and chose to support it (or allowed themselves to be carried along with it) have every reason to remember the war as morally justified. It is only human nature that they should emphasize the factors that lead them to believe that fighting World War II was either morally necessary or practically inescapable or both, and downplay anything that might suggest otherwise.

COs are of course as prone to this temptation as anyone, and they buttress their past choice of objection with whatever re-tellings of history they can make themselves believe, however far these may depart from historical fact. But the same holds true for the mainstream view, and therefore *the* history of World War II is merely one history. If the war was not, as COs tend to imply, the product of the cunning of a few weapons manufacturers and corrupt governments, perhaps it was also not a case of an avenging hero slaying a wicked villain. If it was not a calamity that, as some COs indicate, could have been sidestepped by morally sensitive political leaders, perhaps it was also not the case that the level of destruction that ensued was utterly inescapable and entirely appropriate. By questioning the means of World War II, its stated (and unstated) goals, and its retrospective justification, World War II COs bring us back to the historical rootedness of World War II, to its moral ambiguity. The collective voice of World War II's conscientious objectors may at least dethrone "the good war" and give us the opportunity to learn the lessons it can teach us as we seek to maintain a world at peace.

NOTES

1. C. Wright Mills, "Situated Actions and Vocabularies of Motive," *American Sociological Review,* 5 (1940): 907.

2. T. M. Scanlon, "Contractualism and Utilitarianism," in *Utilitarianism and Beyond,* Amartya Sen and Bernard Williams, eds. (Cambridge: Cambridge University Press, 1982), 117.

Appendix A

Obtaining the Interview Sample

My initial contacts with World War II conscientious objectors came from a listing of alumni of Brethren Civilian Public Service (CPS) camps given to me by Hazel Peters of the On Earth Peace Assembly in New Windsor, Maryland. I was later given a similar listing of alumni of Friends CPS camps by Mel Zuck of the American Friends Service Committee. Because many COs spent years together in CPS camps, close friendships were formed, and today there are occasional CPS reunions and newsletters which serve to gather World War II COs and collect current address information on them. This was the primary source for the Brethren and Friends CPS lists to which I had access. By cross-referencing the listed COs with the *Directory of Civilian Public Service* compiled by the National Service Board for Religious Objectors in 1947, I was able to find their stated religious affiliations during World War II, and also to obtain some clues about their CPS service (e.g., what units they served in, if they left CPS prior to regular demobilization, etc.). In order to broaden the pool of religious affiliations, I wrote to approximately twenty denominations asking them to refer me to any of their members who served as COs in World War II.

Finding COs who were in prison or who served as noncombatants was considerably more difficult. One source of information was the aforementioned letter to various denominations, in which I emphasized my interest in contacting men who were imprisoned or in the military as noncombatant COs. A more common source of information was personal referral; I asked all my interviewees if they knew of COs I might be able to interview who were not in CPS, or who had particularly interesting or unusual religious or political affiliations. In a further effort to broaden the sample beyond CPS, I took special care to interview any COs I could find who left CPS, either for the military or for prison, or who were imprisoned prior to their CPS service.

I conducted the majority of the interviews in person, though in order to include particularly interesting interviewees who lived where I could not afford to travel,

I used several other methods for obtaining interview information. One was to ask the individual to respond to my questions in writing, which I did in two cases. Another was to interview by telephone, a method which worked very well, but which was prohibitively expensive; three interviews were conducted this way. Finally, three interviews consisted of COs' taped responses to my questions. This preserved some of the flavor of in-person interviews and allowed COs to talk at greater length than they could in writing, but unfortunately did not allow me to follow up interesting comments with additional lines of questioning.

My original plan was to interview between 50 and 100 COs. The decision to quit with a sample of sixty was motivated by two factors: first, I had access to approximately 100 interviews with World War II COs conducted by other people, and this enlarged my sample considerably. (Details on these oral history collections can be found in Chapter 1 and in the Bibliography.) Second, I found after about forty-five interviews that the material was becoming quite repetitive. More and more I heard slight variations on a theme, but no new themes. At this point, I made a concerted effort to interview only those COs who had unusual religious affiliations, who spent time in prison or the military, or who had been strongly recommended as having atypical views.

Though in other contexts a random sample of World War II COs might be informative, for my study it is unnecessary. The effort was not to discover what percentage of World War II COs held what views, but to maximize my chances of hearing the full range of pacifist arguments present in the World War II CO population. In order to have achieved the same degree of variation present in my interview sample by means of a random sample, the size of the interview group would have had to be multiplied many times over, and the project would have become unmanageable.

Appendix B

Religious Affiliation and Wartime Status of Interview Sample

Name	Religious Affiliation*	Wartime Status†
Anonymous	German Baptist Brethren	CPS
Anonymous	Unitarian/Quaker	CPS
Anonymous	Theosophy/none	CPS
Anonymous	Methodist	CPS, military
Paul Ashby	Methodist/none	CPS, military
Charles Baker	Brethren	CPS
Don Baker	Methodist/none	CPS, prison
Fred Barnes	Amish/Jehovah's Witness	prison
Donald Beachler	German Baptist Brethren	CPS
Gil Bertochini	Seventh-Day Adventist	noncom
Henry Blocher	Brethren	CPS
Howard Bogen	Evangelical and Reformed	CPS
Aretas Boone	German Baptist Brethren	CPS
James Bristol	Lutheran/Quaker	prison
George Brown	Methodist	CPS, military
Richard Brown	Methodist/Quaker	CPS, prison
Hubert Brubaker	German Baptist Brethren	CPS

*"None" indicates lack of religious affiliation; when it follows a specific religious affiliation, it indictes that the CO in question was raised in a religious group, but is not currently affiliated with one.

†CPS = Civilian Public Service; noncom = noncombatant military service.

Name	Religious Affiliation	Wartime Status
George Brumley	Jehovah's Witness	prison
Arthur Bryant	Baptist	CPS, noncom
Eugene Carper	Old Mennonite/Brethren	CPS
Robert Cary	Methodist	CPS
Sigmund Cohn	Jewish/none	CPS
Bill Colburn	Baptist/Seventh-Day Adventist	prison, CPS
Fred Convers	none	CPS
Joe Dell	Brethren	CPS
Paul Delp	Disciples of Christ	CPS
Wesley Doe	Baptist	CPS
Cal Edinger	Methodist/Quaker	CPS
George Fischer	Advent Christian	CPS
Caleb Foote	Unitarian/none	prison
Seth Gifford	Quaker	CPS
Gilbert Grover	German Baptist Brethren/Grace Brethren	CPS
Dwight Hanawalt	Brethren	CPS
Albert Herbst	Brethren	CPS
Herbert Hogan	Methodist/Brethren	CPS
Russell Jarboe	Brethren	CPS
J. Edwin Jones	Brethren	CPS
Gordon Kaufman	General Conference Mennonite	CPS
Charles Klaffke	Nazarene	CPS, military
Lyle Krug	General Conference Mennonite/Brethren	CPS
Samuel Liskey	Associated Bible Students	CPS
James Lowerre	Episcopal	CPS
Roy Mast	Old Order Amish/Amish Mennonite	CPS
Saburo Mizutani	Methodist	CPS
Gale Nutson	Methodist/Brethren	CPS
Gordon Nutson	Methodist/Brethren	CPS
Malcolm Parker	Congregational/none	prison
Carl Paulson	Catholic	prison, CPS
R. Paul Phillips	Christadelphian	CPS
Rudy Potochnik	none/Quaker	CPS
Harry Prochaska	Christian Science/Quaker/none	CPS
G. Hayes Reed	Dunkard Brethren	CPS

Name	Religious Affiliation	Wartime Status
Gerald Rubin	Jewish/none	CPS
Leland Sateren	Lutheran	CPS
Delmar Stanley	Brethren	CPS, noncom
Bob Stocksdale	Congregational/none	CPS
Howard TenBrink	Methodist/Brethren	CPS
Robert Vogel	Evangelical and Reformed/Quaker	CPS
Harmon Wilkinson	Disciples of Christ	CPS
Duane Windemiller	Church of God (Anderson, Indiana)	CPS, noncom
Gordon Zahn	Catholic	CPS
Tate Zytkoskee	Seventh-Day Adventist	noncom

Appendix C

Interview Guide

BACKGROUND

1. When and where were you born?
2. Were you raised in any particular religious organization?
3. Did you receive any pacifist training through your church/synagogue?
4. Did you participate in any pacifist organizations before the war?
5. How did your parents feel about your decision to be a CO?

THE DRAFT

1. How old were you and what were you doing when you were drafted?
2. Did you have any problems in getting CO status from your draft board?
3. Did you have to appear before your draft board in person?
4. What sorts of questions did they ask you?
   (Depending on what form a man's objection took, I asked the relevant two of these three questions):
   a) Did you ever consider not registering for the draft? Why or why not?
   b) Did you ever consider CPS? Why or why not?
   c) Did you ever consider being a noncombatant in the army? Why or why not?
5. Was this a difficult decision for you to make, to be a CO?
6. What people, books, or organizations influenced your thinking?

WAR YEARS

1. Where did you go when you were first drafted (i.e., which CPS camp, which military unit, which prison)? What was it like?

2. (For CPS only) How did you feel about the lack of pay in CPS?
3. (For CPS only) Did you feel that the churches should have become involved in administering CPS? Do you feel they did a good job?
4. (For CPS only) Would you have preferred service in camps financed and administered directly by the government?
5. Do you believe the government has a right to conscript its citizens for service, whether military or alternative?
6. Was there ever a time during the war when you reconsidered your decision (e.g., thought of going into active military service, walking out of CPS, going noncombatant)?
7. What did you feel people's attitude was towards you as a CO during the war years? Do any specific incidents come to mind?
8. Did Pearl Harbor have any effect on your CO convictions?
9. Do you remember hearing about the Holocaust during the war? What was your reaction?

POST-WAR

1. What was your occupation after the war?
2. Did you experience any difficulty in finding or keeping work? Did anyone react negatively to your CO status?
3. Would you consider yourself a pacifist now?
4. Have your reasons for objecting to war changed over the years?
5. Do you maintain a religious affiliation now?
6. Have your religious beliefs changed over the years? Did your World War II experiences have any effect on your religious beliefs?
7. Have you been involved in any pacifist organizations since the war?
8. How would you respond now to the classic draft board challenges:
   a) What about Hitler? Wasn't this a just war?
   b) What would you do if the United States were invaded by an enemy?
   c) What would you do if someone were attacking your family?
9. Can you imagine any circumstances that would persuade you to fight in a war? Any circumstances that would make a war "just"?
10. Knowing what you know now, would you take the same position regarding World War II?

Bibliography

PUBLISHED MATERIALS

ABC-Clio, Inc. *World War II from an American Perspective: An Annotated Bibliography*. Santa Barbara, CA: ABC-Clio, Inc., 1983.

American Civil Liberties Union. *Conscience and War*. New York: American Civil Liberties Union, 1943.

American Friends Service Committee. *The Experience of the American Friends Service Committee in Civilian Public Service under the Selective Training and Service Act of 1940: 1941–1945*. Philadelphia: American Friends Service Committee, n.d. [circa 1946].

______. *An Introduction to Friends Civilian Public Service*. Philadelphia: American Friends Service Committee, 1945.

Anderson, Martin. *Conscription: A Select and Annotated Bibliography*. Stanford, CA: Hoover Institution Press, 1976.

Bainton, Roland H. *Christian Attitudes toward War and Peace: A Historical Survey and Critical Re-evaluation*. Nashville, TN: Abingdon, 1960.

______. "The Church and War." *Social Action* 11 (January 1945): 5–71.

______. "Technology and Pacifism." *The Christian Century* 55 (May 1938): 618–19.

Barnes, Harry Elmer. "Conscientious Objectors as a Correctional Problem in the Second World War." *Prison World* 6 (July-August 1944): 12, 27–31.

______. "Here is the Truth About Springfield." *Prison World* 6 (May-June 1944): 4–5, 21, 23–25.

Bates, Francis. "Bates Leaves C.O. Camp to Protest War Conscription." *The Catholic Worker* 9 (May 1942): 1, 6.

Baum, Willa K. *Transcribing and Editing Oral History*. Nashville, TN: American Association for State and Local History, 1977.

Bayliss, Gwen. *Bibliographic Guide to Two World Wars: An Annotated Survey of English-Language Reference Materials*. New York: Bowker, 1977.

Bell, Daniel. "First Love and Early Sorrows." *Partisan Review* 48, no. 4 (1981): 532–51.

Bellah, Robert N., Richard Madsen, William M. Sullivan, Ann Swidler, and Steven M. Tipton. *Habits of the Heart: Individualism and Commitment in American Life.* Berkeley and Los Angeles: University of California Press, 1985.

Board of Christian Education of the Southern District of Pennsylvania. *Studies in the Doctrine of Peace and Suggestions for Their Use.* Elgin, IL: Church of the Brethren, 1939.

Boisen, Anton T. "Conscientious Objectors: Their Morale in Church-Operated Service Units." *Psychiatry* 7 (August 1944): 215–24.

Bosley, Harold. "Illusions of the Disillusioned." *The Christian Century* 58 (January 1941): 14–16.

Bowie, Walter Rusell. *What a Pacifist Can Contribute.* New York: Episcopal Pacifist Fellowship, n.d. [circa 1942].

Bowman, Paul H., and Harold S. Guetzkow. *Men and Hunger.* Elgin, IL: Brethren Publishing House, 1946.

Bowman, Rufus D. *The Church of the Brethren and War.* New York: Garland, 1971 [originally 1944].

Boyle, Beth Ellen, ed. *Words of Conscience: Religious Statements on Conscientious Objection.* 10th ed. Washington DC: National Interreligious Service Board for Conscientious Objectors, 1983.

Brax, Ralph S. "When Students First Organized Against War." *New York Historical Society Quarterly* 63 (July 1979): 228–55.

Brinton, Howard H. *Sources of the Quaker Peace Testimony.* Pendle Hill Pamphlet Series, no. 27. Wallingford, PA: Pendle Hill, n.d. [circa 1940].

Brock, Peter. *Twentieth-Century Pacifism.* New York: Van Nostrand Reinhold Company, 1970.

Brown, Dale W. *Biblical Pacifism.* Elgin, IL: Brethren Press, 1986.

Cadoux, Cecil John. *Christian Pacifism Re-examined.* Oxford, England: Basil Blackwell, 1940.

Camus, Albert. *Neither Victims nor Executioners.* Translated by Dwight Macdonald. New York: Continuum Publishing Corporation, 1980 [originally 1946].

Cantine, Holley, and Dachine Rainer, eds. *Prison Etiquette: The Convict's Compendium of Useful Information.* Bearsville, NY: Retort Press, 1950.

Chatfield, Charles. *For Peace and Justice: Pacifism in America, 1914–1941.* Boston: Beacon Press, 1973 [originally 1971].

Cook, Blanche Wiesen, ed. *Bibliography on Peace Research in History.* Santa Barabara, CA: ABC-Clio, 1969.

Cornell, Julien. *Conscience and the State: Legal and Administrative Problems of Conscientious Objectors, 1943–1944.* New York: John Day, 1945.

______. *Conscientious Objection and the Law.* New York: John Day, 1943.

Crespi, Leo P. "Attitudes Toward Conscientious Objectors and Some of Their Psychological Correlates." *Journal of Psychology* 18 (July 1944): 81–117.

______. "Public Opinion Toward Conscientious Objectors: II. Measurement of National Approval-Disapproval." *Journal of Psychology* 19 (April 1945): 209–50.

______. "Public Opinion Toward Conscientious Objectors: III. Intensity of Social Rejection in Stereotype and Attitude." *Journal of Psychology* 19 (April 1945): 251–76.

______. "Public Opinion Toward Conscientious Objectors: IV. Opinions on Significant CO Issues." *Journal of Psychology* 19 (April 1945): 277–310.

______. "Public Opinion Toward Conscientious Objectors: V. National Tolerance, Wartime Trends, and the Scapegoat Hypothesis." *Journal of Psychology* 20 (October 1945): 321–46.

Cronbach, Abraham. *The Quest for Peace*. Cincinnati, OH: Sinai Press, 1937.

Dahlke, Otto. "Values and Group Behavior in Two Camps for Conscientious Objectors." *American Journal of Sociology* 51 (July 1945): 22–33.

David, Cullom, Kathryn Back, and Kay MacLean. *Oral History: From Tape to Type*. Chicago: American Library Association, 1977.

Day, Albert Edward. Answer to editor's question, "If America Is Drawn into the War, Can You As a Christian, Participate in It Or Support It?" *The Christian Century* 57 (December 1940): 1611–13.

______. *The Terrible Meek*. Elgin, IL: Brethren Publishing House, n.d. [circa 1939].

DeBenedetti, Charles. *The Peace Reform in American History*. Bloomington, IN: Indiana University Press, 1980.

de Ligt, Bartelmy. *Conquest of Violence*. Translated by Honor Tracy. New York: Dutton, 1938.

Dick, Everett N. "The Adventist Medical Cadet Corps as Seen by its Founder." *Adventist Heritage* 1 (July 1974): 18–27.

Doty, Hiram. *Bibliography of Conscientious Objection to War*. Philadelphia: Central Committee for Conscientious Objection, 1954.

Dougall, Lucy, comp. *War and Peace in Literature: Prose, Drama, and Poetry which Illuminate the Problem of War*. Chicago: World Without War Publications, 1982.

Droba, D. D. "Churches and War Attitudes." *Sociology and Social Research* 17 (July 1932): 547–52.

Dunaway, David K., and Willa K. Baum, eds. *Oral History: An Interdisciplinary Anthology*. Nashville, TN: American Association for State and Local History, 1984.

Dyson, Freeman. *Weapons and Hope*. New York: Harper and Row, 1984.

Eddy, Sherwood. "Must We Face the War Problem Again?" *The Christian Century* 55 (November 1938): 1363–65.

Edelstein, Leonard. *We Are Accountable: A View of Mental Institutions*. Pendle Hill Pamphlet Series, no. 24. Wallingford, PA: Pendle Hill, 1945.

Eisan, Leslie. *Pathways of Peace: A History of the Civilian Public Service Program Administered by the Brethren Service Committee*. Elgin, IL: Brethren Publishing House, 1948.

Enser, A. G. S. *A Subject Bibliography of the Second World War, 1939–1974*. Boulder, CO: Westview Press, 1977.

______. *A Subject Bibliography of the Second World War, 1975–1983*. Brookfield, VT: Gower Publishing Company, 1985.

Fairbairn, R. Edis. "Judgment Day for Jesus Christ." *The Christian Century* 58 (April 1941): 524–25.

Fellowship of Reconciliation; Peace Section, American Friends Service Committee; Brethren Board of Christian Education; Friends Book Committee; General Conference Commission on World Peace, Methodist Church; The Mennonite Peace

Society; War Resisters League; and Women's International League for Peace and Freedom. *Pacifist Handbook: Questions and Answers Concerning the Pacifist in Wartime*. Nyack, NY: Fellowship of Reconciliation, 1940.

Flynn, George Q. "Lewis Hershey and the Conscientious Objector: The World War II Experience." *Military Affairs* 47 (February 1983): 1–6.

Forest, James H. *Catholics and Conscientious Objection*. New York: Catholic Peace Fellowship, 1981.

Fosdick, Harry Emerson. Answer to editor's question, "If America Is Drawn into the War, Can You As a Christian, Participate in It Or Support It?" *The Christian Century* 58 (January 1941): 115–18.

______. *Living under Tension*. New York: Harper Brothers, 1941.

______. "Putting Christ into Uniform." *The Christian Century* 56 (December 1939): 1539–42.

Frankena, William K. *Ethics*. 2d ed. Englewood Cliffs, NJ: Prentice-Hall, Inc., 1973.

Frazer, Heather T., and John O'Sullivan. "Forgotten Women of World War II: Wives of Conscientious Objectors in Civilian Public Service." *Peace and Change* 5 (Fall 1978): 46–51.

Freeman, Ruth. *Quakers and Peace*. Ithaca, NY: Pacifist Research Bureau, 1947.

French, Paul C. *We Won't Murder*. New York: Hastings House, 1940.

Funk, Arthur L. *The Second World War: A Bibliography of Books in English Since 1975*. Claremont, CA: Regina Books, 1985.

Gara, Larry. *War Resistance in Historical Perspective*. New York: War Resisters League, 1983.

Gibson, George M. "The Flight of Moral Leadership." *The Christian Century* 58 (June 1941): 829–30.

Gingerich, Melvin. *Service for Peace: A History of Mennonite Civilian Public Service*. Akron, PA: Mennonite Central Committee, 1949.

Glaser, Barney, and Anselm Strauss. *The Discovery of Grounded Theory*. Chicago: Aldine Publishing Company, 1967.

Glen, John M. "Secular Conscientious Objection in the United States: The Selective Service Act of 1940." *Peace and Change* (Spring 1983): 55–71.

Gory, Adrian E., and David C. McClellan. "Characteristics of Conscientious Objectors in World War II." *Journal of Consulting Psychology* 11 (September-October 1947): 245–57.

Gray, Harold Studley. *Character "Bad": The Story of a Conscientious Objector, as told in the letters of Harold Studley Gray*. Edited by Kenneth Irving Brown. New York: Harper and Brothers, 1934.

Gray, J. Glenn. *The Warriors: Reflections on Men in Battle*. New York: Harper and Row, 1970 [originally 1959].

Green, Marguerite. *Peace Archives: A Guide to Library Collections of the Papers of American Peace Organizations and of Leaders in the Public Effort for Peace*. Berkeley, CA: World Without War Council, 1986.

Gregg, Richard. *A Pacifist Program in Time of War, Threatened War, or Fascism*. Pendle Hill Pamphlet Series, no. 5. Wallingford, PA: Pendle Hill, 1939.

______. *The Power of Nonviolence*. Ahmedabad, India: Navajivan Publishing House, 1949 [originally 1935].

______. *Training for Peace: A Program for Peace Workers.* Philadelphia: J.B. Lippincott Company, 1937.

Grele, Ronald J., ed. *Envelopes of Sound: Six Practitioners Discuss the Method, Theory, and Practice of Oral History and Oral Testimony.* Chicago: Precedent Publishing, 1975.

Hamilton, Wallace. *Clash by Night.* Pendle Hill Pamphlet Series, no. 23. Wallingford, PA: Pendle Hill, 1945.

Harkness, Georgia. "Are Pacifists Romantics?" *The Christian Century* 55 (June 1938): 693–94.

______. "The Christian's Dilemma." *The Christian Century* 58 (August 1941): 977–79.

______. "A Pacifist Ecumenical Witness." *The Christian Century* 58 (July 1941): 859–60.

______. "What Can Christians Do?" *The Christian Century* 57 (May 1940): 699–701.

Harris, Mark Jonathan, Franklin D. Mitchell, and Steven J. Schechter. *The Homefront: America During World War II.* New York: G.P. Putnam's Sons, 1984.

Harrison, Barbara Grizzuti. *Visions of Glory: A History and a Memory of Jehovah's Witnesses.* New York: Simon and Schuster, 1978.

Hartigan, Richard S. "War and Its Normative Justification: An Example and Some Reflections." *Review of Politics* 36 (October 1974): 492–503.

Hartmann, George W. "Motivational Differences Between Pacifists and Non-Pacifists." *Journal of Social Psychology* 14 (August 1941): 197–210.

______. "Pacifism and Its Opponents in the Light of Value Theory." *Journal of Abnormal and Social Psychology* 36 (April 1941): 151–74.

______. "The Strength and Weakness of the Pacifist Position as Seen by American Philosophers." *Philosophical Review* 53 (March 1944): 125–44.

Hassler, R. Alfred. *Conscripts of Conscience: The Story of Sixteen Objectors to Conscription.* New York: Fellowship of Reconciliation, 1942.

______. *Diary of a Self-Made Convict.* Nyack, NY: Fellowship of Reconciliation, 1958.

______. "Slaughter of the Innocent." *Fellowship* 10 (February 1944): 19–21.

Haynes, Carlyle B. *Studies in Denominational Principles of Noncombatancy and Governmental Relationships.* Washington D.C.: Seventh-Day Adventist War Service Commission, 1943.

Henige, David. *Oral Historiography.* London: Longman, 1982.

Herndon, Booton. *The Unlikeliest Hero.* Mountain View, CA: Pacific Press Publishing Association, 1967.

Hershberger, Guy. "The Christian's Relation to the State in Time of War: Is Alternative Service Desirable or Possible?" *Mennonite Quarterly Review* 9 (January 1935): 20–36.

______. *The Mennonite Church in World War II.* Scottdale, PA: Mennonite Publishing House, 1951.

______. *War, Peace, and Nonresistance.* Scottdale, PA: Herald Press, 1953 [originally 1944].

Holmes, John Haynes. Answer to editor's question, "If America Is Drawn into the War, Can You As a Christian, Participate in It Or Support It?" *The Christian Century* 57 (December 1940): 1546–49.

______. "Long Thoughts About 1917." *The Christian Century* 58 (October 1941): 1267–68.

______. *Out of Darkness*. New York: Harper, 1942.

______. "A Pacifist Minister to His Brethren." *The Christian Century* 56 (November 1939): 1374–77.

Hoopes, James. *Oral History: An Introduction for Students*. Chapel Hill, NC: University of North Carolina Press, 1979.

Hoopes, Roy. *Americans Remember: The Home Front*. New York: Hawthorn Books, 1977.

Horsch, John. *The Principle of Non-resistance as Held by the Mennonite Church*. 2d ed. Scottdale, PA: Mennonite Publishing House, 1940 [originally 1927].

Hughan, Jessie Wallace. *Pacifism and Invasion*. New York: War Resisters League, 1942.

______. *Three Decades of War Resistance*. New York: War Resisters League, 1942.

______. "What About the Jews in the Ghettoes?" *Pacifica Views* 1 (September 1943): 1–2.

Hurwitz, Deena, and Craig Simpson, eds. *Against the Tide: Pacifist Resistance in the Second World War, an Oral History*. New York: War Resisters League, 1984.

Huxley, Aldous. *An Encyclopedia of Pacifism*. New York: Harper Brothers, 1937.

______. *Ends and Means*. New York: Harper Brothers, 1937.

Ives, Edward D. *The Tape-Recorded Interview: A Manual for Field Workers in Folklore and Oral History*. Knoxville, TN: University of Tennessee Press, 1980.

Jacob, Philip. *The Origins of Civilian Public Service*. Washington D.C.: National Service Board for Religious Objectors, n.d. [circa 1942].

Juhnke, Roger. "The Perils of Conscientious Objection." *Mennonite Life* 34 (September 1979): 4–9.

Kaufman, Gordon. *Nonresistance and Responsibility*. Newton, KS: Faith and Life Press, 1979.

Keim, Albert N. "Service or Resistance? The Mennonite Response to Conscription in World War II." *Mennonite Quarterly Review* 52 (April 1978): 141–55.

Kelley, Ray R., and Paul E. Johnson. "Emotional Traits in Pacifists." *Journal of Social Psychology* 28 (November 1948): 275–86.

Kohn, Stephen M. *Jailed for Peace: The History of American Draft Law Violators, 1658–1985*. Westport, CT: Greenwood Press, 1986.

Lawson, Don, ed. *Ten Fighters for Peace*. New York: Lothrop, Lee, and Shepard, 1971.

Liles, Walter Theodore. *The Shadow of a Great Rock*. Portland, OR: Willamette Printing Company, 1943.

Lindner, Robert M. *Stone Walls and Men*. New York: Odyssey Press, n.d. [circa 1946].

Long, Edward LeRoy, Jr. *War and Conscience in America*. Philadelphia: Westminster, 1968.

Macgregor, G. H. C. *The New Testament Basis of Pacifism*. London: Fellowship of Reconciliation, 1936.

______. *The Relevance of an Impossible Ideal*. New York: Fellowship of Reconciliation, n.d. [circa 1941].

McNeal, Patricia F. "Catholic Conscientious Objection During World War II." *Catholic Historical Review* 61 (April 1975): 222–42.

Marion, J. H., Jr. "Conscience and Circumstance." *The Christian Century* 58 (July 1941): 908–10.

Marrin, Albert, ed. *War and the Christian Conscience: From Augustine to Martin Luther King, Jr.* Chicago: Henry Regnery Company, 1971.

Martin, David A. *Pacifism: An Historical and Sociological Study.* London: Routledge and Kegan Paul, 1965.

Mayer, Milton S. "I Think I'll Sit This One Out." *Saturday Evening Post* 212 (October 1939): 23, 96–100.

Mayer, Peter. *The Pacifist Conscience.* New York: Holt, Reinhart, and Winston, 1966.

Mills, C. Wright. "Situated Actions and Vocabularies of Motive." *American Sociological Review* 5 (December 1940): 904–13.

Milne, A. A. *Peace with Honour.* New York: E.P. Dutton, 1934.

______. *War with Honour.* Macmillan War Pamphlets, no. 2. London: Macmillan and Company, Ltd., 1940.

Mitchell, Hobart. *We Would Not Kill.* Richmond, IN: Friends United Press, 1983.

Morris, Cynthia Hastas. "Arkansas's Reaction to the Men Who Said 'No' to World War II." *Arkansas Historical Quarterly* 43 (Summer 1984): 153–77.

Morrison, Charles Clayton. "The Case for Conference." *The Christian Century* 55 (December 1938): 1538–40.

______. "The Church in Wartime." *The Christian Century* 56 (December 1939): 1535–37.

______. "A Strain on the Tie that Binds." *The Christian Century* 58 (July 1941): 853–55.

Muste, A. J. *Non-violence in an Aggressive World.* New York: Harper and Brothers, 1940.

______. "A Pacifist on Invasion." *The Christian Century* 57 (September 1940): 1116–17.

______. *War Is the Enemy.* Pendle Hill Pamphlet Series, no. 15. Wallingford, PA: Pendle Hill, n.d. [circa 1943].

______. *The World Task of Pacifism.* Pendle Hill Pamphlet Series, no. 13. Wallingford, PA: Pendle Hill, 1941.

Naeve, Lowell, in collaboration with David Wieck. *A Field of Broken Stones.* Denver, CO: Alan Swallow, 1959.

National Service Board for Religious Objectors. *Congress Looks at the Conscientious Objector.* Washington D.C.: National Service Board for Religious Objectors, 1943.

______. *The Conscientious Objector Under the Selective Training and Service Act of 1940.* Washington D.C.: National Service Board for Religious Objectors, 1943.

______. *A Directory of Civilian Public Service.* Washington D.C.: National Service Board for Religious Objectors, 1947.

Nelson, John K. *The Peace Prophets: American Pacifist Thought, 1919–1941.* Chapel Hill, NC: University of North Carolina Press, 1967.

Neibuhr, Reinhold. *Christianity and Power Politics.* New York: Archon Books, 1969 [originally 1940].

______. Answer to editor's question, "If America Is Drawn into the War, Can You As a Christian, Participate in It Or Support It?" *The Christian Century* 57 (December 1940): 1578–80.

______. "Japan and the Christian Conscience," *The Christian Century* 54 (November 1937): 1390–91.

Nuttall, Geoffrey. *Christian Pacifism in History*. Berkeley, CA: World Without War Council, 1971 [originally 1958].

Orser, Edward. "Involuntary Community: Conscientious Objectors at Patapsco State Park During World War II." *Maryland Historical Magazine* 72 (Spring 1977): 132–46.

O'Toole, George Barry. *War and Conscription at the Bar of Christian Morals*. New York: Catholic Worker, 1941.

Pacifist Research Bureau. *Conscientious Objectors in World War II*. Ithaca, NY: Pacifist Research Bureau, 1949.

______. *Five Foot Shelf of Pacifist Literature*. Philadelphia: Pacifist Research Bureau, 1942.

Page, Kirby. *Must We Go to War?* New York: Farrar and Rinehart, 1937.

Palmer, Albert W. Answer to editor's question, "If America Is Drawn into the War, Can You As a Christian, Participate in It Or Support It?" *The Christian Century* 58 (January 1941): 51–53.

Parker, Malcolm. *Prison Privilege*. Kaslo, British Columbia: KLC Publications, 1984.

Peck, Jim. *We Who Would Not Kill*. New York: Lyle Stuart, 1958.

Pickett, Clarence E. *For More than Bread: An Autobiographical Account of Twenty-Two Years' Work with the American Friends Service Committee*. Boston: Little, Brown, and Company, 1953.

Potter, Ralph B. "The Moral Logic of War." Occasional Papers on the Church and Conflict, no. 5. Philadelphia: United Presbyterian Church USA, n.d. [circa 1970].

______. *War and Moral Discourse*. Richmond, VA: John Knox Press, 1969.

Rabin, A. I. "Rorschach Test Findings in a Group of Conscientious Objectors." *American Journal of Orthopsychiatry* 15 (October 1945): 514–19.

Reeves, George B. *Men Against the State*. Human Events Pamphlet, no. 9. Washington and Chicago: Human Events, Inc., 1946.

Richards, Edward C. M. *They Refuse to Be Criminals: Parole and the Conscientious Objector*. Nur Mahal Publication, no. 1. N.p. 1946.

Roop, John D., and Daniel C. Moomaw, eds. *Christianity versus War*. rev. ed. Ashland, OH: Brethren Publishing Company, 1949.

Sappington, Roger E. *Brethren Social Policy, 1908–1958*. Elgin, IL: Brethren Press, 1961.

Satterfield, Archie. *The Home Front: An Oral History of the War Years in America: 1941–45*. Chicago: Playboy Press, 1981.

Scanlon, T. M. "Contractualism and Utilitarianism." In *Utilitarianism and Beyond*, edited by Amartya Sen and Bernard Williams, 103–28. Cambridge, U.K.: Cambridge University Press, 1982.

Schlissel, Lillian, ed. *Conscience in America: A Documentary History of Conscientious Objection in America, 1757–1967*. New York: E.P. Dutton, 1968.

Scott, Marvin B., and Stanford M. Lyman. "Accounts." *American Sociological Review* 33 (February 1968): 46–62.

Shinn, Roger. *Wars and Rumours of Wars*. Nashville, TN: Abingdon Press, 1972.

Shridharani, Krishnalal. *War Without Violence*. New York: Harcourt Brace, 1939.

Sibley, Mulford Q. *The Political Theories of Modern Pacifism.* Philadelphia: Pacifist Research Bureau, 1944.

______., and Ada Wardlaw. *Conscientious Objectors in Prison, 1940–45.* Pacifist Research Bureau Pamphlet, series V, no. 2. Philadelphia: Pacifist Research Bureau, 1945.

______., and Philip E. Jacob. *Conscription of Conscience: The American State and the Conscientious Objector, 1940–1947.* Ithaca, NY: Cornell University Press, 1952.

Sitton, Thad, George L. Mehaffy, and O. L. Davis, Jr. *Oral History: A Guide for Teachers and Others.* Austin, TX: University of Texas Press, 1983.

Smith, Jonathan Z. *Imagining Religion: From Babylon to Jonestown.* Chicago: University of Chicago Press, 1982.

______. *Map is Not Territory: Studies in the History of Religions.* Leiden, The Netherlands: E.J. Brill, 1978.

Smucker, Donovan. "Who Are the C.O.s?" *Fellowship* 7 (February 1941): 22–24.

Solomonow, Allan, ed. *The Roots of Jewish Nonviolence.* Nyack, NY: Jewish Peace Fellowship, 1981.

Sprunger, Keith, and James Juhnke. "Mennonite Oral History." *Mennonite Quarterly Review* 54 (July 1980): 244–47.

Stafford, William E. *Down in My Heart.* Elgin, IL: Brethren Publishing House, 1947.

Steele, Richard W. "American Popular Opinion and the War Against Germany: The Issue of Negotiated Peace, 1942." *Journal of American History* 65 (December 1978): 704–23.

Stuart, Jeb. *Objector.* New York: Doubleday, 1950.

Swalm, Ernest J. *Nonresistance Under Test: Conscientious Objectors in Two Wars.* Nappanee, IN: Evangel Press, 1949.

Taft, Charles P. Answer to editor's question, "If America Is Drawn into the War, Can You As a Christian, Participate in It Or Support It?" *The Christian Century* 58 (January 1941): 11–13.

Terkel, Studs. *The Good War: An Oral History of World War Two.* New York: Ballantine Books, 1984.

Thompson, Paul. *The Voice of the Past: Oral History.* Oxford, U.K.: Oxford University Press, 1978.

Thoreau, Henry David. "On the Duty of Civil Disobedience," [originally 1848] in*Walden and Civil Disobedience.* New York: Harper and Row, 1965.

Tipton, Steven M. *Getting Saved From the Sixties: Moral Meaning in Conversion and Cultural Change.* Berkeley and Los Angeles: University of California Press, 1982.

Tittle, Ernest Fremont. "God and National Policy." *The Christian Century* 55 (November 1938): 1462–65.

______. Answer to editor's question, "If America Is Drawn into the War, Can You As a Christian, Participate in It Or Support It?" *The Christian Century* 58 (February 1941): 178–80.

______. "The Present Crisis." *The Christian Century* 55 (November 1938): 1365–67.

Tolstoy, Leo. *Christianity and Patriotism.* Translated by Constance Garnett. London: Jonathan Cape, 1922.

______. *The Kingdom of God Is Within You: Christianity Not as a Mystic Religion but as a New Theory of Life.* Translated by Constance Garnett. Lincoln, NE: University of Nebraska Press, 1984 [originally 1894].

______. *My Confession and the Spirit of Christ's Teaching.* New York: Thomas Y. Crowell and Company, 1887.

Trueblood, Elton. "Vocational Christian Pacifism." *Christianity and Crisis* 1 (November 1941): 2–5.

U.S. Director of Selective Service. *Selective Service and Victory.* Semiannual Report, vol. 4. Washington D.C.: Government Printing Office, 1948.

______. *Selective Service as the Tide of War Turns.* Semiannual Report, vol. 3. Washington D.C.: Government Printing Office, 1945.

______. *Selective Service in Peacetime.* Semiannual Report, vol. 1. Washington D.C.: Government Printing Office, 1942.

______. *Selective Service in Wartime.* Semiannual Report, vol. 2. Washington D.C.: Government Printing Office, 1943.

U.S. Selective Service System. *Conscientious Objection.* Special Monograph no. 11, 2 vols. Washington D.C.: Government Printing Office, 1950.

______. *Report on Conscientious Objection.* N.p., 1944.

U.S. Senate, Committee on Military Affairs. "Conscientious Objectors' Benefits: Hearings on S. 315 and S. 675," 78th Congress, 1st Session. Washington D.C.: Government Printing Office, 1943.

Van Dusen, Henry Pitney. Answer to editor's question, "If America Is Drawn into the War, Can You as a Christian, Participate in It Or Support It?" *The Christian Century* 58 (January 1941): 146–48.

Wallach, Glenn. "The CO Link: Conscientious Objection to World War II and the San Francisco Renaissance." *Brethren Life and Thought* 27 (Winter 1982): 15–34.

Wallenberg, Harry A., Jr. *Whither Freedom?: A Study of the Treatment of Conscientious Objectors in the United States During World Wars I and II and Its Relation to the Concept of Freedom.* New York: Fellowship of Reconciliation, 1954.

Walzer, Michael. *Just and Unjust Wars: A Moral Argument with Historical Illustrations.* New York: Basic Books, 1977.

______. "World War II: Why Was This War Different?" In *War and Moral Responsibility.* Edited by Marshall Cohen, Thomas Nagel, and Thomas Scanlon, 85–103. Princeton, NJ: Princeton University Press, 1974.

Weber, Max. "Religious Rejections of the World and Their Directions." In *From Max Weber.* Edited by H. H. Gerth and C. Wright Mills, 323–59. London: Kegan Paul, 1946.

Wells, R., ed. *The Wars of America: Christian Views.* Grand Rapids, MI: William B. Eerdmans, 1981.

Whiteman, A. Wilson. *The Christian Scientist and the Way to Peace.* Portland, OR: Pacifist Principle Fellowship, 1944.

Wieand, Albert C. *The Prince of Peace According to the Example and Teaching of Christ.* Elgin, IL: Brethen Service Commission, 1952 [originally 1940].

Wilson, Bob. *Of Human Importance: Civilian Public Service 26.* Chicago: Alexian Brothers Hospital, 1946.

Wilson, E. Raymond. "Evolution of the Conscientious Objector Provisions in the 1940 Conscription Bill." *Quaker History* 64 (Spring 1975): 3–15.

Wittner, Lawrence S. *Rebels Against War: The American Peace Movement, 1933–1983*. Philadelphia: Temple University Press, 1984.

Yoder, John Howard. *Nevertheless: The Varieties and Shortcomings of Religious Pacifism*. Scottdale, PA: Herald Press, 1971.

Young, Michael. "Facing a Test of Faith: Jewish Pacifists During World War II." *Peace and Change* 3 (Summer-Fall 1975): 34–40.

Zahn, Gordon C. *Another Part of the War: The Camp Simon Story*. Amherst, MA: University of Massachusetts Press, 1979.

______. "The Catholic CO of World War II." *The Catholic World* 179 (August 1954): 340–46.

______. "Peace Witness in World War II." *Worldview* 18 (February 1975): 48–55.

______. *War, Conscience, and Dissent*. New York: Hawthorn Books, 1967.

Zeitzer, Glen. "The Fellowship of Reconciliation on the Eve of World War II: A Peace Organization Prepares." *Peace and Change* 3 (Summer-Fall 1975): 46–51.

Zook, Mervin D. "How U.S. Magazines Covered Objectors in World War II." *Journalism Quarterly* 48 (Autumn 1971): 550–54.

UNPUBLISHED MATERIALS

American Civil Liberties Union—National Committee on Conscientious Objectors, 1940–1947. Document Group 22. Swarthmore College Peace Collection, Swarthmore, Pennsylvania.

American Friends Service Committee—Civilian Public Service, 1940–1946. Document Group 2. Swarthmore College Peace Collection, Swarthmore, Pennsylvania.

Anonymous World War II CO. Letter to friends, 4 February 1944. Privately held.

______. Special Form for Conscientious Objector. Privately held.

Bristol, James. Letter to draft board, 15 October 1940. Privately held.

______. Letter to draft board, 14 April 1941. Privately held.

______. Sermon (never preached), 13 October 1940. Privately held.

______. Statement to federal judge, 31 October 1941. Privately held.

Brown, George E. Address at New Windsor, Maryland, On Earth Peace Assembly, 12 April 1986. Privately held.

Brumley, George. Letter to author, 4 June 1987.

Civilian Public Service Personal Papers, 1941–1950. Document Group 56. Swarthmore College Peace Collection, Swarthmore, Pennsylvania.

Collective Document Groups A (United States). Swarthmore College Peace Collection, Swarthmore, Pennsylvania.

Conscientious Objectors in New York State, 1940–1945: Scrapbook. Swarthmore College Peace Collection, Swarthmore, Pennsylvania.

Davis, Roger Guinon. "Conscientious Cooperators: The Seventh-Day Adventists and Military Service, 1860–1945." Ph.D. dissertation, George Washington University, 1970.

Doe, Wesley. Letter to author, 14 January 1987.

______. Letter to parents, n.d. [during World War II]. Privately held.

______. Letter to Private Berry, 16 October 1941. Privately held.

Ewing, Emerson Keith. "The Pacifist Movement in the Methodist Church During World War II: A Study of Civilian Public Service Men in a Nonpacifist Church." Master's thesis, Florida Atlantic University, 1982.

Fosdick, Harry Emerson. "Dare We Break the Vicious Circle of Fighting Evil with Evil?" Sermon preached at the Riverside Church, New York, 19 February 1939.

Grover, Gilbert. "The Christian and the State." Unpublished essay. Privately held.

Hafer, Harold F. "The Evangelical and Reformed Church in World War II." Ph.D. dissertation, University of Pennsylvania, 1947.

Hampton, John. Letters from prison. War Resisters League. Document Group 40. Swarthmore College Peace Collection, Swarthmore, Pennsylvania.

Jarboe, Russell. Special Form for Conscientious Objector, 30 June 1942. Privately held.

McLean, Franklin A. Memorandum to the Executive Camp Directors, Camp Operations Division, Selective Service System, 1942.

McNeal, Patricia F. "The American Catholic Peace Movement, 1928–72." Ph.D. dissertation, Temple University, 1974.

Miller, Tom Polk. "Civilian Island: Some Aspects of Alternative Service for Conscientious Objectors, 1941 to 1946." Paper presented before the Denton Forum, 16 February 1985. CPS subject file. Swarthmore College Peace Collection, Swarthmore, Pennsylvania.

Nagel, Thomas. "The Limits of Objectivity." The Tanner Lecture on Human Values, Brasenose College, Oxford University, 4, 11, and 18 May 1979.

Nutson, Gordon, and Gale Nutson. Letter to friends, 5 February 1945. Privately held.

Phillips, R. Paul. Letter to author, 19 December 1986.

Potochnik, Rudy. "Autobiography." Privately held.

Potter, Ralph B. "The Structure of Certain Christian Responses to the Nuclear Dilemma, 1959–1963." Th.D. dissertation, Harvard University, 1965.

Sawatsky, Rodney. "The Influence of Fundamentalism on Mennonite Nonresistance, 1908–1944." Master's thesis, University of Minnesota, 1973.

Templin, Lawrence. Papers. Mennonite Library and Archives, North Newton, Kansas.

Wachs, Theodore Rickard. "Conscription, Conscientious Objection, and the Context of American Pacifism, 1940–45." Ph.D. dissertation, University of Illinois, Champaign-Urbana, 1976.

Weiss, Lorell. "Socio-Psychological Factors in the Pacifism of the Church of the Brethren During the Second World War." Ph.D. dissertation, University of Southern California, 1957.

Zahn, Gordon C. "A Descriptive Study of the Sociological Backgrounds of Conscientious Objectors in Civilian Public Service During World War II." Ph.D. dissertation, Catholic University of America, 1953.

______. "A Study of the Social Backgrounds of Catholic Conscientious Objectors in Civilian Public Service During World War II." Master's thesis, Catholic University of America, 1950.

Zeitzer, Glen. "The American Peace Movement During World War II." Ph.D. dissertation, Bryn Mawr College, 1978.

INTERVIEWS

In addition to my own interviews, I consulted three other sources for interviews. Their full citations, and the way they will be abbreviated in this listing, are as follows:

Hurwitz, Deena. Interviews for *Against the Tide: Pacifist Resistance in the Second World War, an Oral History*. Two interview transcripts. Privately held. [Abbreviated as "Hurwitz interview"]

Polner, Murray. "An Oral History of American Jews who Chose to Become Conscientious Objectors or Resisted Serving in the Military from World War II—Korean War." Ten cassette tapes. Swarthmore College Peace Collection, Swarthmore, Pennsylvania. [Abbreviated as "Polner interview"]

Sprunger, Keith, and James Juhnke, coordinators. "Schowalter Oral History Collection—World War II Conscientious Objectors." One hundred twenty-two casette tapes. Mennonite Library and Archives, North Newton, Kansas. [Abbreviated as "SOH interview"]

The author's taped interviews and their transcripts are deposited in the Swarthmore College Peace Collection, Swarthmore, Pennsylvania.

Ashby, Paul. Interview with author. San Francisco, California, 30 September 1986.

Baker, Charles W. Interview with author. Modesto, California, 24 September 1986.

Baker, Don. Interview with author. San Francisco, California, 1 October 1986.

Barnes, Fred. Telephone interview with author. Brooklyn, New York, 13 May 1987.

Bartel, Peter. Interview by Kurt Goering, 10 May 1976. SOH interview no. 54.

Beachler, Donald G. Interview with author. Modesto, California, 26 September 1986.

Bertochini, Gil. Interview with author. Washington D.C., 1 June 1987.

Blocher, Henry D. Interview with author. La Verne, California, 10 September 1986.

Blosser, Vernon. Interview by Kurt Goering, 27 September 1975. SOH interview no. 33.

Bogen, Howard L. Interview with author. Pasadena, California, 9 September 1986.

Boone, Aretas. Interview with author. Modesto, California, 24 September 1986.

Bristol, James. Interview with author. Philadelphia, Pennsylvania, 27 May 1987.

Brookmyer, Edward. Interview by Kurt Goering, 29 December 1975. SOH interview no. 46.

Brown, George E., Jr. Interview with author. Washington D.C., 1 June 1987.

Brown, Richard A. Interview with author. Berkeley, California, 2 October 1986.

Brubaker, Hubert L. Interview with author. Modesto, California, 25 September 1986.

Brunner, Paul. Interview by Kurt Goering, 29 October 1975. SOH interview no. 40.

Bryant, Arthur P. Self-interview answering author's questions. San Mateo, California, May 1987.

Carper, Eugene G. Interview with author. La Verne, California, 10 September 1986.

Cary, Robert. Interview with author. San Francisco, California, 1 October 1986.

Claassen, Henry. Interview by Kurt Goering, 9 May 1976. SOH interview no. 81.
Cohn, Sigmund S. Interview with author. Berkeley, California, 30 September 1986.
Colburn, Bill. Interview with author. Concord, New Hampshire, 5 May 1987.
Convers, Fred L. Interview with author. Berkeley, California, 2 October 1986.
Deckert, Harvey. Interview by Kurt Goering, 4 November 1975. SOH interview no. 44.
Dell, Joe. Interview with author. Modesto, California, 27 September 1986.
Delp, Paul. Interview with author. Orange, California, 3 March 1987.
Ediger, Elmer. Interview by Roger Juhnke, 9 October 1978. SOH interview, stored in Ediger biography section nos. 1–3.
Edinger, Cal. Interview with author. San Gabriel, California, 25 February 1987.
Fischer, George S. Interview with author. Danvers, Massachusetts, 22 April 1987.
Foote, Caleb. Telephone interview with author. Point Reyes, California, 28 February 1987.
Gerber, William. Self-interview answering Murray Polner's questions, n.d. [circa 1980]. Polner interview no. 30.02.
Gifford, Seth. Interview with author. Providence, Rhode Island, 30 April 1987.
Glixon, Neil. Self-interview answering Murray Polner's questions, n.d. [circa 1980]. Polner interview no. 30.03.
Goering, Milton. Interview by Roger Juhnke, 29 November 1974. SOH interview no. 21.
Goering, Paul L. Interview by Kurt Goering, 26 December 1975. SOH interview nos. 47–48.
Grover, Gilbert. Interview with author. Modesto, California, 24 September 1986.
Grunau, Allen. Interview by Tim Schrag, 24 November 1975. SOH interview no. 36.
Guhr, Samuel. Interview by Myron Voth, 23 October 1975. SOH interview no. 34.
Habegger, Loris. Interview by Keith Sprunger, 13 August 1974. SOH interview no. 15.
Hanawalt, Dwight. Interview with author. La Verne, California, 10 September 1986.
Hein, Marvin. Interview by Tim Schrag, 4 November 1975. SOH interview no. 35.
Herbst, Albert F. Interview with author. La Verne, California, 6 September 1986.
Hogan, Herbert. Interview with author. La Verne, California, 11 September 1986.
Holsinger, Justus. Interview by Deb Janzen, n.d. [circa 1976]. SOH interview no. 41.
Hostetler, John Y. Interview by Joseph Miller, 22 December 1977. SOH interview no. 78.
Hostetter, C. Nelson. Interview by Joseph Miller, 22 December 1977. SOH interview no. 79.
Jarboe, Russell. Interview with author. La Verne, California, 25 February 1987.
Jones, David D. Interview by Tim Schrag, 23 September 1975. SOH interview no. 32.
Jones, J. Edwin. Interview with author. La Verne, California, 6 September 1986.
Juhnke, John. Interview by Jim Juhnke, 24 November 1973. SOH interview no. 16.
Juhnke, Walter. Interview by Jim Juhnke, 4 January 1977. SOH interview no. 61.
Kampelman, Max. Self-interview answering Murray Polner's questions, n.d. [circa 1980]. Polner interview no. 30.04.
Kaufman, Gordon. Interview with author. Cambridge, Massachusetts, 29 April 1987.
Keeney, William. Interview by David Haury, 14 June 1973. SOH interview no. 5.

Klaffke, Rev. Charles A. Interview with author. Duarte, California, 23 February 1987.

Kleinbaum, Max. Self-interview answering Murray Polner's questions, n.d. [circa 1980]. Polner interview 30.07.

Krug, Lyle. Interview with author. Mission Viejo, California, 28 August 1986.

Liskey, Samuel W. Interview with author. Ontario, California, 11 September 1986.

Loganbill, Varden. Interview by Roger Juhnke, 1 November 1978. SOH interview no. 86.

Lowerre, James D. Interview with author. Orange, California, 3 March 1987.

Mast, Roy. Self-interview answering author's questions. Millersburg, Ohio, May 1987.

Miller, J. John J. Interview by Roger Juhnke, 22 November 1978. SOH interview no. 90.

Mizutani, Saburo. Interview with author. Sacramento, California, 29 September 1986.

Nelson, Wallace. Interview by Deena Hurwitz, 11 February 1982. Hurwitz interview.

Nightengale, Herman. Interview by Tim Schrag, 2 April 1975. SOH interview no. 29.

Nutson, Gale O. Interview with author. Modesto, California, 27 September 1986.

Nutson, Gordon W. Interview with author. Modesto, California, 25 September 1986.

Parker, Malcolm. Telephone interview with author. Kaslo, British Columbia, 28 February 1987.

Paulson, Carl. Interview with author. Upton, Massachusetts, 23 April 1987.

Peachey, Laban. Interview by Joseph Miller, n.d. [circa 1977]. SOH interview no. 82.

Peretz, Don. Self-interview answering Murray Polner's questions, n.d. [circa 1980]. Polner interview no. 30.09.

Phillips, R. Paul. Interview with author. Ontario, California, 11 September 1986.

Potochnik, Rudy. Interview with author. Modesto, California, 26 September 1986.

Prieb, Wesley. Interview by Tim Schrag, 24 November 1975. SOH interview no. 36.

Prochaska, Harry. Interview with author. San Francisco, California, 1 October 1986.

Reed, G. Hayes. Interview with author. Modesto, California, 25 September 1986

Richert, Irvin. Interview by Keith Sprunger, 29 September 1979. SOH interview no. 92.

Rodgers, Lloyd. Interview by Kurt Goering, 31 October 1975. SOH interview no. 28.

Rubin, Gerald M. Interview with author. Corte Madera, California, 2 October 1986.

Sateren, Leland. Interview with author. Edina, Minnesota, 9 February 1987.

Spaulding, J. Lloyd. Interview by Deb Janzen, n.d. [circa 1976]. SOH interview no. 43; Interview by Joseph Miller, 11 October 1977. SOH interview no. 59.

Stahly, Delmar. Interview by Joseph Miller, 22 December [1977]. SOH interview no. 77.

Stanley, Delmar S. Interview with author. La Verne, California, 24 February 1987.

Stocksdale, Bob. Interview with author. Berkeley, California, 1 October 1986.

Templin, Lawrence. Interview by William Keeney, 28 January 1975. SOH interview no. 37.

Ten Brink, Howard. Interview with author. Modesto, California, 24 September 1986.

Thiermann, Ian. Interview by Deena Hurwitz, 22 March 1982. Hurwitz interview.

Vogel, Robert. Interview with author. Pasadena, California, 15 September 1986.

Weaver, Joseph A. Interview by Kurt Goering, 29 December 1975. SOH interview no. 51.

Wilkinson, Harmon. Interview with author. Whittier, California, 23 February 1987.

Windemiller, Rev. Duane. Interview with author. Hampton Beach, New Hampshire, 22 April 1987.

Wright, Frank L. Interview by Keith Sprunger and John Waltner, 7 May 1972. SOH interview no. 4.

Yoder, Gene. Interview by Kurt Goering, 24 May 1976. SOH interview nos. 23 and 55.

Yost, Emery. Interview by Tim Schrag, 7 March 1975. SOH interview no. 30.

Zahn, Gordon C. Interview with author. Charlestown, Massachusetts, 29 April 1987.

Zwickel, Abraham. Self-interview answering Murray Polner's questions, n.d. [circa 1980]. Polner interview no. 30.10.

Zytkoskee, Tate. Self-interview answering author's questions. Luray, Virginia, May 1987.

In addition, four interviewees wished to be kept anonymous, and no listing is given for their interviews.

Index

ABOUT THE AUTHOR

Cynthia Eller is teaching in the philosophy department at Fairleigh Dickinson University, Teaneck, New Jersey. She received her Ph.D. in religion and social ethics from the University of Southern California. Her other projects include a comparison of Buddhist and Christian nonviolence and a forthcoming sociological study of the feminist spirituality movement.